MEDITATIONS
on
MONEY

A 365 Day Devotional Quest Through the Bible

DEBORAH EHRFURTH

ACW Press
Ozark, AL 36360

Meditations on Money
Copyright ©2005 Deborah Ehrfurth
All rights reserved

Cover Design by Alpha Advertising
Interior design by Pine Hill Graphics

Packaged by ACW Press
1200 Hwy 231 South #273
Ozark, AL 36360
www.acwpress.com
The views expressed or implied in this work do not necessarily reflect those of ACW Press. Ultimate design, content, and editorial accuracy of this work is the responsibility of the author(s).

Publisher's Cataloging-in-Publication Data
(Provided by Cassidy Cataloguing Services, Inc.)

Ehrfurth, Deborah.

   Meditations on money : a 365 day devotional quest through the
Bible / Deborah Ehrfurth. -- 1st ed. -- Ozark, AL : ACW Press, 2004.
      p. ; cm.
      Includes bibliographical references and index.
      ISBN: 1-932124-40-3

      1. Finance, Personal--Biblical teaching. 2. Money--Biblical
teaching. 3. Devotional calendars. 4. Bible--Meditations.
5. Devotional literature. I. Title.

BS680.M57 E47 2004
241/.68--dc22   0409

Printed in the United States of America.

This book is dedicated with great love and respect to
Brian T. Anderson,
Senior pastor of Vineyard Christian Fellowship
of North Phoenix
who has taught me so much
of what the Bible has to say about money

Acknowledgments

◈　◈　◈

This book would not exist except for some extraordinary people who encouraged me to keep going. First, Glynnis Whitwer, the catalyst behind my taking up writing in the first place. You have changed my life, and I thank you from the bottom of my heart. Lequetta and Brian Bramer, Karen Waer—without you always asking, "How's the book coming?" I may have given up. Thanks, guys.

Janet Drez, for all your enthusiasm and help. Lynda Evans, for your incredible motivation and cheeriness. The members of our small group—you know who you are. Thank you for your prayers.

I owe a debt of gratitude to all the wonderful Christian authors who stimulated my thinking and inspired many of the ideas presented here: Larry Burkett, Ron Blue, Dave Ramsey, Mary Hunt, and Richard Foster among them. I heartily recommend all their books.

My teenagers—Brandon, Ryan, and Kristin—who tolerated a preoccupied mother for the two years it took to birth this. I am so blessed you three are in my life.

And to my husband Len, who supported me and helped with my computer disability. Without his gift for money management, we would never be where we are today. He truly is one of the smartest people I know. Thank you, honey. I love you.

Above all, to my Lord and Savior Christ Jesus, who has never failed me and always assures me of His presence. To Him be all the glory.

Foreword

◆　◆　◆

This book is informative and extremely practical, but best of all highly Biblical. What Debbie has done in these pages is examine what the Bible has to say about money and possessions and present it in a way that will challenge us daily to rethink our attitude about them.

Other than salvation, stewardship is the greatest theme in the entire Bible. Jesus talked more about it than any other subject. Therefore, it is extremely important we get it right!

One of the things I have found in pastoral ministry over the years is that Christians don't always understand the true definition of "stewardship." They don't understand it goes beyond giving and money to include everything God has given us.

Meditations on Money is broad in scope in that it goes beyond the mechanics of tithing and money management to probe at the heart of what God really wants from us as his people. He wants us to trust him, and he wants no other gods before him. We need to be frequently reminded of these fundamental facts. By putting them in the form of a daily devotional, we can keep God's truth about stewardship before us on a regular basis.

I am very excited to recommend this book to anyone who is seeking to deepen their understanding of what the Bible teaches on this subject! I have known Debbie and her family for many years. One of the things I love about her is the fact that she not only understands the subject of stewardship, but she also lives these principles in her daily life.

Brian T. Anderson
Founding and senior pastor,
　　Vineyard Christian Fellowship of North Phoenix
Southwest Regional Overseer,
　　Association of Vineyard Churches USA

Preface

The Bible is the Christian's manual for life, but did you know that also includes your finances? The Scriptures are a gold mine of information on this subject. From Genesis to Revelation, we can find approximately 2,350 verses referring to money. I have pulled together a few hundred of these teachings and presented them in a format that offers bite-sized morsels to be digested a little each day.

I have a great love for the Bible and I hope that passion comes across in my writing. I have tried to be true to the interpretation of Scripture; in most cases God's Word speaks for itself. In instances where my insights may be in error, I refer you to the passages themselves to draw your own conclusions.

A great need exists today for God's people to know and apply his truths about money. If we claim to be disciples of Jesus Christ, we are to obey his commands. He tells us plainly we cannot serve two gods; we must choose our allegiance to one or the other. This book lays out that choice clearly and convincingly.

My prayer is that this devotional guide will lead you to a greater understanding of God's Word and transform your thinking towards your material possessions. And may you know the joy and fulfillment that comes from "godliness with contentment" (1 Timothy 6:6).

Deborah Ehrfurth

Be Transformed By the Renewing of Your Mind

"Do not conform any longer to the pattern of this world, but be transformed by the renewing of your mind. Then you will be able to test and approve what God's will is—his good, pleasing and perfect will."
Romans 12:2

You may have picked up this book as part of a New Year's resolution to get your financial affairs in order this year. Surveys tell us that getting out of debt ranks close to losing weight as the top priorities of Americans every January 1. Both are certainly worthwhile endeavors, so why does this resolution seem to fall apart by January 8?

Perhaps we're not as committed or motivated as we'd like to be, or maybe the task turns out to be more overwhelming than we had initially thought. But most likely the reason we fail is that we're trying to do by will power and acts of the flesh what can only be done by the renewing of our minds.

We need a new approach. We've heard the axiom: "Sow a thought, reap an action. Sow an action, reap a habit. Sow a habit, reap a character. Sow a character, reap a destiny." It all begins in our thought life. We need to reprogram our minds with the truth of God's Word. We need to know it, agree with it, and believe in it—then let that truth work within to change us.

Change does not come about by willpower. It comes from turning our minds around. I know of no other area where Christians are so conformed to the world than in their finances. The Bible is filled with teaching on this subject. Once we begin to *think* correctly about money, we will then *act* differently with money. As we read God's Word, our minds will be transformed. Let the process begin!

Father, I don't want to be conformed to this world. I want your truth to be made manifest in my life. I commit to regularly reading the Scriptures. Give me a teachable spirit. I ask in Jesus' name. Amen.

God Owns It All

"The earth is the LORD's, and everything in it, the world, and all who live in it." Psalm 24:1

The astronauts who have orbited the earth and viewed it from outer space all report being humbled by the sight. I can only imagine what it must be like to gaze out at our fragile planet and marvel at all the life it supports. This is God's creation. It belongs to him, he sustains it, and he wants us to enjoy it. But we must never forget that we are just tenants.

This is true of not only the earth, but all our money and possessions. Everything we have is on loan from the Lord. They are not ours to do what we please. We need to get this truth straight; really believing it would make such a difference in our attitudes when we experience material loss. God has the right to take things back. He's the owner.

Understanding that God owns it all will keep us from segregating our money into categories of sacred (the money I give) and secular (what I keep that goes towards everything else). It *all* comes out of his resources.

If you own property, your name may be on the title or deed, but it really isn't yours. Think about the person who had it before you, and the person who had it before them. How many generations have passed over this particular piece of land? How many will come after you? Since he spoke it into existence, and as long as the earth endures, it is the Lord's.

Our government is fond of telling us that the national parks belong to us and our children. It's a nice thought, but the next time you visit one of these natural wonders, remember who the true landlord is.

Father God, your creation is awesome. Thank you for allowing us to enjoy it. Help me to remember everything I have is really yours. In Jesus' name I pray. Amen.

Stewardship

"Again, it will be like a man going on a journey, who called his servants and entrusted his property to them." Matthew 25:14

Now that we have acknowledged that God owns it all, we are ready to be his managers. This is the definition of a "steward"—one who manages another's property. The manager has responsibilities towards the owner he serves; the owner has the ultimate authority over what the manager is or is not doing with what has been entrusted to him. Stewardship is such a key principle. If you don't understand it, you don't understand the Christian life!

You and I were made to manage the resources God put on earth. This includes the environment, our physical bodies, our time, and of course the money and possessions he has blessed us with. If he called us in for a divine audit, how would we do? Would he find us squandering funds on foolishness and excess? Are we wasteful or negligent in some areas? Are we lazy when it comes time to pay the bills? Can God trust us with more or have we proven we can't handle what he's already given us?

These are sobering thoughts, but the reality is that we will be called someday to give an account to God for what we have done with the finances we were given. Let's make it our goal to stand before him unashamed as wise and worthy stewards. It's all too easy to waste our lives if we fail to take stewardship seriously.

Dear Lord, thank you for all you have entrusted me with. The fact that I have anything at all in my care shows you trust me with it. Help me to be worthy of that trust. Show me the areas where I need improvement. Guide me to the information I need that will help me in my weak areas. Give me ears to hear and feet quick to obey in response to what you tell me. For Jesus' sake. Amen.

Knowing the Truth

"Then you will know the truth and the truth will set you free." John 8:32

Does the truth set us free? No, but *knowing* the truth sets us free. The truth has always been with us. We may have been ignorant of it, so we remained in bondage to whatever wrong patterns of thinking or bad habits had us in their grip.

The purpose of this book is to shed light on the truth so you can experience freedom in your finances. Not in the sense of being financially "independent," but free from the enslavement to debt, the ruthless taskmaster which is mammon, and the sense of being out of control and worried about money all the time.

Far too many people are in denial over their finances. They don't want to know how much they spend or how much they owe, compared to how much they actually earn. As long as they remain unaware, they can avoid facing the feelings of guilt and anxiety that would surface by owning up to their true situation. Ironically, by keeping themselves in the dark, they only create *more* guilt and anxiety.

The problem with knowing the truth is that now you *know*. No more excuses. No more rationalizing. The truth is threatening because it exposes actions we must take to correct our problems. Many people are too paralyzed by fear to make changes, yet change we must.

God does not want us ignorant. Those who will study and glean from the Scriptures all that he has to say about money, and then actually apply it to their lives, can expect all the freedom that comes from operating according to God's principles.

Father, give me the courage to face the truth about my financial situation. Guide me in the changes I will be making. I ask in Jesus' name. Amen.

The Mammon Spirit

"No one can serve two masters. Either he will hate the one and love the other, or he will hold to the one and despise the other. Ye cannot serve God and mammon." Matthew 6:24 (KJV)

Mammon is a unique word, used only four times in the New Testament: the above verse, its parallel in Luke 16:13, and Luke 16, verses 9 and 11. It's unfortunate that the newer translations substitute the words "money" or "worldly wealth" as they really aren't interchangeable.

"Mammon" is a Greek word for "wealth personified" or "avarice deified." What Jesus is saying in this passage is that mammon is a rival god. Money is not just an innocent "neutral form of exchange"; there is a spirit behind it, animating it, that seeks to dominate over us. And it certainly will if we are not aware of it and vigilantly on guard against it.

How can we tell if we are serving mammon? Well, who makes our financial decisions—God or money? When God tells us to do something, do we immediately obey, or do we consult the amount of money available—or not available—to us? When we want something, do we pray about it first or do we just go ahead and get it based on our ability to pay for it? Is all our money available to God at all times? If not, we have some repenting to do.

Dear Father in heaven, I have been guilty of serving mammon. I haven't always let you be Lord of my finances, but I want to change how I regard my money decisions. I want no rival gods in my life; no idols that would make me violate the first commandment. I want you to reign supreme in every area. Help me to put to death the spirit of mammon in my life. Thank you, Father, for forgiving me and loving me as I am. In Jesus' name. Amen.

Taking Our Thoughts Captive

"We demolish arguments and every pretension that sets itself up against the knowledge of God, and we take captive every thought to make it obedient to Christ." 2 Corinthians 10:5

We cannot hope to align our thinking about money with the Word of God without taking control of our thoughts. We need the input of Scripture first, with daily reading and study, and then we need to make decisions based on that Word and not our own feelings on the matter. As we do this, God supernaturally renews our minds. We need to be so grounded in the truth that when a thought pops into our heads that goes against the Bible, we will cast it aside.

Some thoughts Satan may sling your way in regard to your finances may include: "That doesn't apply nowadays!" Or, "Tithe if you want, you'll never make it." Or the old standby, "God wants you to be happy, go ahead and buy it." No, God wants us *holy*. Satan knows if he can gain control of your thought life, he can control you. God's Word is the greatest weapon you can use over demonic thoughts shot into your mind. But to do that, we need to know what the Word says! Ask the Holy Spirit to guide you to scriptures that pertain to your particular struggles with money and memorize them. Quote them to yourself when tempted; post them where you'll see them often.

All this lays the foundation for real and lasting change in your life. It won't happen by osmosis; you will have to put forth effort to see results. The best part is, this will affect more than your finances; it will touch every area of your life.

Begin now to learn to think biblically. It's the key to demolishing the satanic lies that would deceive us.

Father, point me to scriptures that will meet me where I'm at and minister to me. Give me revelation so I can start working into my life what you're teaching me. Thank you for the Holy Spirit to guide me into all truth. In Jesus' name. Amen.

The Love of Money

"For the love of money is a root of all kinds of evil. Some people, eager for money, have wandered from the faith and pierced themselves with many griefs." 1 Timothy 6:10

The love of money is the root of all evil." Do you recognize this verse as one of the most misquoted and misunderstood in all of Scripture? Unfortunately, too many Christians accept the shortened rendering and use it as an excuse to shirk their financial responsibilities. Dealing with money is too unspiritual; it corrupts us; it's a hassle. It's easier to ignore it, except money won't be ignored. It demands to be dealt with on a daily basis.

The power of money is very real. People will lie, steal, and kill for it. They are willing to destroy relationships over it. Eighty percent of divorces occur because of money. It truly is a root of all kinds of evil, but not the source. It is a terrible master but a useful servant. We need to put it in its rightful place, not controlling our emotions and actions. Money cannot and will not meet our emotional needs. When we use it that way we fall into a terrible trap. Money will never love us back, but it will enslave us if we allow it.

God uses money as a spiritual test in our lives. How you spend your money is very revealing. Would anyone be able to tell you are a Christian by looking at your checkbook? Would you be comfortable showing anyone your checkbook? Examine yourself before the Lord. The love of money can be a very subtle thing.

People who set being rich as their goal end up betrayed when at the end of their lives they realize it wasn't worth it, and now it's too late. Having money isn't wrong; it's only wrong when we attach too much importance to it. God will not tolerate any rivals to him in our hearts.

Almighty God, search my heart. I want to be free of the love of money. I will have no other gods before you. I will look to you, not money, to meet all my needs. I pray in the name of Jesus. Amen.

Do You Know Where You Are?

"Be sure you know the condition of your flocks, give careful attention to your herds." Proverbs 27:23

Where are you financially? Do you know the balance of your checkbook at all times, how much you're earning, how much you're spending? Or are you one of those freewheeling souls who breeze through life confident that everything will turn out okay at the end of the month? It's a carefree way to live until (and there's always an "until") the power is shut off because you forgot to pay the bill; you bounce checks; you accumulate late fees; and the stress levels rise. Suddenly, flying by the seat of your pants isn't much fun anymore.

In the agrarian culture of the Old Testament, wealth was measured by the livestock one had. It was important to know what was going on with each animal, because your livelihood was bound up in them. We don't worry about having enough goat's milk to get through the winter today, but do we have a grocery budget? Do we know the months the insurance premiums come due so we aren't caught short of the amount needed?

No one ever just "drifted" into having a plan for their financial affairs. It takes much diligence and careful attention, but the freedom and peace of mind it brings are well worth the effort.

Dear Lord, you are a God of order and of peace. Because I am made in your image, I have the seeds of order and peace within me, even if it doesn't look that way at times! As part of my goal of being a faithful steward, I desire to cultivate these qualities in my life with your help. Reveal to me the areas where I need to pay more attention and put forth effort and discipline in keeping my "flocks and herds" in good condition for you. In Jesus' name I pray. Amen.

Contentment

"But if we have food and clothing, we will be content with that." 1
Timothy 6:8

Do you have food and clothing? Most of us do. Yet how many of us are content? The Bible tells us we should be, if we have those basic needs met. The word "clothing" can be extended to shelter as well, meaning "covering." So if we have some sort of roof over our heads, clothes on our backs, and food in our stomachs, we should be happy and grateful. But we're not. The roof we reside under isn't grand enough, our clothes don't have the "right" labels, and we would rather eat out.

God takes our grumbling against his provision very seriously. He was ready to destroy the Israelites for their complaining (see Numbers 11), and he can't possibly be pleased with our attitudes today. Young couples just starting out believe they're entitled to have the things right away it took their parents thirty years to accumulate. No wonder we owe trillions on credit cards.

The truth is this: More and better stuff will not make you happy. If it were true the residents of Beverly Hills would be delirious with joy; instead they have the highest suicide rate per capita in the world. More stuff means more drain on your energies; every additional item you buy beyond what you need adds stress to your life in one way or another.

Let's get back to basics. I challenge you to go thirty days without buying anything but absolute needs. See how freeing it feels. You don't need clutter in your life to be content.

Lord, you have blessed me so abundantly; I am ashamed of the times I've grumbled about what you have provided for me. Help me to cultivate a grateful heart; open my eyes to the people who live with a fraction of what I have. I want to please you by my contentment. In Jesus' name. Amen.

Well Done, Good and Faithful Servant

"His master replied, 'Well done, good and faithful servant! You have been faithful with a few things; I will put you in charge of many things. Come and enter your master's happiness!'" Matthew 25:21

The parable of the talents has meaning and relevance on many different levels. The commended stewards were called "faithful." Even though they were not given the same amounts, they handled wisely what had been entrusted to them. It didn't matter how much they had been given; what mattered is what they did with it.

They were proactive; they took the initiative. They sought out opportunities to put the money to work for their master. They knew it was expected of them to show an increase. What motivated them? Fear? The desire to please their master? The hope of a reward? Or were they just doing their duty? Regardless, they were faithful in the execution of their stewardship.

We can't always control the amount of resources God gives us, but we can show ourselves faithful in good management with what we do have. That's what our rewards are based on—faithfulness. The smallest amount, used wisely and well, will earn our Master's commendation.

Father, I want to be pleasing to you in my management of your property. Give me your wisdom; I know I can't do this on my own understanding. I struggle at times to put your kingdom before my own wants. Help me to be faithful so that someday I will hear your "Well done!" I pray in the name of Jesus. Amen.

The Wicked Lazy Servant

"Then the man who had received the one talent came. "Master," he said, 'I knew that you are a hard man, harvesting where you have not sown and gathering where you have not scattered seed. So I was afraid and went out and hid your talent in the ground. See, here is what belongs to you."' Matthew 25:24-25

The stunning thing about the way this parable ends is the severity of the master's reaction to what this servant did. First the master calls him wicked and lazy; then he calls attention to the fact that the servant *knew* he was a hard man. And there's the rub—why the master was so angry. This servant had not behaved in ignorance. He knew, but he did nothing. He was lazy; by his own admission he was afraid. Yet he had a very low risk option available to him: simply deposit the money with the bankers and let it earn some interest. Because he failed to do even that, his one talent was taken away and he was cast aside.

How many of us know what we ought to do, but we don't because of the fear of making a mistake? If we live by our feelings, doing only what we feel good about, we will live out our financial lives in either mediocrity or disaster. Obviously, this is not what God wants for us. He wants us to be successful, and he's willing to show us how through the Scriptures.

Go humbly before the Lord, admitting that you don't know what to do and that you're afraid. Confess your failures and ask for a fresh start. As the Lord reveals his plans for your unique stewardship to you, by faith take action and be obedient to what he shows you. You won't be able to plead ignorance any longer, and it sure beats the fate of the wicked, lazy servant.

Father, I confess that at times I have not been a good steward with your resources. But now I want no more excuses in my financial affairs. Give me conviction where I need it, and strengthen me to obey. In Jesus' name. Amen.

Keeping Free From Earthly Entanglements

"No one serving as a soldier gets involved in civilian affairs—he wants to please his commanding officer." 2 Timothy 2:4

How free are you to serve God? If he asked you to move across the country or to another country, would you be able to consider doing it, or are you so deeply in debt it would be unthinkable? Must you work two jobs just to keep the collection agency away from your door? Are you unavailable to God because of your financial obligations?

The King James version of 2 Timothy 2:4 reads, "No man who warreth entangleth himself with the affairs of this life…" The Hebrew word for "borrow" means to entangle, to intertwine. We have entangled and intertwined ourselves with our creditors to the point that we've lost our freedom. We have so much stuff we need to take care of, pay for, insure, organize, fix, worry about, and keep track of, we've lost sight of what God saved us for. It wasn't just so we could go to heaven when we die. It was also to love and serve him now, here on earth. We're to be *in* the world but not *of* the world, and when the world looks at us who proclaim the name of Christ, do they see a difference in how we live, or do they see a people caught up in the same rat race as themselves?

It's not wrong to own a home and have a mortgage, unless it's a hindrance to what should be your first priority—pleasing the one who enlisted you.

Lord, if I call you Lord it's because you are the commanding officer of my life. I am serving in your army and I am to obey your orders at all times, not just when it's convenient. Keep me free from earthly entanglements so I can love and serve you fully. Show me the areas I need to free myself from, and give me the courage to do it. In Jesus' name. Amen.

The Bondage of Debt

"The rich rule over the poor, and the borrower is servant to the lender."
Proverbs 22:7

Other than being in a rocky marriage or having a terminally ill family member, I know of no other life situation more anxiety-inducing and energy-draining than living under a heavy load of debt. In fact, being deep in debt can produce a rocky marriage!

Debt is bondage because you've already spent money you haven't yet earned. You thought you were raising your standard of living by getting what you wanted now and paying for it while you enjoyed it, but what you've done is condemned yourself to a lower standard of living in the future.

The first priority of your next paycheck is now debt repayment. Not only do you have to earn enough to pay back what you owe plus your normal living expenses, you have to do it on after-tax dollars. You're working only to satisfy Mastercard's minimum monthly payments. Your money is not your own, nor is it available to further God's kingdom. You have indeed become a slave—to a financial institution that's hoping you don't ever pay them off. If you keep making only the minimum payments, the interest can roll on for the next thirty years— and that's only if you stop charging! Your house could be paid off before your leather jacket will be.

Debt is a dangerous trap that we slide into little by little, like quicksand. Then one day we find ourselves up to our necks and we realize we can't get out on our own.

Heavenly Father, let these truths about the dangers of debt affect me to the point where I will refuse to be in bondage to a lender. Let me not enter into any kind of loan without prayerfully consulting you first and being obedient to what you tell me, even if it means doing without something I desperately want. I will trust you to meet my needs, Lord, not my credit card. In the name of Jesus I pray. Amen.

Pay As You Go or Don't Go

"The kingdom of heaven is like treasure hidden in a field. When a man found it, he hid it again, and then in his joy went and sold everything he had and bought that field." Matthew 13:44

The point of this parable is that God's kingdom is worth everything we have to obtain, but there's an important financial principle here as well. Notice what this guy did. He sold all his assets and obtained the cash first before he bought the field. Credit is not a twentieth-century concept; he could have gotten a loan somewhere, I'm sure. In today's business schools, OPM (Other People's Money) is so hammered into us that we would accuse the man of being a fool for selling out. Have your cake and eat it, too! Why give up anything? So says the world.

Saving up before we buy something makes more sense in so many ways; for one, time has a way of sifting out our true wants from our impulses. The object of our desire tends to lose its grip on us when it takes many months to put aside the purchase price. We either will realize we don't want it after all, or we find that it is important enough to save up for. Paying cash keeps us from foolish, expensive mistakes and it keeps us out of debt!

There is so much stuff I would not own today if I'd only been willing to wait. Now it's too late; the money is gone and the whatever-it-was has lost not only its retail value but also its worth and appeal to me. So unlike the kingdom of heaven.

Father, give me discernment and wisdom in everything I purchase. I resolve I will not use credit from this day forward for the items I want; I will exercise patience and prudence and discover I really can live without a lot of the trappings of modern life. I want to pursue your kingdom, not my own. For Jesus' sake. Amen.

Lead Us Not Into Temptation

"And lead us not into temptation, but deliver us from the evil one."
Matthew 6:13

Our Lord does not tempt us, and we should not accuse him of doing so. James 1:14 tells us that "each one is tempted when, by his own evil desire, he is dragged away and enticed." The enemy of our souls excels at dangling the bait before us, hoping we'll bite and be hooked, but the truth is, we're very good at leading ourselves into temptation. I've learned to immediately toss unsolicited catalogs into the recycle bin without looking at them. If I don't know what's in them, I won't want any of it!

"Window shopping" is a dangerous pastime for many of us. It can stir up coveting in our hearts for things we weren't aware even existed until we saw them in the mall. We can begin to experience dissatisfaction with our lives simply by exposure to the world's goods. If this is a problem for you, you have to take steps to limit that exposure as much as possible. I once canceled a magazine subscription for a time, because every month it lured me to the nearest cosmetic counter to try something new that I didn't need. You know your own personal triggers. Remember, you can't be tempted by what you don't see!

Father, I do ask that you put a hedge about me and keep me from temptation. Fence me in so I can't wander into places I have no business being. Help me to guard my eyes and my heart from every form of coveting. Let me die to the world and its clamor to spend, spend, spend. In the strength of Jesus I ask this. Amen.

Keep Your Eyes Directly Before You

"Let your eyes look straight ahead, fix your gaze directly before you."
Proverbs 4:25

I used to joke that this was my "shopping" verse—get into the store, get only what I came there for, and get out. No looking around. No innocent browsing. Just grab what I need and go. If my eyes strayed and I did see something I liked, I might be able to avoid buying it that day, but more than likely I would go back in the near future to get it. I recognized that this was a real problem for me, and I decided to put the power and authority of God's Word to bear on this area of my life. I'm happy to say it worked; the Lord honored my commitment to break this bad habit and I am now safe in a store.

Since then I've realized this verse is also useful in achieving financial goals. You want to save money for a down payment on a house? "Let your eyes look straight ahead, fix your gaze directly before you" on the amount you'll need and don't let anything deter or pull you off course. It takes concentrated focus to stay with a savings goal for a long period of time; so many alluring alternative uses for that money seem to come along. We rationalize, "I really need a vacation, and it's such a great price for this cruise." Then we beat ourselves up over our lack of discipline when we fall short of our goal.

In a race, the winners run looking straight ahead. To look around is to be distracted, slowed down, and ultimately lose the contest. The same is true of our financial goals.

Father, I'm so easily distracted. My eyes dart every which way, keeping me from focusing on what I need to do. I know where to direct my gaze; give me the discipline and concentration to sustain it. And above all, let me keep my eyes fixed on Jesus. In his name I pray. Amen.

The Cost of Credit

"Saying, 'When will the New Moon be over that we may sell grain, and the Sabbath be ended that we may market wheat?'—skimping the measure, boosting the price, and cheating with dishonest scales, buying the poor with silver and the needy for a pair of sandals, selling even the sweepings with the wheat." Amos 8:5-6

Think about this: What would happen to the prices we pay for things if credit cards suddenly vanished from the earth; a Visa rapture, so to speak? What items would be left sitting forlornly in the department stores, now that people couldn't purchase them with plastic? How long would it take for their true value to appear?

I noticed on my own odyssey with credit cards that I could rationalize the price of something a lot easier if I were putting it on the card instead of paying cash. So I learned to ask myself, "If I were paying cash for this, would I still buy it?" Shockingly, 99 percent of the time the answer was NO. It wasn't enough to deter me from charging the thing, but 50 percent of the time my guilty conscience would drive me to return it. After riding that see-saw for awhile, I finally got to the point where if I didn't want to go with the green, it wasn't worth having.

But realize: The easy availability of credit has driven up prices on most all consumer items. In fact, when people default on their store charge cards, department stores pass their losses on to you in the form of higher prices. We also pay for the skyrocketing bankruptcy rate in this country. We all participate in the credit game no matter how we choose to pay. And so I continue to dream of a world with no credit cards and lower prices for all. Now that truly would be priceless.

Oh, Lord, your kingdom come! It's frustrating to live in a world system that makes such financial demands on us. Show me how I can make a difference in the way I pay for things and use me as a testimony to your grace and power in my life. For Jesus' sake. Amen.

Count the Cost First

*"Suppose one of you wants to build a tower. Will he not first sit down
and estimate the cost to see if he has enough money to complete it? For
if he lays the foundation and is not able to finish it, everyone who sees
it will ridicule him, saying, 'This fellow began to build and was not
able to finish.'" Luke 14:28-29*

Jesus is talking about the cost of being a disciple, but he compares it
to a building project. He tells us we'd better figure out the full price
before we begin, to avoid embarrassment later. In fact, we're to "sit
down," this isn't an impulsive decision. We are to carefully calculate
and estimate any hidden costs yet unforeseen as well. Anyone who has
ever built a house knows how unanticipated expenses can throw a
budget totally out of whack. The one house we had built cost us an
extra $1200 in just *rock* when it was discovered the soil contained too
much organic material to support the basement.

This is wise counsel in any financial transaction: Determine the
full price first before your emotions get involved. Have you ever fallen
in love with something, and then checked the price and been dis-
mayed? The problem is, now you want it and you begin to scheme how
you can buy it anyway. Even if you're successful at talking yourself out
of it, you turn away feeling disappointment.

A wiser strategy is getting the price first, then you can drop it like a
hot potato as the sticker shock hits you full in the face! Or you may be
pleasantly surprised at how inexpensive it is. (Does that ever happen,
really?) This discipline will not only save you money but it will reduce
the stress in your life as it helps curb any materialistic impulses you are
inclined towards.

Always know what you're willing to pay for something and don't
violate that figure. You won't avoid every unpleasant surprise but you
will be much closer to experiencing financial peace.

*Lord, I need to make a new habit of counting the cost before I make my financial
choices. Remind me to "sit down" first so I don't do anything rash. I ask in Jesus'
name. Amen.*

The Seduction of Advertising

"'You will not surely die,' the serpent said to the woman. 'For God knows that when you eat of it your eyes will be opened, and you will be like God, knowing good from evil.'" Genesis 3:4-5

How hard was it for Satan to get Eve to sin? She had everything: A garden paradise as her home, a perfect husband (!!), plenty of good food. All her needs were met. Yet Satan was able to create in her a sense of something missing. The tactics he used on her are the very same ones used on us every day by advertisers. My pastor, Brian Anderson, shared these insights in a sermon many years ago.

First, he came to her as a serpent—"shining one" in Hebrew, a very beautiful creature. Ads always use appealing models and images to attract us. He came to the woman, not the man—ads go after those under authority, to put pressure on the authority figure. Haven't our kids nagged us for stuff they had pitched to them between cartoons?

Next, Satan created a doubt about established rules. "Indeed, has God really said?" Godly standards are questioned, ridiculed, or ignored. He outright rejects warnings and focuses on the benefits: "You surely shall not die! You will be like God!" He directed her attention to what she didn't have. Ads present products as being able to fill our needs apart from God, encouraging us to find love, acceptance, and security in things. Satan uses partial truths and incomplete statements; so does Madison Avenue. Advertisers ask us to accept their conclusions with no analysis.

Before we come down too hard on Eve, think of all the times we have been led astray by advertising. We are affected, whether we're willing to admit it or not. But at least now we're not ignorant "…in order that Satan might not outwit us, for we are not ignorant of his schemes" (2 Corinthians 2:11).

Father, I confess that I have allowed advertising to manipulate me. I repent, and ask your help to make me more aware of how the world seeks to conform me to its mold. In Jesus' name. Amen.

The Shrewd Manager

"The master commended the dishonest manager because he had acted shrewdly. For the people of this world are more shrewd in dealing with their own kind than are the people of the light." Luke 16:8

Here we have an employee mishandling his employer's assets. Perhaps he was embezzling; we do know he was wasteful. And when his boss got wind of it, he gave him his pink slip. But first his boss demanded a final accounting, and the dishonest manager took advantage of the opportunity. Because he knew he would not be hired as a manager again due to his now-damaged reputation, and feeling unqualified to do anything else, he devised a plan.

He went to his master's debtors and reduced their bills. He may have been able to do this because, according to Mosaic law, Jewish businessmen were not allowed to charge interest to fellow Jews. This was easily gotten around with creative accounting practices. The dishonest steward may have been suspending the hidden interest charges. Because the charges were not legal, there was really nothing his master could do about it. He commended his now ex-employee not because he was pleased, but because he was impressed at his cleverness. The shrewd steward had achieved his goal of having friends to turn to when he was turned out on the streets, yet he hadn't done anything unlawful.

"Shrewd" in the Greek means "to act with foresight." It's used in other places in Scripture; for example, the wise virgins were shrewd (Matthew 25:1-13), and the man who built his house on the rock was shrewd (Matt. 7:24). As disciples of Jesus Christ, we are to look to the future with foresight, keeping our eyes on eternity and how we can best use our resources to expand the kingdom of God. Although the dishonest steward is no hero, we can and should emulate this one quality he demonstrated.

Heavenly Father, the work I do for you here on earth will follow me long after I've gone to be with you. May I never be put to shame for squandering those resources or cheating you in any way. For Jesus' sake. Amen.

Using Unrighteous Mammon

*"I tell you, use worldly wealth to gain friends for yourselves, so that
when it is gone, you will be welcomed into eternal dwellings." Luke 16:9*

This verse continues the parable of the shrewd manager, who had done this very thing of making friends with his ex-employer's debtors by discounting their bills in hopes of getting the favor returned in the near future. Although the man's motive was purely selfish (looking out for number 1), Jesus was acknowledging that his followers needed to take a lesson from the ousted manager, in using "unrighteous mammon" (which is the better translation) to help fellow believers and to spread the gospel.

When money has been dethroned in our lives and placed under the authority of Christ, it has enormous power to accomplish much good in the world. Ask any laborer in the Lord's service; it's hard to do much ministry without money. Although it's powerful, it's also limited. "When it is gone" means literally "when it fails." This is a reference to death; we can't take money with us, but we can send it on ahead in the form of the good use we put it to. I think of the Ray Boltz song entitled, "Thank You":

> Then another man stood before you
> He said, "Remember the time
> a missionary came to your church?
> His pictures made you cry
> You didn't have much money
> but you gave it anyway.
> Jesus took the gift you gave;
> That's why I'm in heaven today."[1]

That song makes me cry. I urge you to listen to it; it sums up all I've been trying to say here.

Gracious Father, how awesome it is that you would use us to accomplish your purposes here on earth. Sometimes we forget it's the little things we do that matter so much for eternity. No act is too small to be beneath your notice, not even the giving of a cold cup of water. Open our eyes and our hearts to the opportunities all around us. In the precious name of Jesus. Amen.

Money Needs to Flow

"One man gives freely, yet gains even more; another withholds unduly,
but comes to poverty." Proverbs 11:24

The kingdom of God is upside down; it is full of paradoxes. How do you get more by giving away what you have? Logic says that you will now have less; best to hang on to everything you can. But God's Word says doing that will leave us impoverished. How is that possible?

Look at what happens to a body of water when there is no outlet. The water stagnates and becomes scummy; bacteria breeds, and it can barely support any life. This is what happens to us spiritually when we hoard what God gives us. We become unpleasant to be around, no one really cares to be generous towards us, and we turn inward to become selfish people. Just as water needs to flow to be a life-giving, refreshing stream, so money needs to flow through our lives and out into the world to be a blessing. Money stuck in a drawer, never intended to be used, never blesses anyone.

One of the purposes of money is to minister to others, and we can't do that if we hold it with a clenched fist. The same is true of our material possessions. I've known people who have given away their cars to needy families and they themselves are never in lack of anything. Generosity scares us; we've been conditioned by the world that we need to "look out for number one" because if we don't, no one else will. That is a lie from the pit of hell; the One who created the universe and everything in it is looking out for us! If we make ourselves available to him as agents of mercy and blessing to his people, he will richly supply us with more so we can give again.

When we refuse to reach out, we sit and become scummy. Flowing river or stagnant pond; it's our choice.

Heavenly Father, I choose to be a fresh, flowing stream that brings life to others. I recognize you as the source and your supply never runs dry. Help me to understand how your kingdom works. For Jesus' sake. Amen.

In God We Trust

"Some trust in chariots and some in horses, but we trust in the name of the LORD our God." Psalm 20:7

The motto "In God We Trust" has appeared on United States coinage since 1864. The idea was first suggested in a letter to the Secretary of the Treasury by a minister in 1861. An act of Congress approved it and first authorized it to appear on two-cent coins. When it was left off the new gold coins issued in 1907, such an outcry of criticism arose that legislation was passed in 1908 to make it mandatory on all coins it had previously appeared on. By 1955, it was on all coins and paper currency.

In 1956, "In God We Trust" became the national motto of the United States. This has been challenged in federal court in recent years, but met with defeat. Most informal polls show that Americans like "In God We Trust" on their money and don't want it dropped. My heart is gladdened by this, but it begs the question: Does the way we live our lives demonstrate that we do, indeed, put our trust in God? Get out a paper bill, look at the words and reflect on them.

Do we trust God or do we put our trust in money?

God knows all about your financial struggles. What he wants most of all from you is your trust. Will you trust that he cares and will take care of you if you rest in him?

Don't trust in money. Money will let you down. Remind yourself of that every time you handle cash, and read that motto with a joyful heart. I don't think it will be appearing on credit cards anytime soon.

Father, I trust you with my eternal soul, so why shouldn't I also trust you with my finances? You delight in demonstrating your power on my behalf. In Jesus' name. Amen.

Money Doesn't Satisfy

*"Whoever loves money never has money enough; whoever loves wealth is
never satisfied with his income. This too is meaningless." Ecclesiastes 5:10*

I love the book of Ecclesiastes; it's so brutally honest that over the
centuries scholars have questioned why it's even in the Bible. It was
written by King Solomon, and if anyone would know anything about
money's inability to satisfy, it would be him.

Solomon was the richest man the world will ever know. Gold was
so common in his kingdom that his bodyguards sprinkled gold dust in
their hair every day. I once owned five horses; Solomon had twelve
thousand. It's all beyond belief, even in these days of Arab oil sheiks
and their wealth. So when someone that filthy rich talks about money,
we'd be wise to pay attention.

Now it's true that Solomon wrote this from the perspective of life
without God, yet that makes what he says even more reality based.
Whoever loves money never has money enough. You won't hear someone
who loves money say, "That's enough; I'm satisfied." No, it's like asking
a sugarholic if she's sated after one cookie. And you don't have to be
rich to be afflicted by this. I read an article in which the author inter-
viewed four families at four different income levels and, without exception, all felt they would be doing so much better if they were only
earning 10 percent more. This was true of the family earning $20,000
for whom take-out pizza was a huge treat and the family earning over
six figures with his and hers Porsches.

Not much has changed since Solomon's day. Think back to when
you were earning less money than you are now. Did you believe then
that once you achieved the income level of today, you'd be happier and
better off? Has that happened? Or did your expenses increase right
along with the income?

This lie of more money being the answer has been perpetuated
long enough. Listen to Solomon. He's been there, done that, and he's
concluded that it's meaningless.

*Lord, I ask to be released from the lie that I need more money to be satisfied. Help
me to see that satisfaction is found in you alone. In Jesus' name. Amen.*

Guarding Against Greed

"Watch out! Be on your guard against all kinds of greed." Luke 12:15

The setting for this statement of Jesus came in the midst of his teaching his disciples while thronged by a crowd of thousands, all jostling and pushing, trying to get a good position in which to hear. He was telling them the need to be bold and fearless in their witness of him, when someone in the crowd rather rudely interrupts with a personal business matter. The audacity!

Jesus refuses to get involved. It was common at that time then to bring a dispute, such as this one over an inheritance, to an accredited rabbi, but that was not Jesus' mission. Even if the man were being wronged by his brother, he was trying to use Jesus to get what he felt he should have coming to him. Jesus turned the situation into a lesson for the crowd.

"Watch out! Be on your guard!" is a dramatic warning against a sin that can be subtle and go unrecognized in our lives. Greed is "a consuming desire to have more." It is the opposite of contentment. In the not so distant past, people knew this. Greed was considered one of the seven deadly sins. Today it is applauded and venerated. Ivan Boesky, who went to prison for insider trading, was cheered at a business school graduation when he told the class, "Greed is all right. I want you to know I think greed is healthy."

Christians have bought into this line of thinking as well. Is our Lord's warning falling on deaf ears? It's important to note that just because someone is wealthy does not mean they're greedy; we can't make judgments about people based on their net worth. Very poor people are also consumed by the beast of greed. We need to identify areas of our lives where greed could be sneaking up on us and confess and repent. There is no place in the life of a disciple of Jesus Christ for greed in any form.

Father, I will take your warning seriously. I will guard my heart against all forms of greed. I will do whatever is necessary to free myself from it. In Jesus' name. Amen.

Life: Not About Possessions

"A man's life does not consist in the abundance of his possessions."
Luke 12:15

We give lip service to this declaration of Jesus, but we behave exactly the opposite. Bumper stickers proclaim, "He who dies with the most toys wins." I like the counter-one to it, "He who dies with the most toys still dies." In our maddening race to accumulate, do we ever pause long enough to ask why? Do we really believe we'll win some sort of prize for keeping up with the mythical Joneses? Is it a point of pride to have so much stuff the cars have to sit outside because the garage is crammed to overflowing?

People who move frequently are sometimes free of this malady because they recognize that the more possessions they have, the more they have to pack and haul. Or maybe they just never unpack. It's hard to imagine Jesus and the disciples traveling about the countryside trundling cases of stuff with them.

Maybe we're beginning to catch on; the mid 1990s saw a "simplicity movement" begin to gain momentum. People began to see what Jesus knew all along: Accumulating excessive possessions isn't worth it. Life is made up of time, and unlike money, you can't earn more. Each of us is allotted a finite amount and quite frankly, it's just plain stupid to spend vast portions of it acquiring more things. You can't take it with you, and the people you leave it to will argue over it to the point of estrangement.

So think twice before beginning your next collection of whatnots. No one cares you have one in each color. Go through each possession in your home and determine if you feel fulfilled by owning it. If you do, great. It has a place in your life. If not, fill up a box with all the stuff you don't care about and get rid of it. Remember, when you stand before God someday there is no crown for Abundance of Possessions.

Dearest Lord, I want my lifestyle to be aligned with your Word, not what the world says I need. I want wisdom in editing the amount of stuff I have. I ask in Jesus' name. Amen.

Robbing God

"Will a man rob God? Yet you rob me. But you ask, 'How do we rob you?' In tithes and offerings." Malachi 3:8

While it is true that God owns it all and we are only his stewards, he has chosen to depend upon his people to return to him what is rightfully his. If we lend something to a friend, we expect to get it back. When it becomes obvious that our friend has no intention of giving it back to us, we rightfully would call them a thief. If you are not giving at least ten percent of your income back to God, you are stealing from him.

This is not a salvation issue; Jesus Christ's atoning work on the cross accomplished that. This is an obedience issue. Why should we tithe? Because it is biblical. Tithing was practiced by Abraham with the motive of gratitude alone over four hundred years before the law was even given to Moses. New Testament believers were renowned for their generosity and they didn't stop at ten percent; they gave well beyond that. Read the book of Acts and tell me these people needed to be taught to tithe.

So what is our problem? Do we need more evidence to convince us? Only once did Jesus ever proclaim "You must be born again" to Nicodemus in John 3:3, yet I don't hear too many debates on the validity of that! Some of our resistance to this is instigated by Satan; he wants the church to be anemic and ineffective, unable to carry out the work of ministry due to lack of funds. If every Christian were to tithe, would the church be as needy as it is now? I'm convinced such a revival would take place that unbelievers would sit up and take notice.

Our chief motive for tithing should be that we are jealous for God's kingdom and want it to thrive. Let's stop robbing him.

Lord God Almighty, I tremble at your word in Malachi 3:8. I will be a tither; I will deal with all the issues holding me back and by faith turn over to you what is rightfully yours. For Jesus' sake. Amen.

Under a Curse

"You are under a curse—the whole nation of you—because you are robbing me." Malachi 3:9

We don't like to talk much about curses. It brings up connotations of voodoo or witch-craft. Yet God is totally serious when he talks about cursing his people for their disobedience. Deuteronomy 28:15-68 is a grim record of what God would allow to come upon Israel if they disregarded his commands.

To curse means to "invoke evil upon," to "call upon divine or supernatural power to send injury upon," or "evil or misfortune that comes as if in response to imprecation or as retribution." These curses did come to pass in Israel's case. God meant what he said. In Malachi's day, the remnant that had returned to their country from their exile in Babylon were going through the motions but their hearts were not in their worship and they did not take the law seriously. Specifically, they were not tithing. Oh, they were probably giving some, equivalent to our throwing a five dollar bill in the plate as it goes by—"Here's a tip, God"—but not the amount God required. Their small nation was struggling and demoralized, and they were questioning God's covenant promises to them. Through his prophet Malachi, God reveals to them what the problem is and how they could remedy it.

Living under a curse is something we do to ourselves through our disobedience to God. If you're struggling with your finances, and have been for a long time, look at your practices under the light of the revelation given to Israel. Have you been robbing God? Have you failed him in giving of the tithe? The good news is, your obedience will free you. God longs to bless you, but you have been tying his hands. Step out in faith and begin living life in the light of God's favor.

Father, I don't like to think about your having a judgment against my finances. I have no excuse now that I know the truth. I'm sorry, Lord. I want to make things right. Give me the courage to do so. I pray in Jesus' name. Amen.

Proving God

> *"'Bring the whole tithe into the storehouse, that there be food in my house. Test me in this,' says the Lord Almighty, 'and see if I will not throw open the floodgates of heaven and pour out so much blessing that you will not have room enough for it.'" Malachi 3:10*

This verse is one of the most extraordinary in all of Scripture. Nowhere else are we invited by God himself to test him. The Bible makes no attempt to prove God. It states his existence as a given fact, not open to debate. Yet in this area regarding tithing, God puts himself out for us.

Why does he do this? Perhaps in his mercy and grace, he knows what difficulty we have in this area and he wants to motivate us. Who among us can resist a challenge? As my pastor likes to say, "God double-dog dares us!" The first move is ours. We are to tithe to our local church where we fellowship, the modern day "storehouse" replacing Israel's temple treasury.

My husband and I were raised in churches that didn't teach tithing; we didn't learn of it until our third year of marriage. We didn't see how it would be possible, with Len's meager wage trying to support one baby and another on the way, but we did it regardless. It was tight, but we paid all our bills. Len worked in a grocery warehouse, and suddenly truck drivers were giving him cases of damaged boxes of cereal and even disposable diapers! It was miraculous how God provided. Not just material blessings, but innumerable spiritual ones as well. We can honestly say that as we tithed, God was more than faithful. We have no debts. We have three children who are a joy to us. We have a ministry we are passionate about. The floodgates of heaven are open in our lives. God invites you to prove him in this as well. What do you have to lose?

Heavenly Father, you say I can test you in my obedience to the tithe. From this day forth, I will give you ten percent of all I earn and watch you prove yourself faithful and true. In Jesus' name I pray. Amen.

Rebuking the Devourer

*"'I will prevent pests from devouring your crops, and the vines in your
fields will not cast their fruit,' says the Lord Almighty." Malachi 3:11*

Anyone who has ever cultivated a patch of earth of any size in an
attempt to grow something knows exactly what this verse is talking
about. For farmers, especially in the days before pesticides, an invasion
of locusts was a disaster of epic consequences. No harvest, no food.
They were much more dependent upon God to protect their crops
than we are today with our modern technology.

But we have other devourers in our lives, just as insidious. How
about credit card or other consumer loan interest? Nothing can eat up
your earnings quicker than a high interest rate on a debt you can't
afford. And God wants you to tithe? Ha! If that's your response, God
has good news for you. If you are obedient to the tithe, the Lord himself will rebuke the devourer and enable you to meet your debt obligations. You may believe that's impossible, but with God all things are
possible.

In our financial counseling, my husband and I have seen miracles
occur when people got serious about tithing, no matter what shape
their finances were in. God's math does not compute. He can do more
with 90 percent than we can with 100 percent. He can make some bills
go away entirely. He can heal you of medical conditions that are sap-
ping your funds. He can keep your clunky old car running well.

Lift up your eyes and realize what an awesome God we have! It is
the testimony of so many people that not until they began to tithe did
they begin to get out of debt once and for all. No, it won't be easy and
yes, you will have to sacrifice. But God is willing to help you by keeping
away the devourers. Avail yourself of that help today.

*Father God, I want to dare to believe that you can do what you say. Help my unbe-
lief! Show yourself mighty on my behalf, Lord, as I step out in obedience to you. In
Jesus' name I pray. Amen.*

The Un-Pharisees

"Woe to you, teachers of the law and Pharisees, you hypocrites! You give a tenth of your spices—mint, dill, and cummin. But you have neglected the more important matters of the law—justice, mercy and faithfulness. You should have practiced the latter, without neglecting the former." Matthew 23:23

After listening to my husband regale me with the details of another heavy debate with a Christian who believes tithing isn't for believers, I wondered if any argument would convince a confirmed non-tither. These people would wave off angels. As I thought about it being an issue of the heart (and only God can change people's hearts) it occurred to me that the Pharisees, indeed, did tithe. It was actually one of the easiest points of the law to keep because it was such a black-and-white issue. It was measurable; one could surely tell if they were doing it or not. They were so meticulous about it, they even tithed on the tiny herbs they grew. It was the justice, mercy, and faithfulness part they struggled with.

In these last days, we've done an about-face. We pride ourselves in the body of Christ when we exhibit being just, merciful, and faithful, so we're excused from the need to tithe; after all, that's under the law, we're under grace. We've become the un-Pharisees. I find it interesting that Jesus brought the two sides together in Matthew 23:23, the only place in the Gospels he brings up the subject. He commended their scrupulous tithing and commanded they keep it up. If he was going to abolish the tithe, he certainly could have mentioned it here. Yet of equal concern to him was their hard hearts towards the people. They were not practicing love for their brothers. It's pretty obvious that we are to do both.

Lord, I confess that I've been hard on the Pharisees. But by pointing fingers at them, I judge myself. I am guilty of feeling smug about my spirituality. I thank you that you sent Jesus to give us the righteousness we can never obtain by keeping the law. Help me to be faithful in all aspects of my walk with you. For Christ's sake. Amen.

Honoring the Lord with Our Wealth

*"Honor the LORD with your wealth, with the firstfruits of all your crops;
then your barns will be filled to overflowing, and your vats will brim
over with new wine." Proverbs 3:9-10*

The Bible is filled with promises that God will bless those who give.
Why? To motivate us to keep giving! Why else would he continue
to pour in material blessings to people who do not give back? We
honor God when we give back to him in proportion to what he has
given us, and he turns right around and blesses us again!

Understand this: You cannot outgive God. If there were a giving
competition, God would win every time. His very nature is that of a
giver; he gave his only Son to die for us. How can we with a clear conscience withhold anything from the one who has done so much for us?
Honoring him with our wealth is one tangible way of showing him
how much he means to us.

Where do we start? We start with the tithe; giving back to God the
portion that is rightfully his; our "firstfruits." Whatever our income, we
take 10 percent off the top before we do anything else. If you wait until
you can "afford" to tithe, you never will. Be obedient now, right where
you are. If you won't tithe on fifty dollars, you certainly won't on five
hundred. To help us, God never demands obedience without a promise
of blessing, because our obedience touches his heart. He loves to bless
us!

Our obedience unleashes more of his power in our lives. Ask anyone who is a veteran tither and be prepared to hear testimony after testimony of what God has done—and not just in their finances.
Something happens in the spiritual realm when we tithe; it's so powerful even the secular world is beginning to teach it! If you've been
tithing, you know what I'm talking about. If you're just starting, be
ready for a tremendous adventure. You cannot outgive God!

*Lord God, I want to honor and obey you. I will return to you the portion that is
yours. Give me the faith to do that, no matter what the situation in my life. In
Jesus' name I pray. Amen.*

February 2

The Spirit of Poverty

*"I don't have any bread—only a handful of flour in a jar and a little
oil in a jug. I am gathering a few sticks to take home and make a meal
for myself and my son, that we may eat it—and die." 1 Kings 17:12*

This widow was facing starvation. She had already resigned herself
and her son to death when Elijah came along. No wonder she was
hesitant to share with the prophet; there was barely food for the two of
them. She had a very legitimate fear of not having enough.

We may not be living in poverty but there is such a thing as "the
spirit of poverty" that can afflict anyone. It can be defined as "the fear
of not getting that causes you to hold on tightly to what you do have."
People in this bondage act as if every twenty-dollar bill that passes
through their hands will be their last. They have a good job, but they
live in constant fear of losing it. They live two blocks from a grocery
store, but they stockpile food just in case. Because they don't trust God
to meet their needs, they feel they need to scramble for themselves.

This mind-set is a deception, but how do we break free? What did
the widow do? After explaining her plight to Elijah, he said to her,
"Go home and do as you have said. But first make a small cake of
bread for me from what you have and bring it to me, and then make
something for yourself and your son." He tells her: *me first!* Then he
gives her this promise: "The jar of flour will not be used up and the
jug of oil will not run dry until the day the Lord gives rain on the
land" (1 Kings 17:13-14).

She may have doubted, but she obeyed. As a result, "there was food
every day for Elijah and the woman and her family," (1 Kings 17:15).
We are released from the spirit of poverty by giving to the Lord in
faith.

*Lord God, I will not live in fear. I will give, knowing you are more than able to
meet all my needs for the future. In Jesus' name. Amen.*

God Is the Source

"But remember the LORD your God, for it is he who gives you the ability to produce wealth." Deuteronomy 8:18

Remember" is the common theme throughout the book of Deuteronomy, Moses' final address to the nation of Israel. After much hardship following forty years of desert wandering, they are about to enter the Promised Land with "streams and pools of water, with springs flowing in the valleys and hills; a land with wheat and barley, vines and fig trees, pomegranates, olive oil and honey; a land where bread will not be scarce and you will lack nothing" (Deuteronomy 8:7-9). It must have sounded like heaven to them. Yet Moses warns them sternly to not forget where all this bounty came from.

Human nature has not changed since then. We get comfortable in our surroundings, we "eat and are satisfied," we "build fine houses and settle down," our "silver and gold increase," and "all that we have is multiplied" (Deuteronomy 8:12-13). The danger is that our "heart will become proud and [we] will forget the Lord [our] God" (Deuteronomy 8:14).

It's easy to be dependent on God when we're needy. But when we get relief, then what? After pouring out our thanks and praise to God for bailing us out once again, do we continue to live in humble dependence on him? Or do we start to believe our prosperity is the result of our own hard work? While it is true many of us have worked very hard to get where we are, where does this ability to work hard come from? Who gave you the health to be able to do what you do? Who provided the skills you have? Who created your brain?

God, of course. He knows exactly what's best for us. If he's keeping you on a short financial leash, it may be because he knows you need that to stay close to him. In short, everything in our lives comes to us from his hand. Let's thank him even as we continue to enjoy his benefits.

Father God, I praise you and give you thanks for all that you have done. Let me never take any of it for granted, Lord. In the blessed name of Jesus. Amen.

The Value of Work

"The Lord God took the man and put him in the Garden of Eden to work it and take care of it." Genesis 2:15

We were made to work. Work is not part of "the curse" of our fallen nature; God told Adam to work and care for Eden before the Fall. Work was meant to be a blessing; to give us a meaningful purpose in our daily labors. It still can be; God's intention for his creation has not changed. The original command to work was never rescinded. God in his grace allowed now sinful human beings to continue as his caretakers over the earth. Noble labor is important. We are co-workers with God himself.

The problem in our modern era is that we have equated work with money, and that's all. No wonder we often have such a bad attitude towards it, particularly if we feel we're not being paid enough for the work we do. (Some of us may be overpaid for the effort we put forth!) While it is certainly a just principle that we be fairly compensated in our jobs, the value of work goes far beyond that.

Definitions for work include: "activity in which one exerts strength or faculties to do or perform something"; "sustained physical or mental effort to overcome obstacles and achieve an objective or result." The following definition describes what God does: "something produced by the exercise of creative talent or expenditure of creative effort; artistic production."

Notice that none of these definitions connect work with money. Money has a way of cheapening some work; certain activities are beyond putting a price to. How much would a mother get paid if her work could be quantified in dollars? Work is God's plan for us; our responsibility is to do what our gifts and abilities have equipped us for, whether we get paid for it or not. God values highly what you do; you should also.

Father, teach me to value work the way you do. Help me break out of the mind-set that it's all about a paycheck. Continue to give me important, meaningful things to do in this short time I have on earth. And let all I do bring glory to your name. For Jesus' sake. Amen.

Work with Diligence

"Lazy hands make a man poor, but diligent hands bring wealth."
Proverbs 10:4

The Living Bible puts it bluntly: "Lazy men are soon poor; hard workers get rich." There are twenty-eight proverbs praising hard work; it is a virtue God highly esteems. Do you have a reputation for being a hard worker? What would your boss have to say, or your co-workers, or your spouse?

If you are self-employed, you know the truth of this principle as the success of your business is directly correlated to the amount of work you invest in it. There is more motivation for you to work hard than for someone whose pay doesn't correspond with the quantity and quality of work performed. Unfortunately, many people have taken advantage of this to do "as little as I can get by with and not get fired."

Unbelievers may have such an attitude, but Christians are called to a higher standard of service—not just in the work we do for the kingdom, but in *all* we do. It doesn't matter if we work at a nuclear plant or a fast food restaurant, we're to represent Christ and do our jobs to the best of our ability every single day. It means we don't call in sick if we're not, or take extra long lunch breaks.

To be diligent is to be "characterized by steady, earnest, and energetic effort." It connotes perseverance under all kinds of conditions, and let's face it, some jobs are truly awful and don't pay well. But, if you are a hard worker and do your job well, someone will notice. Sometime, somewhere, you will be elevated to a better position. God can give you favor with employers if you truly desire to better your lot. He sees you work even if it seems no one else ever does, and he's the one we seek to please anyway.

Do a self-evaluation. Would you want to have an employee like you? If not, then make the necessary adjustments to be a worker the Lord—and an employer—can be pleased with.

Lord, I want part of my testimony for you to be my reputation for hard work. Give me the courage to apologize to anyone I've hurt by my slacking off. In Jesus' name. Amen.

February

Chasing Fantasies

"He who works his land will have abundant food, but the one who chases fantasies will have his fill of poverty." Proverbs 28:19

You see them every week—in line at the supermarkets, the quick stop convenience stores, every kiosk that promotes "a dollar and a dream"—buying their weekly lottery tickets. They know the odds of them getting struck by lightning are greater than getting five matching numbers, but still they buy, firm in their belief that "you can't win if you don't play." It's harmless fun, some would argue. It's good for the economy; it will give us tax relief. (In actuality, it's a tax on the poor.)

It troubles me that the people who least can afford it will queue up on payday for a ten-million-to-one shot of striking it rich. Some are so deeply imbedded in this mind-set that they're not concerned about trying to improve their lot in life with a better-paying, more highly skilled job. After all, someday they're going to win the lottery! All their problems will be over. They will buy a new SUV for every member of their extended family. They will vacation in the Caribbean. They will eat steak and lobster every night.

While they wait for that happy day, they drag themselves off to work for the required forty hours a week, come home, sit on the sofa with a six-pack, and watch television. They have to; how else will they find out the winning numbers? Week after week, they tear up their ticket in disgust. Oh well. It was only a dollar. Better luck next time. The odds increase the more you play!

Years go by. The kids are grown up, pursuing their own dead-end jobs. But it won't always be this way; someday they're going to win the lottery…

Father, search my heart for any greed or desire for ill-gotten wealth. Help me to understand that it is ultimately you who decides how to distribute the financial resources of the world, not the lottery system. I will turn to you, not gambling, to meet my future needs. In Jesus' name. Amen.

Seek His Kingdom First

"But seek first his kingdom and his righteousness, and all these things will be given you as well." Matthew 6:33

The kingdom of God refers to his rule and reign. It is complete in heaven, but on earth it resembles a picket fence. It's here but not here. Christians are not only to actively seek the kingdom, but to help it manifest through the works we do to serve it.

Jesus is telling us in this passage to get our priorities straight. We are not free to seek and serve God's kingdom if our days are filled with the cares of life. Our biggest concern is supporting ourselves through money. It touches every aspect of our existence. We're all very aware of this, and if we're disciples of Jesus Christ we also know this verse very well, but do we put it into practice?

What will happen to our careers, our very livelihood, if we were truly to put God first in our lives? Read the verse again. Basically, God is telling us that if we look to *his* business, he will take care of *our* business. It's a pretty good deal! God is much wiser and has infinitely more foresight than we do. Many of us are in the process of running our lives straight into the ground by not seeking the kingdom first.

If you're not giving God your time or your money, he is not number one, no matter what you say. You need to spend time with him so he can reveal to you his plans for your life. It may surprise you what he has in store for you. Why do we harbor the belief that God is out to ruin our fun and make us do things we don't want to do?

As we get closer to God, his desires become *our* desires. Our longings for material things will fade away as we seek the Lord first because now we're living in the real world—God's kingdom.

Father, I will reorder my life so that you are my top priority. Help me to put your kingdom before my own. In Jesus' name I pray. Amen.

Do Not Worry

*"Therefore I tell you, do not worry about your life, what you will eat
or drink; or about your body, what will you wear. Is not life more
important than food, and the body more important than clothes?"*
Matthew 6:25

Three little words: Do not worry. Boy, do we have trouble with that
one. Five times in this passage Jesus admonishes us for worrying.
Granted, it's much easier to not worry when your bills are paid and
your health is not in jeopardy. But even if you have all those problems
going on simultaneously in your life, Jesus still commands you not to
worry. Why?

For one thing, worry is sin. It demonstrates a lack of trust in our
heavenly Father. Most of us don't worry about where our next meal is
coming from or if we'll have clothes to put on our backs tomorrow.
No, we worry and fret over our retirement accounts, paying for our
kids' educations, beating inflation—all the "what ifs" of life. Jesus says,
relax. Why spend all that mental energy when God knows what we
need? Most of us have such abundance in the areas of food and clothing alone that a wiser course of action would be in figuring out how to
cut back!

If we live in fear, buying things we don't need now "just in case,"
we end up with things that don't meet the need *if* it ever does arise. I
speak from experience! We need to hear the voice of the Lord saying,
"Trust me." Don't you feel hurt when a loved one demonstrates a lack
of trust in you if you've never done anything to warrant it? It's the
same with God.

Worrying is how we reveal that lack. Worrying never changed anything anyway; it just adds needless stress and anxiety. Lift up your
needs to the Lord and express your faith that he will come through for
you. And he will. No worries!

*Father, I'm sorry for all the times I've worried when I should have prayed; acted in
fear when I should have waited and trusted. You know my needs and have promised to meet them. In Jesus' name. Amen.*

February

Saving

"In the house of the wise are stores of choice food and oil, but a foolish man devours all he has." Proverbs 21:20

Does saving money demonstrate a lack of trust in God? Is it more spiritual to "live by faith"—paycheck to paycheck—and just count on God to come through for us? Some people are called to live exactly like this. I think of George Mueller and his orphanages, how all the needs were prayed in and God never failed. I believe that lifestyle is a calling, however, not a model for everyone.

We may all have seasons in our life when our resources are limited, and God uses these seasons to teach us to heavily rely on him. Periods of unemployment, sudden widowhood, and other situations life throws at us can catch us unprepared and launch us into an adventure with God. That may be exactly where he wants us at that time. The lessons we learn by these experiences are invaluable.

But they are not an excuse for laziness or indiscriminate spending with the belief that "God will take care of me." The Bible is very balanced in its teachings on trusting God and having the wisdom of a savings plan. We can have wrong motives in saving money, however, such as loving money for money's sake, using it as a way of measuring success, being addicted to accumulation (hoarding), as a means of feeling secure, or to prop up self-worth.

Good reasons to save money include: not having to use credit in emergencies, delayed gratification, enables giving, allows for retirement, and helps in accomplishing long-term goals. It is crucial to have a positive cash flow margin every month; basically, spending less than you earn. Without that cushion, you will live as a responder, putting every little unexpected expense on a credit card, buying impulsively, and falling more behind every month.

Having savings is wisdom. Prayerfully consider the areas of your lifestyle you could cut back on to come up with those savings. It's your future.

Dear Lord, I need radical new wisdom in this area of saving money. Purify my motives. I trust you to care for me, but I don't want to be foolish or lazy. In Jesus' name. Amen.

Get Rich Quick?

"A stingy man is eager to get rich and is unaware that poverty awaits him." Proverbs 28:22

Nowhere in the Bible is the concept of get-rich-quick schemes supported. People seek them out because of their "something for nothing" appeal. The underlying motivation behind them is greed. If greed is allowed to run unchecked whenever we are presented with the next great deal, it will blind us to the facts and we will see only what a "terrific" opportunity it is. Usually it's only an opportunity for the person pitching it to us; they get all our money and we are left holding the bag.

The problem is that once our emotions become involved, in our excitement we fail to thoroughly check out an investment and do the actual math. Or we have so much respect and trust for the person selling us that we're blinded by that as well. Enthusiasm sells; it can also get us into trouble with impulsive decisions. "If it sounds too good to be true, it probably is" applies here.

Never be pressured by someone who says, "You have to act on this right now, today!", no matter what reason they give you. If it truly is a great deal, and after prayerfully considering it, you feel God wants you to do this, the deal will still be there next week or next month. God does not pressure or push or create a state of anxiety in us. We once were offered a tremendous deal on 20 acres of raw land, but we waited and prayed for a few days before we gave our decision, knowing that someone else could be buying it while we "dawdled." When we called back, the land was still available, and we knew God wanted us to purchase it.

I've never heard of any get-rich-quick-with-no-money-down seminars that teach patience. It's all hurry-up, do-it-now, hyperactive verbiage that doesn't give us a chance to think it through. The sad thing is that many people who fall for this stuff can't afford to lose the money. So beware! Don't be taken in by "easy" wealth.

Father, I admit I act on impulse sometimes, and it costs me money. Teach me to bring every decision to you first. In Jesus' name. Amen.

Get Rich Slow

"Dishonest money dwindles away, but he who gathers money little by little makes it grow." Proverbs 13:11

I wonder if Solomon had compound interest in mind when he wrote this verse. His wealth wasn't gained that way, but it is one of the best ways for the rest of us to build our net worth. It isn't necessary to save a million dollars to have a million dollars; it just takes self-discipline, patience, and a positive cash flow.

You will never accumulate if you spend more than you earn. If you think you can't possibly cut back on your expenses to have money to save, consider this: Suppose you gave up just one habit that costs you a dollar a day. It could be a soft drink, a candy bar, that quick-stop coffee. With that one dollar a day, invested every day for 45 years at 10 percent interest, you would end up with $274,250. Your original investment would be $16,425, and it would have been a fairly painless sacrifice.

But, you say, I don't have 45 years. Fine, then you need to set aside a larger sum. If you're 45 years old and put $100 a month aside at 10 percent you'll have $71,880 at age 65. Start sooner, at age 35, and you'll have $206,440. Begin at 25; you'll gain $555,454 by age 65. Time creates money. You have to be forward thinking, realizing that a dollar spent today on consumable goods is gone forever.

The only non-consumptive uses for money are giving and saving; our lifestyles swallow up the rest. How much is the stuff you buy really costing you when looked at in this way? Not only in dollars removed from future growth, but in depreciation. It applies to more than cars. I've had the sad experience of selling an item in a yard sale for 1/20 of what I paid for it.

We've all had compound interest working against us; turn that around and let it work *for* you. Start today, with one dollar if you must, but start!

Lord, I ask for wisdom in making my money grow. Show me where to find the seed money to begin and give me the discipline to see it through. In Jesus' name I pray. Amen.

Avoid Becoming a Rich Fool

*"But God said to him, 'You fool! This very night your life will be
demanded from you. Then who will get what you have prepared for
yourself?' This is how it will be with anyone who stores up things for
himself but is not rich towards God." Luke 12:20-21*

The term "fool" used here is very strong language. It is not a description of this rich farmer's mental capacity but of his spiritual discernment. A fool, according to the Bible, is someone who lives his life as if God did not exist. This was the man's fatal flaw.

On the surface, as you read Luke 12:16-19, his actions don't seem that questionable. Building bigger barns appears to be both wise and practical. It was his attitude that condemned him; he was living only for himself. He thought he was a big success, but God had another opinion. Once again, it was not because he was wealthy, or how he acquired it, or that he had a huge increase. God is not opposed to wealth, but what we do with it reveals our heart towards it, and he is deeply concerned about that.

Stockpiling worldly wealth so we can "take life easy, eat, drink, and be merry," epitomizes the pursuit of "the good life" that has no room in the budget or the schedule for the kingdom of God. The way to assure treasure in heaven is by sending it on ahead, because all treasure on earth is left here where it will do us absolutely no good in eternity.

The rich farmer discovered that. No sooner had he made his grand plans when God stepped in and said, "That's enough!" The term "demanded" in Luke 12:20 is the same word used for a loan that has been called. God owns our lives, and he can "call it in" whenever he chooses.

Money and possessions do not go into eternity; only people do. The best use of our wealth is to invest it in people! Let's not build our lives around what can't last and doesn't really matter.

*Father, I choose to invest my treasure in heaven and in people. I want to be rich
towards you above all. In Jesus' name. Amen.*

Does God Want Christians Rich or Poor?

"But it is God who judges; he brings one down, he exalts another."
Psalm 75:7

When we ask if God wants us rich or poor, what we're really wondering is, "What is the appropriate lifestyle for a Christian?" We're disciples of Jesus Christ. Should we live as paupers and be content or earn all we can as good stewards? There is no right answer.

As the above verse shows, it is God who decides. We do have some input, of course. If we choose to be slothful it stands to reason we won't be featured in Fortune 500 anytime soon. We can also pursue wealth to the seclusion of all else and miss out on rewards in heaven. It is our character, our heart attitude that God cares about. Does he want you rich? Well, what would it do to you? Would it allow you to be generous or feed your greed? Would having wealth make you less dependent on God?

Because only the Lord knows us well enough to know what's best for us, he will use our financial circumstances to shape us into the people he wants us to become. He may do that by having you live hand-to-mouth for a season. He may encourage you to give beyond what you're comfortable with. God has dozens of means at his disposal to teach us and form us. We need to stay close to him to better understand the lessons he puts before us, so he doesn't have to repeat them! He is patient, and will keep placing us in the same circumstances until we learn.

The best advice I can give is this: Whatever he shows you, obey immediately. His will is not hidden; he will guide you to the appropriate lifestyle for you. Our occupations determine a great deal of where we are socio-economically; a mechanic and a lawyer are obviously going to be at different levels. And that's good, we're all needed! Rich or poor, God will use us to serve him and others.

Lord, I acknowledge that it is you who exalts me or brings me down, and I trust that you know exactly what it is I need. I pray in the name of Jesus. Amen.

The Power of Giving

*"Do not lay up for yourselves treasures upon earth, where moth and
rust destroy, and where thieves break in and steal. But lay up for yourselves treasure in heaven, where neither moth nor rust destroys, and
where thieves do not break in and steal. For where your treasure is,
there your heart will be also." Matthew 6:19-21*

The Bible is a book about giving. Faith is mentioned 246 times;
hope appears 185 times; love, 733 times. Giving—2,285 times!
Obviously giving is a value very near to the heart of God. Our heart
will follow where our money goes. If we're giving to the work of God's
kingdom, our heart will be there. That's how it works.

The point Jesus makes in this passage is that it's foolish to invest in
a bunch of stuff that deteriorates and won't go into eternity with us.
How much better to have treasure in heaven that will never decay,
doesn't have to be insured, and never has to be cleaned!

Giving is the antidote to materialism. It strikes at the very root of
our selfishness; it takes us out of ourselves and our own little box to
participate with God in his work of redeeming the world.

Money spent in offerings to God is money that will never be
wasted. He multiplies what we give in ways we can't imagine. To para-
phrase Jim Elliot, we give what we can't keep to gain what we can never
lose. So why don't we give more?

We don't give because our hearts are clinging to the things of this
earth. To be a true follower of Jesus means that we obey his commands
(John 14:15) and his commands are not burdensome (1 John 5:3).
Giving blesses *us*! If we could only get our minds around this truth!

Please follow the trail of your treasure and find your heart. Then
you can decide if that is where you should keep it.

*Lord God, I want to be near to your heart. Your word tells me that giving is a way
that I can. I choose to invest in eternity, and send my treasure on ahead. For Jesus'
sake, Amen.*

Extravagance

"Then Mary took about a pint of pure nard, an expensive perfume; she poured it out on Jesus' feet and wiped his feet with her hair." John 12:3

If I could choose to have been any Bible character, it would be Mary of Bethany. Every time she appears in Scripture, she is at the feet of Jesus. Her final act of worship has her breaking a jar of perfume so costly it was worth a year's wages. Yet she willingly poured out every drop over her Master.

It was an act of supreme devotion and sacrifice, and as many such acts are, it was misunderstood by those who observed it. "Why wasn't this perfume sold and the money given to the poor?" one bystander asked. Jesus is quick to her defense. "Leave her alone. It was intended that she should save this perfume for the day of my burial. You will always have the poor among you, but you will not always have me" (John 12:7-8).

Where do we get the notion that God is cheap? Here we see him approving of an act so extravagant it's breathtaking. Sometimes love costs a lot. Sometimes it should. We can get so bent about "waste" that we lose our perspective. The churches built today are nothing like the cathedrals erected in the Middle Ages. Then, God's house was worthy of the finest materials and workmanship, taking decades to complete. I'm sure there were those who stood around complaining about the "excessiveness" of it all, and how the money would be better spent to help the poor village in which it stood. And perhaps they had a point.

But when it came to God selecting the materials to be used in Israel's tabernacle, no expense was spared. When Solomon built the temple, same thing—solid gold everywhere. It would make many of us nervous to even enter a building that extravagant!

There are times in our lives when frugality should be set aside, times when it glorifies God, and when an act of devotion demands the very best we have to offer.

Lord, make my life a broken vase, poured out for you. You alone are worthy of my best. In the glorious name of Jesus. Amen.

Sacrifice Should Cost

"But King David replied to Araunah, 'No, I insist on paying the full price. I will not take for the Lord what is yours, or sacrifice a burnt offering that costs me nothing.'" 1 Chronicles 21:24

Because King David had sinned in taking a census of his fighting men, the Lord sent a plague on Israel. As he was about to destroy Jerusalem, he became grieved and told the angel to withdraw his hand. The angel was standing at Araunah's threshing floor when David looked up from his petitioning and saw him. The angel ordered him to build an altar on the threshing floor and David immediately went to Araunah to request that he sell the threshing floor to him.

Araunah fell all over himself in generosity, offering to give David not only the threshing floor but also the oxen, the wood, and the wheat. Maybe the sight of an angel moved him; maybe it was the love and devotion he had for his king. He certainly wasn't wrong in making the offer, but David knew it would be wrong to accept it.

By very definition, a sacrifice is something surrendered at a loss to us. We really haven't experienced sacrifice in middle-class America today. We speak self-righteously of the "sacrifice" it took to put our kids through school, but what did we really give up to do that? New cars? A bigger house?

Sacrifice to me is one of those holy words I dare not regard lightly. I think of Abraham binding his son Isaac to the altar, of the disciples leaving all to follow Jesus, of Jesus giving his life on the cross. Sacrificial giving is genuinely giving up and going without to give to God.

King David paid six hundred shekels of gold for the threshing floor. It served not only as a one-time altar for the offering to stop the plague, but it became the site of the future temple his son Solomon would build. I'm sure David considered it the best six hundred shekels he ever spent.

Lord God, I confess that I misuse that word sacrifice. Teach me the true meaning of it, and how you would require me to practice it. In Jesus' precious name. Amen.

The Poor Widow's Offering

"As he looked up, Jesus saw the rich putting their gifts into the temple treasury. He also saw a poor widow put in two very small copper coins. 'I tell you the truth,' he said, 'this poor widow has put in more than all the others. All these people gave their gifts out of their wealth, but she in her poverty put in all she had to live on.'" Luke 21:1-4

Jesus was a people watcher. Here he is sitting in the court of women where the treasury boxes were, observing the worshippers drop in their offerings. The rich are possibly making quite a show of it, being sure everyone sees and knows how much they are contributing. Jesus is not impressed. He is drawn to a woman as she quietly slips in two little copper coins, worth half a cent.

Jesus does not care about the amount. He is looking at her heart. He knows what this represents. Wanting to worship God, despite her poverty, she gives it all, trusting that God will somehow meet her needs. Touched by the quality of her gift, Jesus points this out to his disciples.

Why would he evaluate and compare people's giving? Because money speaks! Money reveals the posture of our hearts. Maybe we can fake it to people, but we can't fool God. He knows our capacity to give; he knows when we give from abundance and when we make a true sacrifice. He never begrudges anyone for giving a small gift when it's all they have.

This shatters the excuse that the poor don't need to give since they have so little. Jesus did not rush to stop her, knowing the conditions she was living in. He didn't minister to her in any way that we're told about. He only holds her up as a shining example of the measurement that really counts, that of a willing heart.

Lord, sometimes I lose sight of the truth that it's the proportion of my giving that matters. Show me my giving through your eyes, I ask in Jesus' name. Amen.

February

The Rich Young Ruler

"Jesus answered, 'If you want to be perfect, go, sell your possessions and give to the poor, and you will have treasure in heaven. Then come, follow me.'" Matthew 19:21

We get into trouble with this verse when we fail to consider the full context in which it appears. It is not a broad command given to all believers; it is the response given to a young man who was seeking, but had a big obstacle in his path. The fact that Jesus recognized this is revealed in the commandments he omitted in reply to the man's inquiry: Do not have any other gods, do not make any idols, do not misuse the name of the Lord, do not covet. To the six he did mention, the man could say he had kept them. Yet he instinctively knew that wasn't good enough, because his next question was, "What do I still lack?"

Jesus, in love, pointed out the one area of his heart not fully devoted to God—his wealth. Because that was the one area he was not willing to relinquish, the young man turned away from Jesus in sorrow. Notice Jesus didn't run after him, calling, "Wait! Perhaps I was being a little hard..." in an attempt to soften the blow and gain a disciple. No, Jesus meant what he said, and let him leave. He will not tolerate any halfway devotion. He knows our biggest struggle in surrendering to God involves our money; still he insists that we voluntarily give even this over to him.

This does not mean that all of us should live as Jesus and the disciples did, with only the clothes on our backs. It does mean, however, that if Jesus asks us to uproot and serve him elsewhere that our possessions and personal comfort would not hold us back. We are to hold everything loosely.

So, no you don't have to sell everything you own to gain eternal life. But if Jesus asked you to, would you? Could you?

Lord, this is a hard teaching. How entrenched we are in the material world! Purify my heart, and rid it of every idol. In Jesus' name. Amen.

How Hard It Is for the Rich!

"It is easier for a camel to go through the eye of a needle than for a rich man to enter the kingdom of God." Mark 10:25

Because I struggle with getting a thread through the eye of a needle, I can appreciate the difficulty involved in getting the largest animal in Palestine through one! This remark of Jesus has been explained away as being an exaggeration, or that "the eye of a needle" was a gate into the city that camels had to kneel down in order to enter (demonstrating humility), and other such allegories.

The disciples took him literally. They were amazed, and looked at each other: "Who then can be saved?" To the Jews of their day, the rich were blessed by God; that's why they were rich. If God's favored ones had no hope, what chance did the disciples have? Jesus assures them that anything is possible with God; in fact it is *only* God who can save anyone. What he is saying is that the rich tend to rely and depend on their money. Wealth can exert a negative influence over a person's life that drags him away from a wholehearted pursuit of God.

We need to see it as a grace of God that he is preserving many of us from such an entanglement that has caused the fall of so many. We all know of people who have changed for the worse after amassing their fortunes. It doesn't have to be that way, of course, but it is a danger the wealthy need to be aware of and guard against.

Despite what the first-century Jews thought, the rich do not have an "in" with God. Neither do the poor. The ground is level at the foot of the cross. All of us have to come with nothing but ourselves, willing to offer everything to the one who made it possible for all—rich, poor, and everything in between—to enter the kingdom of God.

Father, break me of any belief that I am "better" than anyone else because of my bank balance. Humble me and make me see my need of you in everything. I pray in Jesus' name. Amen.

*February*

Godliness with Contentment

"But godliness with contentment is great gain." 1 Timothy 6:6

To be content is a value that seems all too elusive in our society today. We are a nation of *dis*contents in pursuit of more/bigger/better. The average person owes $8,000 to a credit card institution. We constantly upgrade our computers so we don't get stuck with last month's technology. We trade in our cars for a new one every two years.

If you've been able to stay off the consumer treadmill, congratulations. But are you content? Are you satisfied with what you have, right now, today? Or do you find yourself engaging in thinking that goes, "I'll be happy when I have a (fill in the blank)." When we do acquire the object of our desire, we up the ante and find something else we want.

Contentment is not complacency. We need to have goals and strive to better ourselves. Contentment is not laziness. We need to work on having orderly lives. The flip side of contentment is covetousness which leads to complaining and demonstrates ungratefulness to God for all that he has given us. We all have what we need; it's our wants that get us into trouble.

Contentment is a state of mind. It's every day telling yourself, "I have everything I need. God is good. When I do have a need, God promises to provide for it. I will not knock myself out trying to provide for all my wants."

Will it be easy? Of course not. We live in a restless culture that is never satisfied and we are constantly being bombarded with advertising that programs us to believe we can't possibly be happy if we don't have whatever-it-is they're selling. Contentment is a choice. You make the decision to be content; you don't fall into it, like falling into a ditch. Pair contentment with godliness (a good and holy life) and you will have greater riches than the millionaires of this world will ever know, and no one can ever take that away from you.

Father, like the apostle Paul, I want to learn to be content. I will give thanks to you on a daily basis for your many blessings to me. In Jesus' name. Amen.

February

The Concept of "Enough"

"Keep falsehood and lies far from me; give me neither poverty nor riches, but give me only my daily bread. Otherwise, I may have too much and disown you and say, 'Who is the Lord?' Or I may become poor and steal, and so dishonor the name of my God." Proverbs 30:8-9

In his prayer Agur is asking God for just enough to sustain him one day at a time. This is a foreign idea to us; we've been trained to stockpile food (in case of emergency), clothing (so the fashion police won't arrest us for being seen in the same thing twice), and paper products (we live in fear of running out of toilet paper). Daily bread? Not for us Sam's Club members!

While it can sometimes make sense to buy in bulk, do we really need to lay in a ton of supplies in case war breaks out or another unexpected disaster occurs? There's always a sale on, somewhere. You won't miss out. You'll also find you have much less waste. When my kids were little they'd go on food sprees where they would eat the same thing four times a day for months, but as soon as I bought it in bulk, they decided they were sick of it and never touched it again. The local food banks profited, but from then on, I decided our grocery buying would be week to week.

How much is enough? It's different for everyone, but for most it's a lot less than what we're accustomed to. The Great Depression has left its legacy on some of us who didn't even live through it, but we "heard the stories." Consequently, we live in fear of suffering serious deprivation if we don't continue to fill our homes to the bursting with all the flotsam of consumer America.

Try to imagine life without buying a single thing you don't need or truly want. Wouldn't you feel free? Wouldn't your bank account benefit? Wouldn't you have more time without the need to shop so much?

Enough. It's a concept I can live with.

Father, you know what I need and you have promised to supply it. Give me this day my daily bread, I ask in Jesus' name. Amen.

How to Decrease Your Goods

"As good increase, so do those who consume them. And what benefit are
they to the owner except to feast his eyes on them?" Ecclesiastes 5:11

I really regret not learning this truth sooner: There is such a thing as a fulfillment ceiling, and beyond that point, the more material things we have only bring us frustration and anxiety. My husband was born knowing this. He has no consumer vices. The definition of *consume*, by the way, isn't pretty: "To spend wastefully; squander; use up; to do away with completely." *Consumer goods* is telling: "Goods that directly satisfy human wants."

I would argue that they *don't* satisfy human wants—they only make us want more. I developed a list of questions to ask myself before bringing anything new home. Run all your purchases through this grid:

- Do I need it?
- Do I need it now?
- Can I buy it later?
- Can I get it cheaper?
- Can I ask for it as a gift?
- Will this simplify my life?
- Does it fit my lifestyle?
- Is this adding to the quality of my life or is it just taking money from me?
- Do I love it? Does it make my heart leap?
- Why do I want this? (Honestly!)
- Is it clutter?

And the clincher...

- Will this end up in the yard sale?

Anything that can survive this list is probably a worthy purchase, unless I'm lying to myself! Yard sales, by the way, are an excellent means of decluttering. Give it all away otherwise, but by all means, free yourself from the stuff that doesn't satisfy and weighs you down from enjoying the stuff that does!

You'll find that as the clutter is eliminated from your home, the clutter in your soul drops away as well. There is a peace that comes with knowing you have everything you need and nothing you don't. Less *is* more.

Father, with your help I desire to change my consumer behavior. Help me to clear
away the debris around me so I can be free, I ask in Jesus' name. Amen.

Loving Pleasure

"He who loves pleasure will become poor; whoever loves wine and oil will never be rich." Proverbs 21:17

We could all find exceptions to this verse, but the principle remains: Spend too much on lavish living and you will end up in want in your later years. A penchant for luxury goods exercised without restraint will have us living elevated lifestyles we will find difficult to give up should our financial situation suffer any kind of setback.

There are families whose finances are in jeopardy because of someone's (usually the husband's) obsession with a hobby. They are funding a pleasure they financially have no business indulging. Other habits are even more money consuming. Gambling is a huge industry in this country; you no longer have to go to Vegas to lose your shirt. Folks have racked up huge debts to casinos and now there are extended lines of credit, cash advances on credit cards, and ATM machines with overdraft protection right next to the slot machines.

Love of travel is another area where people tend to indulge, blowing thousands of dollars on a once-in-a-lifetime vacation. Nothing is wrong with seeing the world and having a hobby, *if you can afford it.* Examine your lifestyle and look for those areas where you can cut down.

What is your heart attitude towards these indulgences? Can you shrug and say, "Okay, we could save money if I didn't do this anymore," and leave it at that? Or are you addicted to your pleasures? We may feel we're entitled to eating at the best restaurants, owning a fancy car, and living in a large house. Oddly enough, though, studies have shown that millionaires don't live this way. They tend to be very frugal, traditional people, disciplining their appetites for the finer things in life while they were building their net worth.

Regrettably, many of us have perhaps subconsciously bought into the hedonistic motto, "You only go around once, so live it up!" Yes, but at what price?

Father, reveal to me any love of luxury that should not be there. Release me from any addiction to pleasures that are not honoring to you. For Jesus' sake. Amen.

Driving Out the Enemy

*"When the Lord your God has delivered them over to you and you have
defeated them, then you must destroy them totally. Make no treaty
with them, and show them no mercy." Deuteronomy 7:2*

Have you made some progress in your quest to master your money?
Maybe you've downscaled in some areas; perhaps you have a plan
to get yourself out of debt, or you could be tithing for the first time.
Whatever changes you have implemented, guard them zealously or you
will find yourself slipping back into old habits and practices.

When the Israelites entered the Promised Land, the Lord told them
they were to utterly destroy its inhabitants as he knew if they were
allowed to remain, it would be flirting with disaster. The temptation to
adopt the inhabitant's lifestyle and customs, especially their idolatrous
religious practices, would be too great.

If we have struggles with money, we should see this as an area of
weakness in which we can allow no compromise. If we truly want to be
free, we must eliminate everything that would cause us to stumble. If
you can't handle credit cards responsibly, cut them up. Don't think you
can keep them around for an emergency. And you must be faithful to
the tithe. You must never tell yourself, "I'm a little short this month,"
and rob God. Kill that kind of thinking!

We must destroy all the "carved images and cast idols" and demolish all the "high places" that exist in our financial landscape. Know the
places that give you trouble and bring them down. Drive that prover-
bial stake in the ground and say to the Lord, "I'm done with this. I've
put it to death."

Maintaining change over the long haul is where your commitment
will really be tested. Don't think Satan doesn't know all the cracks in
your armor. It's difficult to do this on your own willpower. Get on your
knees and ask your heavenly Father to provide the strength you lack.

*Lord God, I commit to driving out the enemies I've allowed to hang around in my
finances. Go ahead of me and destroy them so I can be free. In Jesus' name. Amen.*

Seeking Wise Counsel

"A wise man has great power, and a man of knowledge increases strength; for waging war you need guidance, and for victory many advisors." Proverbs 24:5-6

If people would only seek wise counsel *before* making a major financial decision, they would avoid much grief and hardship. In our experience as financial counselors, couples come in for help a month too late—*after* they've just signed that four-year lease on the new minivan, bought a house they can't afford, or taken on the furniture store's offer of no payments until New Year's. They soon realize they're in over their heads, and come to us for help in bailing them out. There's nothing we can do at that point; they'll have to live with their mistakes for years to come.

We've concluded that often such people have already made up their minds as to what they're going to do, and no one is going to tell them otherwise. They don't want to hear that their dream house is out of reach at this point in their financial lives. They *need* a new vehicle, and because they have no down payment, well, to them a lease seems the reasonable thing to do. But God's Word is filled with admonition to seek counsel—not only in money matters but in every area of our lives.

If we struggle with money, it makes sense to talk to people who are experienced and have proven to be good stewards. Even if you feel you totally understand a situation, other people may see it from an angle that never occurred to you. They may see things in the fine print that you missed, or be able to foresee a potential problem down the road. If so, wouldn't you want to know about it before you commit to something that you can't extricate yourself from?

Please, seek wise counsel first. Learn from the mistakes of others. It's much cheaper than making them all yourself.

Lord God, please give me the grace to humble myself and seek counsel before I act. Provide sources that are biblical and that I can trust. I ask in Jesus' name. Amen.

Cosigning? Don't!

"Do not be a man who strikes hands in pledge or puts up security for debts; if you lack the means to pay, your very bed will be snatched from under you." Proverbs 22:26-27

Here is one financial decision you will not ever have to seek counsel about—cosigning on a loan for someone. The Bible is very clear we are not to do it.

- "He who puts up security for another will surely suffer, but whoever refuses to strike hands in pledge is safe" (Proverbs 11:15).
- "A man lacking in judgment strikes hands in pledge and puts up security for his neighbor" (Proverbs 17:18).

Not yet convinced?

- "My son, if you have put up security for your neighbor, if you have struck hands in pledge for another, if you have been trapped by the words of your mouth, then do this, my son, to free yourself, since you have fallen into your neighbor's hands; go and humble yourself; press your plea with your neighbor!" (Proverbs 6:1-3.)

It's simply a very foolish thing to do. If a creditor does not trust this person to repay a loan, why should you? It doesn't matter if it's a relative or your best friend—no exceptions. If you think refusing to help them will strain your friendship, what kind of relationship do you think you will have if you end up having to cover this person's financial obligation?

Too many sad testimonies abound of people who really got cleaned out after co-signing for a "dear friend" who defaulted. In Bible times, to take on responsibility for someone's debt could end in slavery, as when Judah offered himself to Joseph so Benjamin could be safely returned to Jacob (see Genesis 44:32-33). The risk we run today is losing all our savings and possibly even our homes. Protect yourself. Be wise, not sorry.

Father, I ask now for the courage to refuse if anyone asks me co-sign a loan for them. I want to obey your word in all things. In Jesus' name. Amen.

Bankruptcy Is *Not* An Option

"The wicked borrow and do not repay, but the righteous give gener-
ously." Psalm 37:21

Seventy couples attended a budget workshop we held; corporately, they owed around $2 million in consumer debt. Many of these people wanted to make their financial problems go away by simply declaring bankruptcy. But not so fast. Laws have changed so that all that gets discharged are credit card debts. Mortgage payments, student loans, and car loans all continue on. Not much of a solution, is it? Not to mention what declaring bankruptcy does to your life for years to follow.

If you're forced into involuntary bankruptcy by your creditors, you can't do anything about it, but you are still obligated to pay the debt in full. The evil is not in declaring bankruptcy, but in doing so to escape paying back what you owe. That is being a cheat—not only to the financial institution that lent you the money in good faith, but to the rest of us who have to pay for your folly through higher costs in consumer goods and services.

Most people can work out an alternative as creditors want to be paid and are willing to work with you. It takes honesty and communication, along with sacrifice. God is capable of redeeming any situation. What he cares about most is the attitude of your heart. Are you assuming responsibility for your actions and are you willing to do whatever it takes to get out of this mess?

Bankruptcy is legal but it's not moral. It is a black mark on your credit report for seven to ten years. And what does it do to your testimony? Catastrophic medical expenses or lawsuits can put us into financial stews not of our own making, but "convenience bankruptcy" has no place in the life of a Christian.

Lord, if my situation seems hopeless, I will turn to you for mercy. Make a way where there seems to be no way. I ask in Jesus' powerful name. Amen.

Debt Free Living

"Let no debt remain outstanding, except the continuing debt to love
one another, for he who loves his fellowman has fulfilled the law."
Romans 13:8

In the verse previous to this one, Paul tells his listeners to give every-one what they are owed; he acknowledges that debt might exist, but it is not a normal situation. Some teach that any debt over six years is forbidden in Scripture, putting home ownership out of reach of many sincere Christians who want to be obedient. I believe God's Word doesn't prohibit borrowing, but we have to stop thinking of long-term debt, such as 30-year mortgages, as acceptable. The solution is to pay your mortgage off early by making principal only payments.

The problem comes when you can barely manage the payment itself, let alone anything above and beyond. This is a case of more house than you can afford. To avoid this, borrow no more than double your annual gross salary. This will keep your payments reasonable, and paying an extra $100 a month could cut fifteen years off the life of the loan. Bi-monthly payments save thousands in interest, usually shaving off seven years.

So while it may not be possible to purchase a home with cash, it is very possible to own it free and clear quite quickly. If you commit to it, you'd be amazed at what God can do. We retired the mortgage on our current home in five years. Forget the tax deduction; any time you pay interest you lose.

Imagine life without debt! Carrying debt weighs us down in our souls. It may not make economic sense if we have a low interest rate, but I believe in the spiritual realm it is far better to be free of the psy-chological burden debt lays on us. I've heard people say, "You will always have a house payment, and you will always have a car payment." Yes, you will—if you believe it, it becomes a self-fulfilling prophecy.

Debt free living is possible, and it is available to everyone.

Father, reprogram my mind from a society that says debt is necessary and unavoid-
able. Help me to bring my desire level down to my income level. I ask in Jesus'
name. Amen.

Who Are the Poor?

"Is it not to share your food with the hungry and to provide the poor wanderer with shelter—when you see the naked, to clothe him, and not to turn away from your own flesh and blood?" Isaiah 58:7

Is a person poor if they don't have enough money to pay their bills? Think carefully. It's a trick question! The answer is no. The inability to pay your bills does not make you poor. Plenty of people with six-figure incomes can't meet their expenses each month.

So how do we define the poor in our society today? The unemployed? The homeless? Those who live on the wrong side of the tracks? The incarcerated? Can we make a sweeping generalization as to who qualifies as poor?

Yes—if you don't have enough to supply yourself and your family with food, clothing, and shelter, then you're poor. This is not "living in a bad neighborhood" or driving an old beater car. We've extended the idea of being poor to include those who ride the city bus or live in a trailer park, and we tend to look down on those people. We blame their poverty on personal laziness, lack of education, or lack of jobs, and we often fail to see them as people who matter to God.

We live in a fallen world, filled with injustice, oppression, crime, and disease. Until Jesus comes again to this earth, these conditions are not going to go away. We will continue to have to deal with the poor; not ignoring them or looking away in embarrassment, or saying they are someone else's problem, not ours. Much of Jesus' ministry was to the poor. He had compassion on them and made them an object of his special concern.

We need the heart of Jesus in regard to the underprivileged and we must never forget that "rich and poor have this in common: The LORD is the Maker of them all" (Proverbs 22:2).

Father, give me your heart towards the poor, that I would see them as valuable human beings who matter. Show me how I can make a difference in their lives. For Jesus' sake. Amen.

Lending to the Lord

"He who is kind to the poor lends to the Lord, and he will reward him for what he has done." Proverbs 19:17

Did you know that God regards it as a gift to him when we help the poor? "He who oppresses the poor shows contempt for their Maker; but whoever is kind to the needy honors God" (Proverbs 14:31). When we are sensitive to their needs, we lock arms with God, for he is on their side.

What are some practical ways we can show the love of God to the poor? Our church has what we call "Compassion Block Parties" where a group will go out to a park in a underprivileged neighborhood on a Saturday and serve food, hand out bags of groceries and clothing, provide a live worship band and games for the kids (including a "bounce" room), and of course, proclaim the gospel and pray for people. As an individual, you can volunteer at a homeless shelter, donate food to your local food bank, or get involved with Habitat for Humanity. You also can donate clothing and other needed household supplies to families in need.

If you really want to make a difference in the life of a child, consider sponsorship through a worthy organization such as Compassion International. We are sponsoring our third child now, and the letters we have received from them over the years are truly precious. It has been one of the most rewarding things we've ever been involved in.

Get your kids involved with you, and encourage them to think of others less fortunate than themselves. We can stem the tide of selfishness if we begin modeling love and care for the poor for the next generation. If we really love God, we can do no less.

Lord, you are the God of the poor and downtrodden, and your heart beats with concern for them. I want to be part of the solution; give me opportunities to show your love to them in my own city, in my nation, and around the world. Use what I have, Father, however small that might be, but bless the poor through me. For Jesus' sake, Amen.

Faithful in Little Things

"Whoever can be trusted with very little can also be trusted with much, and whoever is dishonest with very little will also be dishonest with much. So if you have not been trustworthy in handling worldly wealth, who will trust you with true riches? And if you have not been trustworthy with someone else's property, who will give you property of your own?" Luke 16:10-12

Hopefully, starting when we're very young, we have learned the importance of hard work, diligence, and being trustworthy. If we have not, Jesus says that this will prevent us from being truly effective in his kingdom.

God uses money and possessions as a tool to test us. Things as simple as paying your bills on time—all your bills, no matter how small the amount. I once wrote a check for 61 cents to pay off a credit card. I felt foolish; I felt even more foolish putting a 34-cent stamp on it to mail it. But I owed the money, and wanted to cancel the account. *Faithful in little things.* God was pleased; he certainly would not have been had I just blown it off as being too miniscule to bother about.

We have to stop assigning different values of importance to our obligations; they are *all* important. If we borrowed something from someone (especially a book!), we need to return it in a timely fashion. If we don't, and our friends are reduced to either begging or threats to get it back, how soon do you think they'll lend us anything again? If you rent, are you a good tenant? Or will the landlord keep your security deposit to clean up your mess when you move out? Being irresponsible or untrustworthy can cost us.

By your behavior with money, can God trust you with true riches—the things of highest value with eternal consequences, like a fruitful ministry or a position of spiritual authority? Wake up to all those little details in your finances you've dismissed as trivial. They're not trivial to God.

Father, forgive me for all the little indiscretions I've made with money over my lifetime. Bring to mind anyone I need to make restitution to. For Jesus' sake. Amen.

To Whom Much Is Given

"From everyone who has been given much, much will be demanded;
and from the one who has been entrusted with much, much more will
be asked." Luke 12:48

I knew a couple who understood this verse very well—and shrank from it. They stated, in essence, that it was a relief for them to always be broke, because then they didn't have to tithe ("there's no way we could tithe") and they could escape from the accountability they felt would be theirs if they were not living hand to mouth. They did not want to have "much demanded" of them, even though they were living under considerable financial stress. They were so fearful of being required to give, they pushed money away and kept themselves in need.

Still, they're not off the hook. The great thing about tithing is that 10 percent is always 10 percent, whether it's $5 or $5,000. How would you feel if you received $50,000 a month? Elated? Would you write that check to your church for $5,000 faithfully? If you gasp, "That's a lot of money!" remember, from everyone who is given much, much will be demanded. Perhaps your income level is directly tied in to your level of comfort in giving!

If God blesses you with abundance, he expects a return on his investment. He does not send financial increase into the lives of his children for them to squander on their pleasures. He expects that money to be available for kingdom work and helping the needy. Keeping ourselves needy by choice is a rather perverse way of thwarting God's intentions to bless us and others through us. He can, and does, bless us by giving us peace, joy, and righteousness when we are walking in the light, but even these gifts make demands on us spiritually.

We are accountable, whether we want to be or not. In that we have no choice, but we can choose to reward God for his faith in us.

Lord, I do believe the truth in this verse, and I know it to be a kingdom principle. I release to you any areas I've selfishly held back. In Jesus' name I pray. Amen.

Put Your Hope in God

"Command those who are rich in this present world not to be arrogant nor to put their hope in wealth, which is so uncertain, but to put their hope in God, who richly provides us with everything for our enjoyment." 1 Timothy 6:17

You may not think of yourself as rich, but if you live in the United States, on a global scale you most certainly are. The apostle Paul is addressing *us*. Throughout history, affluence has repeatedly led people away from God. It is more dangerous from a spiritual standpoint to be prosperous than it is to be in poverty. The poor know they are dependent on God, and they have learned not to put their security in things. It doesn't take a lot of faith for God to provide for you when you're sitting on an ample bank account.

When life is going well for us, we have a tendency to forget the source. Our ego can become inflated as we slide into thinking that somehow we are responsible for our success. We must realize we have no reason to be arrogant about anything; to put our hope in wealth is to build on a very shaky foundation.

If you don't think wealth is uncertain, ask anyone who was involved in dot com stocks. They were millionaires—briefly. They staked their hopes and dreams on Wall Street, and it all came crashing down around them. Some committed suicide. Their hope was in wealth, and wealth let them down.

Paul reminds us that God will not let you down. He will be there for you no matter what the markets do or if you lose your job. We don't have to live in fear of recessions or inflation or even depressions. God want us unshakable, looking to him, not to our 401k plan. God is not poor, nor is he stingy. He "richly provides us with everything for our enjoyment." With a heavenly Father like that, we can be confident that our hope is not in vain.

Lord, you are my rock, my sure foundation; in you I put my trust. I know I will always need you, no matter how successful I become. In the name of Jesus I pray. Amen.

Who Wants to Be a Millionaire?

"People who want to get rich fall into temptation and a trap and into many foolish and harmful desires that plunge men into ruin and destruction." 1 Timothy 6:9

Who wants to be a millionaire? Just about everyone, if we look at the media and observe our society. The game show of that name is one of television's most popular offerings, and more and more outrageous contests are being invented to see how far people are willing to go to get rich. Books on how to accumulate wealth fill the best-seller lists. People will travel across state lines and line up for blocks in hopes of purchasing the winning ticket when the lotto jackpot climbs to an astonishing nine figures. Stories and data on millionaires fascinate us; the sports news focus more on athletes' salaries than stats, and even the church has fallen into the "prosperity movement."

What does God think of all this? From New Testament teaching, it would seem our Lord is down on wealth. Actually, it is the *pursuit* of wealth that ruins us. It can begin as innocently as playing the stock market; if we experience some success we're suddenly willing to take more risks, either by short-selling or buying on margin. People have lost their homes this way, leveraging the equity they have in speculation.

The things people will do for money! In the mid 1840s they were willing to pack up and go west because there was gold in California. In the 1980s they were willing to work 70 hour weeks. Today they're willing to make a total fool of themselves on national television, even marry a stranger, for an opportunity to be rich. We need to examine our own hearts; how far are we willing to go? Are there any money-chasing activities we're engaging in that compromise our relationship with God? Be honest. Do you want to be a millionaire?

Father, thank you for your warnings about where the pursuit of wealth can end. Guard my heart, Lord, and let me not fall into the trap of desiring riches above godliness. Make me more like Jesus. In his name I pray. Amen.

Don't Set Your Heart on Riches

"Do not trust in extortion or take pride in stolen goods; though your riches increase, do not set your heart on them." Psalm 62:10

This is a theme woven throughout all the Scriptures: Do not place your trust, your hope, your security, your comfort, or your faith in money. What is the allure of money that it can drive us to do things so contrary to what the Bible teaches?

It's not money itself that attracts us; it's what money can do—at least the *illusion* of what it can do. Money holds out false promises that appeal to our fallen natures. We think having enough of it will give us god-like sovereignty; we won't need anybody or anything. Money claims it will lead us to a place of inner satisfaction. It offers us feelings of self-worth and importance, even power. As we look at the world around us, we can't deny that it is the wealthy who are respected, who control things, who have every material desire met. Then we look at ourselves—struggling to pay bills, not being able to take a day off, afraid of Social Security not being there for us when we need it, and longing to buy some object of our desire without guilt just because we want it. It would seem that money is the answer to our problems.

We honestly believe that money will make us happy. If we won't listen to King Solomon when he tells us it doesn't, perhaps we'd listen to David Geffen, a Hollywood producer, who made the statement, "Those who believe that money will make them happy have never had any." There are always those who are "surprised by success" and suddenly find themselves millionaires several times over who will honestly admit they were happier when they were nobodies with modest means.

Satan pushes this money thing so hard because it's a proven device to pull us away from God and an eternal perspective. That's the deception of money. It's not the savior it claims to be.

Lord, prevent me from setting my heart on anything except you. Equip me to handle it properly should my riches increase. I ask in Jesus' name. Amen.

Trembling at God's Word

"This is the one I esteem: he who is humble and contrite in spirit, and trembles at my word." Isaiah 66:2

How seriously do you take what the Bible says about money? Do you see it as commands from the mouth of the Lord that are to be heeded, or do you have the attitude that it's just more friendly advice in a self-help addicted society? Sometimes we seem to put more stock in what Oprah's guests have to say on the subject than our sovereign Lord. Why is this?

Do we believe the creator of the universe is out of touch with current market trends? Do we subconsciously think he is not as intelligent as Bill Gates? Maybe our own intelligence gets in the way and we think we're smarter today than when the Bible was written. Whatever our reasons, God will have none of it.

"I am the LORD Almighty!" he thunders in Malachi, "for I am a great king, and my name is to be feared among the nations" see (Malachi 1:14). God did not lay out his righteous precepts in Scripture for us to decide whether or not they sound good to us. They are there to be obeyed. We are to agree with God on what he says and live our lives accordingly.

When he says debt puts us into bondage, we must believe that to be true and avoid debt. When he says we cannot serve both God and mammon, we know we must make a choice. Yet I see so much of this attitude of "I'll think about that," as though God's commands were optional. It's as though money and finance do not fall under God's domain.

God understands everything there is to know about money. Why wouldn't you want to listen to someone like that? It's high time Christians woke up and started taking God at his word. So many believers' financial lives are in a state of shipwreck because they've been listening to the world and not to the Lord. If that's you, repent! Start trembling and begin obeying.

Almighty God, I come to you with reverence and awe. You are infinitely wiser than any mere human being, and I will obey what you say. In Jesus' name. Amen.

Give to Everyone Who Asks

"Give to everyone who asks you, and if anyone takes what belongs to you, do not demand it back." Luke 6:30

This is one of those hard sayings of Jesus we draw back from. Give to everyone who asks? Every homeless beggar? Every worthy charity that calls to solicit donations? He can't possible mean that! What if we can't afford to? Are there exceptions?

As I was pondering this verse, I realized there is no noun there. Give *what?* Money is the first thing that comes to mind, but it doesn't state that. The Lord brought to my attention Peter and John's experience in Acts 3. On their way to the temple, a lame beggar accosts them asking for alms. They have no money to give, so what do they do?

Peter states, "Silver and gold I do not have, but what I do have I give you: In the name of Jesus Christ of Nazareth, rise up and walk" (Acts 3:6). The man received a healing! What the Lord gave him through Peter was what he needed, not the handout he had asked for. Oftentimes just giving money is the easy way out for us.

Peter and John ended up getting arrested for their service to the lame beggar. Our good deeds usually don't cost us in that way, but they cost us time, which is actually more precious than money since we have such a limited amount available to us. In some situations, a donation of money is exactly what is needed. Other times, offering to pray for someone is worth more than the "silver and gold [we] do not have."

I have found the Lord to be present and directing my actions in such instances. Develop a sensitivity to the Holy Spirit and you will find that obeying this verse isn't as daunting as it seems. As we learn to hold our possessions with an open hand, they become more available to use for the kingdom in ministering to others.

Father, enlighten me to understand what the command of "give to everyone who asks you" is demanding of me. I look forward to what you will do through me, in the name of Jesus. Amen.

Who May Dwell in the Lord's Sanctuary

"Lord, who may dwell in your sanctuary? Who may live on your holy hill? He whose walk is blameless and does what is righteous, and speaks the truth from his heart and has no slander on his tongue, and does his neighbor no wrong and casts no slur on his fellowman, who despises a vile man but honors those who fear the Lord, who keeps his oath, even when it hurts, who lends his money without usury and does not accept a bribe against the innocent. He who does these things will never be shaken." Psalm 15:1-5

This psalm is a list of requirements for those who wish to have access to God in his temple. It spells out the character of a person who would feel at home in God's presence. The one overriding virtue throughout is *honesty*—honesty in speech, in relationships, in keeping our word; honesty in business dealings. Our integrity is to be so sterling that nothing should be able to move us to compromise.

Money tests our integrity like nothing else, in dozens of ways every day. How honest are we when it comes to things like filling out our tax returns, bringing it to a clerk's attention when they've undercharged us, turning in a lost wallet? Is lying a method we employ if it will help bring money our way? Do we fudge the numbers on an expense account, or fail to disclose important information when filling out an application? We can get away with doing them, but not in the eyes of the Lord.

How close to God do we want to be? Do we want to be above reproach, able to dwell on his holy hill? Then we must be scrupulously honest in our handling of money and our financial affairs. In determining how trustworthy we are, money is the acid test.

Almighty God, you are so pure and holy, how can I ever approach you? Only by the blood of Jesus! I claim his cleansing power in my life. Point out to me any places where I stumble in my financial integrity so that I may repent. In Jesus' name. Amen.

Use It or Lose It

"For everyone who has will be given more, and he will have an abundance. Whoever does not have, even what he has will be taken from him." Matthew 25:29

In the parable of the talents, the master has just condemned the lazy servant for burying his talent. He commands that his one talent be given to the servant who doubled his five talents. "But he already has ten!" cried those who were looking on. In other words, "Unfair!" If that's your reaction as well, you need to understand this isn't about equality. It isn't about social justice. It's one of the laws of God's kingdom, which I like to describe as "use it or lose it." It's a principle God has built into the universe and it works in all areas of life.

Everyone has learned algebra in school, but if your job doesn't require that knowledge after graduation, what happens? You forget all those formulas you once had memorized; you "lost" it. On the other hand, if you go on to become an engineer, not only do you use all that x=y stuff, you learn even more complex math theorems.

Apply this principle to anything you wish—money, skills, abilities—and God tells us that if we are willing to use what he has given us, we will be given more. But if we "bury" it, it will be taken from us. God views our use of his gifts very seriously. It's all about stewardship.

How we handle God's truth is another place to see if we are using the revelation we've been given. Are you walking in the light of the truths that you know? Until you are, there will be no more forthcoming. If your thinking about finances isn't starting to be conformed to what God says about them, you won't progress in maturity towards being a good steward.

If you aren't already doing so, just start doing what you do know. Even the smallest efforts will lead to greater things. Work on building your financial muscles. Use them or lose them!

Father, help me put to use all you have given me so I will not suffer loss. In the name of Jesus I pray. Amen.

The Origin of Tithing

"Then Abram gave him a tenth of everything." Genesis 14:20

We cannot get a third of the way through the first book of the Bible before tithing makes an appearance. Apparently the first tither was Abram but for all we know Abel tithed. How fitting that Abram is also our model of justification by works as well as our example of justification by faith.

In Genesis 14, Abram has won a great victory in rescuing his nephew Lot, who had got caught in the middle of a war between the kings of the area. After he has plundered the defeated kings, out of nowhere a priest named Melchizedek appears and blesses Abram. With no prompting or instruction, Abram gives this mysterious priest one tenth of all the plundered goods. Why?

He had never met this man before. Melchizedek's words were apparently enough: "Blessed be Abram by God Most High, creator of heaven and earth. And blessed be God Most High, who delivered your enemies into your hand" (Genesis 14:20). The priest affirmed what Abram surely must have realized—it was the Lord who gave him this incredible victory. Out of gratitude, then, Abram tithed to express what he felt. He'd been asked by God to do some very difficult things, but this act of giving one tenth of everything was done completely voluntarily.

Why one tenth? Why not a third, or twenty percent? There really isn't an explanation, except that God did validate the ten percent when he gave the law later. He himself may well have put the ten percent figure in Abram's mind.

Under the Mosaic law, tithes were to be paid to the priests to support their work in the tabernacle. Melchizedek was a figure of Christ, our great High Priest, and Abram's giving of the tithe to him demonstrates to whom our tithes should be given today—to the body of Christ, our local church. It is not "under the law" now; we are to return to our model Abraham and tithe because of the great blessings God has given us.

Almighty God, you have blessed me so much. I give you my tithes but they are a mere token of my love and thankfulness to you. In Jesus' name. Amen.

Can God Be Against Our Finances?

"You rebuke and discipline men for their sin; you consume their wealth like a moth—each man is but a breath." Psalm 39:11

One way God punishes those who violate his word is to cause them to lose money. His goal in this, of course, is to bring us to the end of ourselves so that we will turn to him. Money is a great attention-getter. Because God wants no competition for our hearts, it shouldn't surprise us when our worship of money brings on divine discipline. If he has to hit us in our wallets to humble us and wake us up, he certainly won't hesitate to do so.

This is different from reaping the consequences of what we've sown. Our own laziness and procrastination can certainly drain our financial resources, but what I'm talking about here is direct discipline from the Lord over outright sin in our lives.

God is not willing to leave us comfortable in our sin. If our consciences are seared so we no longer heed his warnings, he is faithful to not leave us in that condition. He will do whatever it takes to bring us back, even striking us where we are sure to feel it quickly and painfully—in our income. We will be brought to a alert realization of where the source of our wealth really is, and it's not in our jobs or skills. We can lose those things in a moment.

Of course, sometimes it's not due to sin at all; just the Lord doing a new thing in our life. He may want to teach us greater dependence on him, increase our faith, or any of a myriad of reasons only he knows. But we must be aware of our spiritual condition so we can discern if we need to repent.

If we come to him with an open heart and a contrite spirit, he will make known to us what action to take, and he will quickly receive us back.

Heavenly Father, I thank you for your discipline in my life. Show me my sin and give me the courage to turn from it. In Jesus' name I ask. Amen.

Is Money the Answer for Everything?

"A feast is made for laughter, and wine makes life merry, but money is the answer for everything." Ecclesiastes 10:19

My first reaction to this verse is to laugh; it's so outrageous. It actually says that in the Bible? What is Solomon getting at here? Is he being sarcastic? How are we to make sense of this?

It's easy in a situation like this to pull a verse out of context and make a doctrine out of it that the writer never intended. This is one of those instances. Here, Solomon is referring to the dissolute nobles he introduced in verse 16: "Woe to you, O land, when your king is a child, and your princes feast in the morning!" These rulers demonstrate their irresponsibility by partying into the early hours of the day; their only concern is to have a good time. What's worse, says Solomon, is the position of authority these rulers occupy; it gives them a platform for making ridiculous statements like the above.

Do you remember the campaign slogan that made the rounds in the 1990s—"It's the economy, stupid"? Money is the answer to everything! As if nothing else mattered. Many people bought that philosophy, judging by the results at the balloting booths.

So are we take this statement at face value? Of course not! In the larger frame of the entire book of Ecclesiastes, Solomon exerts a great amount of ink in telling us that money is *not* the answer.

It's difficult to follow Solomon at times; he vacillates between cynicism and optimism until we wonder just where he is going. But this wisdom book is so invaluable in presenting life as it really is, it is well worth the effort required in understanding it. I am grateful Solomon's spiritual journey is preserved in the Scriptures so that all of us can learn without making his mistakes ourselves.

Lord God, as I read your Word, help me to discern what is your truth and what is being presented as someone's opinion. Thank you for the wisdom that shows me the way to live a joyful, purposeful life. In Jesus' name I pray. Amen.

Rich Oppressors

"Now listen, you rich people, weep and wail because of the misery that is coming upon you. Your wealth has rotted, and moths have eaten your clothes. Your gold and silver are corroded. Their corrosion will testify against you and eat your flesh like fire. You have hoarded wealth in the last days. Look! The wages you failed to pay the workmen who mowed your fields are crying out against you. The cries of the harvesters have reached the ears of the Lord Almighty. You have lived on earth in luxury and self-indulgence. You have fattened yourselves in the day of slaughter. You have condemned and murdered innocent men, who were not opposing you." James 1:5-6

I had been reading a commentary on some of the practices of slaughterhouses in this country. Workers are forced to work at a fast, dangerous pace under the most horrifying conditions imaginable. Many of these employees are immigrants, hired to do a job no one wants because of the low wages and high risk. The injuries these people endure include deep lacerations from dull knives, loss of limbs, even decapitation and death. All this misery so a corporation can fatten its bottom line. I opened my Bible and there was James 5. I was stunned. What a perfect description of the situation! And I was comforted by the realization that yes, the Lord does see, and he cares. God's justice for the oppressed may not be as swift as we'd like, but it is sure. Their tormentors are accountable, and they will stand before the Lord one day to be judged. I found it interesting, in light of this particular instance, that God compares these rich oppressors to cattle being fattened for slaughter! They are bloated on their wealth, not knowing it will cost them their eternal lives.

Can we make any difference to change things? Of course we can pray, and we can refuse to give our money to any industries that we know exploit their workers. Whatever you give money to, you enable— whether it's a segment of the food industry or clothing manufacturers who use sweatshop labor. You don't have to make yourself crazy over this, but be informed. And if you're an employer, pay your people what they're worth. Remember, the Lord sees.

Father, there is so much injustice and oppression in this world. Show me the difference I can make by changing my consumer habits. In Jesus' name. Amen.

A Reason to Be Rich

"You will be made rich in every way so that you can be generous on every occasion, and through us your generosity will result in thanksgiving to God." 2 Corinthians 9:11

Why would the Lord give a Christian more wealth beyond what he or she needs? The answer is in the above verse: to be a blessing to others. Nowhere in the Bible are we taught to pile up money for our own selfish ends. Yet look at how the majority of us live—working ourselves to death to accumulate for the first half of our lives, and then spending the next half trying to protect the surplus from taxes. Is that any way to live?

Materialism has such a grip on us that we don't even question it anymore. We need to! How can we justify our enormous homes and three cars and stuff, stuff, and more stuff when needs are all around us? How can we excuse ourselves from giving because we are drowning in debt from our consumerism? One day we will stand before God and give an account. What did we do with our wealth? Did we support the church, the body of Christ? Did we help the poor—not a one-time handout, but regularly, consistently?

There is no greater fulfillment than to hear someone giving praise to God for meeting their need and knowing that you played a part in it. Allow yourself to be used! A new electronic toy for you has no eternal value, but money spent on the kingdom, invested in people, has value not only in this life but in the life to come. That's the reason to be rich!

Father God, free me up from money and possessions so that when I do receive them I am equipped to handle them appropriately, sharing them with those who are in need. Make me rich in righteousness, in faith, in mercy—the true riches that last forever. I ask in Jesus' name. Amen.

Pretenders

"One man pretends to be rich, yet has nothing; another pretends to be poor, but has great wealth." Proverbs 13:7

Appearances are deceiving; we all realize that. In this credit driven society when we see someone driving around in a luxury car, we are less apt to think they're wealthy as we are to think they can afford the lease payment. Either way, we are making a judgment based on externals.

People like to create façades that are not really representative of their status. We all know of folks who live way beyond their means to give the illusion of an affluent lifestyle when they're actually one paycheck away from homelessness. There are also people who live very modestly, even miserly, and yet are millionaires. Both groups usually are trying to hide their true condition from the world, due to pride or greed.

What do you think of people who try to look prosperous but actually aren't? Is that something you engage in? If so, why? To stroke your ego? Have you bought into the world's creed of "If you look, think, and act successful, you'll be successful"? You can go bankrupt trying to look successful! Live according to the place God put you for now. It's good to have goals to work towards, but we are not to be hypocrites telling untruths to ourselves and those around us while we're on our way to our goals. Give your dissatisfaction to the Lord and allow him to deal with it.

If you're rich and pretending you're not, why? Are you uncomfortable being well-off because of childhood messages you received about the wealthy being snobs? Are you afraid people will befriend you simply because you have money? Seek the Lord and ask him to show you the root cause of your behavior.

It is important that our financial lives are built upon a foundation of truth. Giving false impressions can eventually destroy us. In the spiritual realm, someone with great wealth can be destitute but a poor person can be rich in eternal treasure. Inwardly or outwardly, our pretense never fools God.

Father, I want to be genuine. Make me transparent in who I really am, whether rich or poor. In Jesus' name I ask. Amen.

The Witness of the Early Church

"Selling their possessions and goods, they gave to anyone as he had need." Acts 2:45

What was it that captured the attention of the citizens of Jerusalem following the Day of Pentecost? Were they talking about the signs and wonders of people speaking in other tongues? Were they marveling at Peter's powerful preaching? Maybe. But the one action of these new believers that spoke louder than any words was the selling of their possessions and giving the proceeds to the needy.

Imagine in Los Angeles if a large portion of the population were having huge yard sales, selling off their excess belongings and using the money to help the homeless. Do you think the community would notice? You bet they would!

It was the same way in Israel 2,000 years ago. God's people had a track record of oppressing the defenseless. But now Jesus had come and paid the price for sin. Risen from the dead, he sent the Holy Spirit to empower all who believe on him. It was this power that broke the spirit of materialism.

Now notice, they weren't selling their homes; they were meeting in their homes for fellowship (Acts 2:46). There's no mention of communal living. They were simply moved to dejunk their lives of everything unnecessary so they could carry on the work of Christ, ministering to the poor and needy. It was this very visible change of heart that was the true testimony of the difference Jesus makes in a person's life.

The result of it all was this: "They enjoyed the favor of the people. And the Lord added to their number daily those who were being saved" (Acts 2:47). Would this work in our day? Christians have been accused of being no different in their lifestyles than non-Christians, and rightly so. We have conformed to this world, and we cling pathetically to our possessions. We need a visitation from the Holy Spirit, to proclaim Christ in how we live and represent him accurately to a cynical world. That will be our greatest witness.

Lord God, I repent of anything in my lifestyle that is misrepresenting you to a lost world. Put to death the power of materialism in my life. I ask in Jesus' name. Amen.

God Controls the Economy

*"This is what the Lord says: 'About this time tomorrow, a seah of flour
will sell for a shekel and two seahs of barley for a shekel at the gate of
Samaria.' The officer on whose arm the king was leaning said to the
man of God, 'Look, even if the Lord should open the floodgates of the
heavens, could this happen?' 'You will see it with your own eyes,'
answered Elisha, 'but you will not eat any of it!'" 2 Kings 7:1-2*

Israel's sins had become so great that the covenant curses had come
to pass; the famine was so severe women were eating their own children. King Joram was blaming the disastrous circumstances on Elisha
and on God himself, not on the disobedience and idolatry of himself
and his nation. He was seeking to kill Elisha when the prophet gave
him the above message.

We shouldn't be surprised at the officer's response. A seah of flour
for a shekel was about double the normal cost, but in a country with
no food, it would be a miracle. And only 24 hours from then?
Impossible! But he forgot that nothing is impossible for God, and he
disregarded who was speaking this word. Elisha was God's mouthpiece;
to doubt his word was to doubt God. Because of that, the next day,
when the people went out of the city to gather the plunder of the scattered Armean army, this officer was trampled in the gateway, "and he
died, just as the man of God had foretold when the king came down to
his house" (2 Kings 7:17).

God takes our unbelief personally and seriously. How seriously do
we take him? Do we believe prophetic words that come out of our own
time concerning the economy? If God warns us that financial disaster
is coming, do we wave it off? As this scripture shows, circumstances
can change overnight, for good or bad. God is sovereign; he is not limited by world conditions.

We aren't to live in fear, but in trust of the one who knows what
the future holds.

*Almighty God, you are in control. I trust you and I know with you I am safe no
matter what the economy does. In Jesus' name I pray. Amen.*

What's a Second Paycheck *Really* Worth?

"Yet when I surveyed all that my hands had done and what I had toiled to achieve, everything was meaningless, a chasing after the wind; nothing was gained under the sun." Ecclesiastes 2:11

Why does a married mother leave her home to go to work? Most often it's a need for income; at least a perceived need for income. There are mothers who work to meet emotional needs, but I'm addressing the mother of young children whose heart breaks every morning when she drops off her kids at the day care center or the sitter's. She wants to be home with them but believes it is financially impossible to do so.

Have you ever sat down and figured out in bottom line dollars and cents what she is actually contributing to the family's net income? The tax bite is usually 33 percent, then there's the tithe, so maybe half the paycheck is left. Now take out all the expenses associated with working—transportation, meals, wardrobe, child care—the obvious stuff. But then what about convenience foods and fast food because she's too tired to cook, expensive alternatives to cleaning, repairs, and other things you don't do because no one has the time or energy; illnesses caused by stress; extra escape entertainment to try to relieve the pressure; treats bought for the kids to make up for feelings of guilt. The list could go on.

What expenses do you have that would go away if Mom stayed home? A teacher in one of our classes did this exercise and was shocked to find she was clearing $300 a *year*; some women are *paying* to go to work. Others are living a fast-track lifestyle because they look at the figure on the paycheck and assume it's all gravy money. It's not.

If you're jolted by this, and you want to be at home, begin now to make changes that would enable you to do so. Don't miss out on raising your children full-time; no paycheck will ever compensate your loss if you do.

Lord, I feel so trapped. I want to be with my family, but I can't see how to make it happen. Move in the circumstances of my life for change. In Jesus' name I ask. Amen.

Is It Wrong for a Mother to Work?

*"Then they can train the younger women to love their husbands and
children, to be self-controlled and pure, to be busy at home, to be kind,
and to be subject to their husbands, so that no one will malign the
word of God." Titus 2:4-5*

Verses like this one have been known to send tempers flaring among
women who consider its counsel to be sexist and demeaning. But
let's take a closer look at who Paul is referring to here. *Young* married
women *with* children, which tells us the children would be young as
well. Other translations use the terms "keepers at home" and "home-
makers." We can agree on this much: All mothers work; a stay at home
mom does not have it easy. Children are very demanding; they need
constant nurturing.

However, nowhere in Scripture are women told to bury their gifts
and talents for the sake of their families, but to use them construc-
tively. Working from home makes this possible. There are hundreds of
ways this can be done without an enormous time commitment; it has
become a very popular option for many women who are exhausted
from the rat race of the corporate world.

It doesn't matter so much what a woman *does*; what God cares
about is who she *is*. It is not wrong for a mother to work, but if what
you're doing makes you feel guilty, try to figure out why. Is it conviction from the Holy Spirit or is it the voice of the world telling you what
you should do and be? Different seasons in your life will also determine any vocation you may pursue. What wouldn't work when your
kids are toddlers may be perfect when they're teenagers. I didn't do any
writing when my kids were small.

Go to God with an open mind and heart and pour out all your
aspirations and longings to him. He knows exactly what's right for you
at this time.

*Father, I surrender all my plans and dreams to you. If you want me to stay at home,
I will. If you want me to be employed, show me in what capacity. I trust you with
what's best for me and my family. In Jesus' name. Amen.*

A Warning for Workaholics

"Do not wear yourself out to get rich; have the wisdom to show restraint. Cast but a glance at riches and they are gone, for they will surely sprout wings and fly off to the sky like an eagle." Proverbs 23:4-5

The Bible is wonderfully balanced in its teachings between working hard and being slothful. Although it condemns the latter, it encourages the former—to a point. There is a line between being industrious as a good provider and working to the exclusion of everything else.

Why are some people workaholics? The drive for wealth is an obvious reason, and this scripture points out that even if it is attained, riches are not certain. I wonder if the U.S. Treasury was thinking of this verse when they decided to put an eagle on our paper bills! Money does seem to fly out of our wallets, doesn't it? That's why it's so tempting to work harder and longer.

Becoming wealthy won't bring us contentment, as now we have to worry about trying to hang on to it. One of the saddest commentaries is a life that was lived in pursuit of fortune, ignoring the importance of relationships with family and friends, neglecting spiritual disciplines, even sacrificing personal health and well-being, only to end up in retirement years (the time they were slaving all their life to enjoy) alone, broken in body and spirit. This is the danger of an unbalanced life.

Putting all our eggs in the basket of "getting rich" leaves us with nothing to show for it in the end but a pile of money. Few people, on their deathbeds, express regret that they didn't make more money.

Only two things on this earth will go into eternity—people and God's Word. That's what we need to invest our lives in. Time is life. We have to earn a living, but we shouldn't squander time living just for work. That's making a dying.

Father, I desire to live a balanced life. Impress on me the importance of time to rest and be with the ones I love. In Jesus' wonderful name. Amen.

Good Measure

*"Give, and it will be given to you. A good measure, pressed down,
shaken together and running over, will be poured into your lap. For
with the measure you use, it will be measured to you." Luke 6:38*

This teaching has suffered much abuse at the hands of the prosperity preachers. It is used to justify their "giving to get" doctrine: I'll give money to God, and then he'll give me back three, five, even ten times as much! There are several problems with this theology.

God looks at the motives of our heart when we give, and self-interest as a motivation for giving isn't even mentioned in the Bible. Giving is supposed to be the antidote to greed; applied in this way it doesn't appear to be doing its purpose, does it?

Look closely at this verse. Where is the noun? Give *what*? We associate this scripture solely with money, but money isn't even mentioned. It needs to be interpreted in the context of the entire passage, beginning in Luke 6:37: "Do not judge, and you will not be judged. Do not condemn, and you will not be condemned. Forgive, and you will be forgiven. Give, and it will be given to you…" Somewhere we've made the leap that all we have to give is money. Not so!

Jesus is talking about how we treat others; the larger context of Luke 6 is about loving your enemies. He tells us to return love for hate, to offer forgiveness to those who've hurt or offended us. This establishes the measure which, in time, will be measured back to us.

We can't use Luke 6:38 as a lever for fund-raising. It is very true that we can't out give God in our finances, but our goal shouldn't be for him to make us wealthy when we do give. We should give out of love; that's the heart of Jesus' message. The greater the measure of love you give, the more love will come to you in return. Pressed down, shaken together, and running over into your lap.

Dearest Lord, make me a more loving person. The more I love, the more I'll give—time, money, forgiveness—whatever. Change my heart to reflect more of Jesus. In his name I pray. Amen.

Do Not Love the World

"Do not love the world or anything in the world. If anyone loves the world, the love of the Father is not in him." 1 John 2:15

Since the fall of Adam and Eve, when they introduced sin into God's perfect creation, Satan has been the temporary ruler of this world system. The spirit behind it is the same one that gives money its power over people's hearts. It stands in opposition to God and his ways, and as God's children we are to also stand in opposition to it. If we're not, then John says we don't truly know God.

We try to have it both ways—one foot in the world and the other in God's kingdom, and it doesn't work. A divided heart will serve only to make us restless, unsatisfied, and uneasy in our Christian walk. How do we know if we love the world? There are two sure indicators: our calendar and our checkbook. Where do we spend our time, and on what are we spending our money? If you were to be put on trial for being a Christian, would there be enough evidence to convict you if these items were laid open to the court?

God has not called us to be just like the rest of the unbelieving world. The phrase "everybody does it" will not cut it with the Lord. Polls have shown that in every major lifestyle category, self-proclaimed Christians don't live any differently from non-Christians. They're in just as much debt, they divorce at the same rate, they file just as many lawsuits, and they have many of the same values! "My brothers, this should not be" (James 3:10)!

The abundant life Jesus has called us to is to be radically different from the unbelievers around us. If we are coveting and running up consumer debt on credit cards, it's safe to say that our hearts are cozying up to the world and all it offers. We need to renounce this realm or we will have all eternity to be sorry.

Father, I need to know that your love is in me. Please show me where I'm loving the world. Give me the strength to turn away. In the name of Jesus I pray. Amen.

Satan's Three Basic Plays

*"For everything in the world—the cravings of sinful man, the lust of
his eyes and the boasting of what he has and does—comes not from
the Father but from the world. The world and its desires pass away,
but the man who does the will of God lives forever." 1 John 2:16-17*

Money, sex, and power. These three pursuits categorize just about
everything that humankind has stumbled over since the Garden
of Eden. In football, an offense will keep using the same play over and
over again if the defense can't stop them from advancing the ball.
Satan's playbook contains three basic plays that down through history
have been proven winners for him.

"The cravings of sinful man"—Satan tempts us with things that
appeal to our fleshly nature, such as money and possessions. Once we
have become fixated on material goods, Satan has us neutralized as far
as our influence for God's kingdom goes.

"The lust of the eyes"—Satan will hit us in our appetites. We can
squander our money on too much food, too much drink, too much
entertainment. We haven't much of a testimony for Christ in this condition, either.

"The boasting of what he has and does"—pride was Lucifer's original sin, and we are just as susceptible. Our desire for status has us frantically climbing the corporate ladder or living a lie in order to appear
successful.

This is all part of Satan's grand scheme—to lure us away from
doing God's will and to immerse us in the world system that he controls. He tried these same three plays on Christ in the wilderness, but
Jesus stood firm and overcame him with the Word of God.

Half the battle in beating the other guy is knowing his game plan
and developing an effective defense against it. God has revealed it in
his Word. Study it, obey it, and be victorious!

*Father, thank you that we are not ignorant of Satan's schemes. Thank you for the
offensive weapon of your Word. Teach me to use it to overcome the forces that would
direct my heart away from you. In Jesus' name I pray. Amen.*

The Best Things in Life Are Free

"Come, all you who are thirsty, come to the waters; and you who have no money, come, buy and eat! Come, buy wine and milk without money and without cost. Why spend money on what is not bread, and your labor on what does not satisfy?" Isaiah 55:1-2

When life is beating us up and wearing us down, and bills are threatening to overwhelm us, we need to be pulled over and reminded of what God offers us at no cost. What we need at these times is not a vacation, but spiritual refreshment.

The "resort" God beckons us to is affordable to everyone, because it's free! The only catch is that we have to come. If someone offered us an all-expenses paid week at Canyon Ranch, wouldn't we go? And yet it still wouldn't touch our real need—for God the Father to fill us with his living water and feed us with the bread of heaven.

Wine and milk are symbols of abundance, nourishment, and enjoyment. God has spread a banquet of spiritual blessings for us, why don't we take him up on it? Perhaps because it's so tempting to keep on keeping on in our flesh. Especially if we're deeply in debt, we feel we must keep working overtime to get out from under the crushing payments. Or we're so obsessed with building our net worth that relationships become secondary.

It's easier to take a break when we break down physically. God is calling us to a full stop before that happens. He wants to remind us that life is more than earning a living. He wants us to enjoy the journey, to be aware of his creation all around us, to give thanks for each new day, to breathe deeply and know he is the source of it all.

God longs to feed you with food and drink that will truly satisfy. Go to him; be refreshed. Your life and any financial problems will still be there, but now you will have the inner resources to handle them.

Father, I come to you. Prepare me a seat at your banqueting table and nourish me with the food that will fulfill me for eternity. I ask in Jesus' name. Amen.

A Hidden Consequence of Debt

*"The wife of a man from the company of the prophets cried to Elisha,
'Your servant my husband is dead, and you know that he revered the
Lord. But now his creditor is coming to take my two boys as his slaves.'"*
2 Kings 4:1

Men and women tend to react to debt very differently. For a man, debt can be seen as a smart business decision, a tool to help him get ahead. For his wife, it can be a threat to her security. It may be difficult for men to understand, but in the back of his wife's mind is always the thought of what she would do if he were to suddenly die.

This is not fatalistic, negative thinking. Most married women do end up as widows. Even if they have careers and are bringing in a paycheck, most lifestyles aren't based on just one income.

In Bible times, a woman had no legitimate way of supporting herself. In this incident, the woman's husband had died in debt and the only way to pay it was to hand over her sons as slaves. The boys were her only means of provision, and she would have lost them to the creditor had Elisha not performed a miracle on her behalf.

Debt always causes pressure on dependents. Something happens in the spiritual realm that strongly affects those under the authority of the person who took out the debt. If there isn't a guaranteed way to pay off the debt, either by selling the asset the debt is against or adequate insurance coverage in event of a death, the anxiety it creates for those who will be left to deal with it is significant.

Men, don't dismiss your wife's concerns as foolish or ignorant. Debt can be an enormous threat to a woman whose sole support is her husband. It is crucial to have a financial plan in place so that your wife and family can breathe easier.

Don't let your family end up like the prophet's widow, needing a miracle.

Lord God, open my eyes to the effects debt has on my family. Give me wisdom to keep them out of a position of desperation should anything happen to me. In Jesus' name. Amen.

Peace Over Wealth

"Better a little with the fear of the Lord than great wealth with turmoil." Proverbs 15:6

What do we really value in life? What we say we value doesn't always line up with our actions. Some people claim their family is the most important thing to them, but don't spend any time with them. You can't have close, loving relationships with people you're hardly ever with.

Some of the most turbulent families today are those households where both parents work and the kids are pretty much on their own. Meals are a rushed affair with every eater for themselves; there's no time for heart-to-heart conversation as someone is always on their way to somewhere. There's little prayer and less acknowledgment of the Lord in the home. This is not what God had in mind when he created the concept of family.

And what's all the rush and commotion for? So we can have more stuff, more experiences. Money can bring all the allurements and enticements of this world with the result that we end up being owned by our possessions and our schedules.

This is not peace; this is being weighed down with concerns and worries that a simpler life never considers. We look to the rich as "having it made" and never realize the mental anxieties they bear. Wealth itself is a burden; it brings great responsibilities and pressures as there is so much more of everything to worry about. All that worry doesn't leave much room for spiritual pursuits.

We have this belief that if only we were free from the worry of trying to make ends meet, we'd be free to really go after the things of the Lord. No, we wouldn't. We'd just gather up more stuff to distract us and be in worse condition than before.

God has made it clear: Our first priority is to be him, whatever state our finances are in. Fearing the Lord, trusting in him, serving him is what brings real, lasting peace. If you have Christ, you already have all the wealth you will ever need.

Lord, make me aware of all the riches I have in Christ. Thank you, Father, for giving me what can never be lost or stolen—peace with you. In Jesus' name. Amen.

Priceless

"The law from your mouth is more precious to me than thousands of pieces of silver and gold." Psalm 119:72

The Word of God. Can anyone possibly assess a monetary value to it? I have the first Bible given to me by my mother when I was twelve; it's the first thing I would grab in an evacuation. Its sentimental value makes it irreplaceable. Do you have a Bible you feel that way about? It's true that as mere paper and ink, a Bible is worth only a few dollars, no different than any other book. Still the best-selling volume in the world, decade after decade, it now comes in an astonishing variety of bindings and translations, in a price range for everyone. No longer is owning a copy of God's Word restricted to the affluent and the educated. As the communicator of truth and knowledge of God's love and saving grace through Jesus Christ, its message is available to all, and priceless beyond measure.

We say we value the Bible; the proof is in how we use it. Do we read it each day? Do we apply its teachings to our lives? Do we study it diligently, or are we more faithful to the daily newspaper? A few years back my husband was dealing as a fix-up project on a house that had been ravaged by fire. He'd been told the tenants had salvaged anything valuable and everything left was just junk. Picking through the mess, I found a King James Bible in perfect condition. It appeared to have never been opened; the binding was still stiff. Obviously its owners didn't set great store by it. That Bible sits on our shelf today, not because we needed another Bible, but as a reminder that the Word of God endures, even if it's treated like rubbish.

The Bible is more than letters on paper; it is the power of God to change lives. It's an education with the Holy Spirit as instructor, something that not all the money in the world could purchase.

Thank you, Father, for your holy Word. Let it be as precious to me as it is to the psalmist, worth more than silver or gold. In Jesus' name. Amen.

A Fool and His Money

"Of what use is money in the hand of a fool, since he has no desire to get wisdom?" Proverbs 17:16

A fool and his money are soon departed." That's one Solomon didn't write down, though he could have! A fool, remember, in Bible terminology, is someone who lives as if there is no God. This is different from the "sucker born every minute," according to P.T. Barnum. A fool doesn't believe he is accountable to anyone, so he spends his money as he pleases, without regard for consequences. He is his own god.

Wisdom, as Solomon defines it, is the necessary skills for living. God is the source of all wisdom, so we can see that a fool is cut off from learning how to manage his life well. Go through the book of Proverbs, note all the references to "fool," and you will get a composite picture of all the grief such a person brings upon himself.

One area of ruin in the life of a fool is in his finances. There are as many ways to waste money as there are people, and we've all had the experience of watching someone frivolously squander their resources on junk and junk activities. Examples of this run the gamut from the working poor who spend all their money on liquor and tobacco to multi-millionaires who own five homes but contribute nothing to the world's suffering masses. In either extreme, of what use was their money?

Money can buy you an education, but that won't make you wise. There are plenty of fools with degrees and letters after their names. Interestingly, studies have shown the more education a person has, the more they spend.

Are we being foolish with money? The closer we are to God, the harder it will be for us to justify some of our expenditures. Let's bring our spending under the authority of the Lord and avoid the fate of the fool.

Lord, I do desire to get wisdom; I do want how I spend my money to count for your kingdom. Guide me as I seek your will. In Jesus' name. Amen.

What a Family Really Needs

*"Fathers, do not exasperate your children; instead, bring them up in
the training and instruction of the Lord." Ephesians 6:4*

What is the number one need of a family? Two words: spiritual
leadership! Paul is addressing the fathers since they are the head
of the household and accountable to God for their administration of
this duty. Why am I bringing this up? Because most families, Christians
included, are operating under the premise that the number one priority is to provide a high standard of living.

How else to explain the high incidence of two-paycheck households—often the father holding down the two jobs. He is gone in the
morning before his kids get out of bed and doesn't return until they
are asleep at night. His physical presence is not with them, but his
influence is, as he teaches by example that earning money is more
important than they are.

Kids (and wives, for that matter) spell love T-I-M-E. "Stuff" can
never fill that void in their hearts; they want their parents' attention
more than they do another toy. Toys purchased out of guilt do not
make up for the hurt feelings caused by missing all those athletic contests or musical performances.

Time is life and you can never get it back. You can always make
more money. The main reason men (and women) work the long hours
they do is not to provide necessities but to provide a better lifestyle. If
we pass our temporal values on to our kids, they will develop that
same belief system that says money=fulfillment and ruin their adult
lives in the futile quest of materialism.

What will ultimately happen to all the things we buy with money?
When we die, they are of no further use to us. The only thing we can
take to heaven with us is our family. Shouldn't we be investing our
resources in what will last forever?

Stop sacrificing what really matters on the altar of mammon. You
can't provide spiritual leadership if you're not there.

*Father, help me to keep my priorities straight. Loving you with all my heart and
mind and strength is to be number one in my life, and I need to model that for my
family. I ask in Jesus' name. Amen.*

April **1**

Bring That Offering!

"Ascribe to the LORD the glory due his name; bring an offering and come into his courts." Psalm 96:8

Our worship to God is more than the fruit of our lips and the posture of our hearts; it is also what we bring in our hands. God told the Israelites in Exodus 34:20: "No one is to appear before me empty-handed." They brought their lambs and their goats and their bulls and their oil and their wheat—a portion of their livelihood in that agrarian society. It was to be the *best* portion, something they would have wanted to keep for themselves

We don't always grasp the significance of that. To us one twenty dollar bill is the same as another. We do identify with wanting to keep it. The mammon spirit shrieks at us that we need it more than God does. For some of us, parting with our money in this way is a difficult thing. For others it truly is a sacrifice; it's money they need for rent, for food, for gas. God understands. And he commands that we bring it anyway as an act of worship.

How can this be? Many of us were raised with such a division of what's secular and what's sacred that we have a hard time believing God and money could mix in any meaningful way. But worship itself is an offering; it means giving. Money represents the time and effort it took us to earn it, and we release a bit of ourselves with it when we give. This is what makes it an act of worship.

If we withhold our money, we are withholding ourselves from God. There is no way around that fact. But if we are truly devoted to him, we can come to the place where it is a delight to enter his courts with an offering, and he is delighted to welcome us in. All of us, nothing withheld.

Lord God, I come to you bringing my offering. It is my act of worship to you. I give it because I love you and this is a way I can show you. For Jesus' sake. Amen.

Bring It Weekly!

"On the first day of the week, each one of you should set aside a sum of money in keeping with his income, saving it up, so that when I come no collections have to be made." 1 Corinthians 16:2

Paul is speaking here of a collection he had asked the church in Corinth to take up to give to the church in Jerusalem. I see an important principle here instructing us on *when* we are to give.

I was convicted on this just recently. We had always paid our tithe on the first Sunday of each month on the grounds that it was easier to write just one check. I felt a twinge on those "off Sundays" when the offering plate would go by and we would put nothing into it, but I comforted myself in the knowledge that we were already "paid up" for that month.

There would be the inevitable times when we forgot to bring it because we weren't in the habit of doing it every week. "Oh, *this* was the first Sunday?" Whoops. Better remember next week. We could be sloppy about it, but our one check did make it every month. It was while doing a study on worship that I was staggered by Exodus 4:20, and realized that we were appearing before God three to four times a month empty-handed! "Lord, forgive us," I confessed.

Now what we do is divide the monthly amount by four and give that sum every week with the added benefit of giving an additional 25 percent every quarter when there's a fifth Sunday! And most importantly, we are full participants in the service each week.

After all, we don't treat any other element of worship that way: "Well, I praised God the first Sunday, so I'm done for the month." "I received communion, so I'm good for a few weeks." Ridiculous! It's obvious to me now; the Lord just had to open my eyes.

Every week when the plate goes by now I feel joyful instead of guilty that I've come into his courts with empty hands.

Almighty God, you are a great and awesome king, worthy to be praised. I bring my offering every time I enter through your gates to worship. In Jesus' name. Amen.

April

God Takes Care of His Own

"I was young and now I am old, yet I have never seen the righteous forsaken or their children begging bread. They are always generous and lend freely; their children will be blessed." Psalm 37:25

What a wonderful promise this is! David states that in his long life he has never known a case of a believer in the Lord not having their needs met. In fact, whatever they had they shared with others. I've witnessed this in our ministry to the poor. There are many precious Christians in their ranks, and as God meets their needs for food, clothing, and shelter, they are generous in giving whatever abundance they have to help their families and friends.

As moving as this is to see, it causes me to examine my own heart for selfishness and greed. Do I tend to hoard the things God graciously gives me for myself? If so, why? Do I not trust him to provide again? The homeless live day by day; they concern themselves with one meal, one night's shelter at a time. They trust God will show up right on schedule when they need him.

In North America, we of the middle class aren't satisfied with our daily bread; we think in terms of a month or more. We need to learn a lesson from the poor: God takes care of his own, no matter what socioeconomic class they happen to be in. However, we need to remember this promise is for the righteous, not the wicked. There were plenty of begging children in Jerusalem during the Babylonian siege of the city; God was bringing judgment on an idolatrous people. He takes disobedience very seriously, and if you've wandered away from him, he will use whatever means necessary to bring you back. That in itself is proof we belong to him!

He will never leave us or forsake us, and he is faithful to provide all our needs. What a great God we serve!

Heavenly Father, I can live with confidence knowing I'm never out of your sight, and you know all my needs before I'm aware of them myself! With that in mind, help me to be generous in blessing others out of my abundance. In Jesus' name. Amen.

April 4

Teach Your Children

"These commandments that I give you today are to be upon your hearts. Impress them on your children. Talk about them when you sit at home and when you walk along the road, when you lie down and when you get up." Deuteronomy 6:6-7

If you feel incompetent or ignorant in managing your money, it's not entirely your fault. You were just never taught when you were growing up. We picked up our parents' attitudes and habits about money whether they were verbalized or not.

This is why it is vital if you are a parent to teach your children God's principles on money. They are old enough to learn as soon as they are capable of picking up after themselves. They are old enough to tithe as soon as they begin to make their own money. If you give them an allowance, it should be earned and not a handout or they'll expect the same thing from the working world. And don't give them money to put in the offering at church; this teaches them nothing about giving. Children are naturally greedy and at first you'll have to insist that they tithe. When they're older, they can make their own giving decisions, hopefully following your good example.

Teach them how to budget, to balance a checkbook, to save a portion of what they earn, how banks and lending works, and how interest can help them or hurt them. If you do your own income taxes, involve your older children. Be open and honest about your finances with them. If they see how much it costs to run a household, they'll be more respectful of your income.

If the thought of all this terrifies you, your kids will pick up on that fear and develop unhealthy attitudes towards money. Financial management is a crucial skill they will need in life, more important than learning to drive a car. Who better to teach them than their parents?

Father, I need your help in teaching my children how to handle money your way. I want to be a good example to them. Give me wisdom for the task. I ask in Jesus' name. Amen.

Destroyed By Ignorance

"My people are destroyed by lack of knowledge." Hosea 4:6

This passage of Scripture is an indictment through the prophet Hosea against the priests of that day who had failed to teach God's Word to the people of Israel. As a result, sin abounded and the Lord was not acknowledged among them.

"The speed of the leader is the speed of the team" is a common saying in the business world, and it applies in any situation where people look to their leaders for direction and guidance. In Israel's case, the priests' failure to zealously guard God's laws and supply instruction in his ways had the people under their spiritual watch turning to idols. Yet throughout the book of Hosea, God makes it clear that the priests aren't entirely to blame; the people were accountable for their disloyalty and they would be punished.

Likewise, if poor financial decisions are shipwrecking our lives, we can't point fingers at our parents or our pastors and claim it's all their fault. We are responsible to seek out right paths for ourselves; ignorance is not an excuse. As long as we continue to blame others, we remain stuck in our destructive patterns; we take on a "helpless victim" mentality that does us absolutely no good.

Instead of letting others do our thinking for us and having them spoon-feed us whatever they're dishing out, we need to be proactive in digging into God's Word for ourselves, studying what he has to say about financial management, and letting the Holy Spirit be our teacher. There's nothing wrong in hearing godly men and women expound on the subject; it can be extremely beneficial to learn from gifted Bible teachers, but they should not be our only source of information.

Everything we hear we need to filter through the Spirit's discernment to be sure we're learning the truth and not the current popular ideas. Get to know the Bible so well that you recognize error the moment you come in contact with it. When it comes to handling your money, ignorance is not bliss.

Father, I don't want to be in the dark when it comes to managing money. Lead me to Bible teachers who will speak the truth. I pray in Jesus' name. Amen.

Treasure in Heaven

*"Sell your possessions and give to the poor. Provide purses for yourselves
that will not wear out, a treasure in heaven that will not be
exhausted, where no thief comes near and no moth destroys. For where
your treasure is, there your heart will be also." Luke 12:33-34*

These words of Jesus have a tendency to make us Western Christians
uneasy. We try to rationalize our way through the minefield of his
most radical statements, convincing ourselves that the text must mean
something else, something "deeper," than what it says on the surface.
Other believers have taken this verse literally and own only the clothes
on their backs.

So how do we obey this teaching? First, we are to see this not as a
call to rid ourselves of everything we own and be destitute, but to live
simply. Possessions are a blessing in that they have kingdom value
when we use them to minister to others. You have a home? Practice
hospitality. Host a small group or a Bible study. Let visiting missionaries stay with you. You have a car? Transport yourself and others to a
ministry, or run errands for a shut-in. You have food and clothing?
Share them with those who do not. Have a yard sale and give the proceeds to the benevolence fund at your church. Don't get hung up on
having temporal things; live with your eyes lifted up to heaven and the
things of the earth will no longer seem so attractive.

Second, we are to give knowing that with God as our provider, our
purse will never be depleted. We never really lose anything we give up
for the kingdom's sake. God has promised to reimburse us. The size
and quality of our eternal dwelling will be determined by the materials
we send on ahead. Are we anticipating living in a mansion or on "skid
row"?

We will all be broke at the moment of our death. Our choices
today determine how wealthy we will be in eternity.

*Father, I ask that you change my heart towards the things of this world. They will
all perish; turn my heart towards what will never fail, kept safe by you in the
heavenly places. In Jesus' name. Amen.*

Hundredfold Blessings

"Isaac planted crops in the land and the same year reaped a hundred-fold, because the LORD blessed him. The man became rich, and his wealth continued to grow until he became very wealthy." Genesis 26:12

How much did God bless Isaac? Well, the meaning of "a hundred-fold" is 100 x 100—ten thousand percent! That's a pretty good rate of return on your investment! This was part of God's plan for Isaac, to fulfill his covenant promise to make Isaac a mighty nation. However, we mustn't make the same mistake the Hebrews did, which was to assume that only the wealthy were being blessed by God. They understood that wealth and land, crops and herds, and children came from the hand of the Lord, but they measured their standing with him by the amount of their material goods. If someone was poor and struggling, or a woman was barren, to their way of thinking they must be under a curse. This was why Job's friends came down so hard on him.

We can fall into that same trap today, calculating God's favor by the size of our bank accounts or how well we're succeeding at our jobs. We beat ourselves up if our fortunes take a downturn, sure that God must be displeased with us or we wouldn't be in this predicament. Sometimes it is our sin and disobedience that has brought on God's divine discipline. But often it is a trial God is allowing to mold our character to the likeness of Christ.

We must not make the "hundredfold blessing" the standard for God's stamp of approval on our lives. He blesses us in so many other ways than financially. Do you enjoy good health? A loving family? Good friends? Do you have the peace that comes from having a relationship with God through his Son Jesus Christ? These things are priceless and should never be taken for granted.

"Bless me, Lord" is a very open-ended prayer. His blessings come in ways we don't always expect.

Heavenly Father, you are so good to me! You have blessed me beyond what I deserve, but I will not assume a connection between my prosperity and my spirituality. In Jesus' name. Amen.

What's It All For, Anyway?

*"Man is a mere phantom as he goes to and fro; he bustles about, but only
in vain; he heaps up wealth, not knowing who will get it." Psalm 39:6*

This little verse sums up the entire theme of the book of
Ecclesiastes—that life without God is meaningless. It paints a picture of the human race running in circles, engaged in the frantic activity of amassing an estate only to leave it all to someone else. How
depressing, how futile. How important it is that we spend our few years
here in pursuit of what is really important!

It happened in Solomon's generation and it continues to this day—
the building of fortunes to the neglect of families. The irony of it is
what frequently happens when the will is being drawn up—the inheritance intended for the children cannot be left to them after all. Either
they are estranged from their parents or they are irresponsible,
untrustworthy, or unproductive. The wealthy patriarch poured his life
into his portfolio instead of his posterity. His statement of net worth
brings him little comfort as he prepares to exit this world for the next.

God is not impressed with our empire building. What he will want
to know is: What did you do to influence your family for me? What
kind of spiritual leadership did you provide? What did you do to connect people with my Son?

The danger of wealth is that it can draw us away from our primary
business as Christians. The best investment of our time and money
should be in the form of saved souls. We need to become world-class
Christians, not worldly ones.

Our tombstone will be engraved with two dates—the year of our
birth and the year of our death, with a dash in between. Just a short
line to represent our life on earth. We have no control over the dates,
but what will you do with your dash?

*Father, I confess that sometimes my agenda distracts me from your agenda, that of
winning the lost. Help me to focus on what's really important. In the name of the
Lord Jesus I pray. Amen.*

April

The Sin of Pride

"By your wisdom and understanding you have gained wealth for your-self and amassed gold and silver in your treasuries. By your skill in trading you have increased your wealth, and because of your wealth your heart has grown proud." Ezekiel 28:4-5

Pride is a sin God especially hates. It is an abomination to him because it expresses a heart that is not acknowledging his sover-eignty. It is the original sin of Lucifer before he became Satan (see Isaiah 14:12-14).

Religion is based on man's pride. It says that man can do some-thing to earn God's acceptance. This goes completely contrary to the gospel, which says that man has nothing to offer God, but must receive forgiveness based on Christ's sacrifice. Religion can't stand the truth because it rebukes self-sufficiency and pride.

Having wealth is one of the surest roads to becoming prideful. If we're not careful, we begin to believe that we are self-made. We leave God out. This is one of the principle dangers of riches. It is so grievous to the Lord he would rather keep us poor than to risk us becoming puffed up with pride over our prosperity.

Affluence requires much more maturity to manage than does abasement. If we're not in the habit of thanking God daily for being the source of everything we have, we run the risk of developing the disease of independence. Look at what happened to the prideful king of Tyre: "Therefore this is what the Sovereign Lord says: 'Because you think you are wise, as wise as a god, I am going to bring foreigners against you, the most ruthless of nations; they will draw their swords against your beauty and wisdom and pierce your shining splendor. They will bring you down to the pit, and you will die a violent death in the heart of the seas' " (Ezekiel 28:6-7).

We need to pray that we would cultivate an attitude of humility so we can see ourselves in our true light—fully dependent upon God.

Sovereign Lord, I am dependent upon you for my next breath. Teach me humility; then I can handle however much you choose to give me. In Jesus' name. Amen.

The Purpose of Proverbs

"The proverbs of Solomon son of David, king of Israel; for attaining wisdom and discipline; for understanding words of insight; for acquiring a disciplined and prudent life, doing what is right and just and fair."
Proverbs 1:1-3

The opening verses of the book of Proverbs lays out for us what we can expect from reading it. It is one of the wisdom books of the Bible; indeed the word *wisdom* occurs 41 times throughout. It contains 31 chapters, one for each day of the month, and a good habit to get into would be to read a chapter each day. Not only will the constant review help you memorize Scripture, but it will renew your mind as it teaches you godly principles for conducting your life.

Proverbs is a treasury of sound financial guidelines, I have relied more heavily on this book than any other in gleaning instruction on money matters. Its pages also emphasize *discipline*; you can achieve nothing in your life without it, including getting out of bed in the morning! Discipline is like a muscle; it grows stronger with use. When you develop it in one area of your life, it spills over and affects other areas also. This means if you can stick to and maintain an exercise program, it will become easier to control your impulse spending. Learn to love discipline; it will get you to where you want to go in life. In fact, it's impossible to have an ordered financial life without it.

Do you want to become wise? Become a student of this ancient book. It is as practical and relevant today as it was when it was written 3,000 years ago. Its truths are timeless. It is God's gift to us. Make use of it!

Father, thank you for the book of Proverbs. Thank you for inspiring Solomon and others to write it. As I read it, give me revelation as to how to apply it to my finances. I ask in Jesus' name. Amen.

Withholding Good

*"Do not withhold good from those who deserve it, when it is in your
power to act. Do not say to your neighbor, 'Come back later, I'll give it
tomorrow'—when you now have it with you." Proverbs 3:27-28*

In our counseling, my husband and I have met individual and couples who were deeply in debt, yet were continuing to fund their
retirement account to the maximum. We always advise them to take
those funds and use them to pay their obligations. Most people are
loathe to do this; they protest that this is money they need to retire on.
Our answer is that if they don't retire the debts and stop using credit,
their retirement will be the least of their concerns. They won't even be
able to retire!

Occasionally we see people who have had debts "charged off" and
now are happily accumulating savings due to improved circumstances.
This is cheating the creditor who loaned them money in good faith.

We tend to think of lending institutions as being impersonal and
wealthy so it's okay to default on the bill. God sees no difference
between ripping off your close friend and ripping off a huge corporation—either way you're a swindler. The same principle applies to deliberately paying late when you have the funds available. You agreed to a
due date when you took the loan, and the lender has the right to
expect payment by that date. The mind-set of making your creditor
"sweat" waiting for you to come through every month only hurts yourself—in late fees, in black marks on your credit report, and in higher
interest rates. Did you know that one late payment can cause your
credit card rate to be increased? Treat your landlord this way and don't
expect a glowing reference, either.

So ask yourself: Who do I owe money to? Then arrange to pay
them according to the terms agreed upon. God honors us when we
honor our commitments.

*Lord, convict me where I need it on this issue. Point out even the smallest viola-
tions so I can make things right. In Jesus' name. Amen.*

Finding Joy in Trials

James was writing to Christians who were being killed for their faith, and he opens his letter with an admonition to consider their trials "pure joy"! How were they to have such a supernatural response to their sufferings? By looking to the eventual results.

Let's admit it—none of us really welcomes problems. We tend to fuss and complain and ask, "Why me?" In financial matters it's sometimes our own doing that brought on the trial, but we can also be the victims of unjust lawsuits, medical emergencies, company downsizing, or other circumstances beyond our control. While it's never fun, we need to look at these things through God's eyes. It is the troubles and problems of life that help us to grow. The saying is true, "Smooth seas don't make skillful sailors." God can use a financial trial in a myriad of ways: to make you more dependent on him, to test your commitment to giving, to change the direction of your life, and to develop your faith.

In my own case, God used a trial to teach our family about his timing and to trust him. He told us to move to Phoenix, but then allowed a year to pass before our house would sell. He was not going to release us to go until we learned the lesson, and as painful and maddening as the entire episode was, when I look back I'm very glad he allowed it. It taught us things about God that we could learn in no other manner. He came through for us in many ways, and we truly did experience joy in the end.

Untested faith isn't really faith at all. Remember that in the midst of your next trial, and rejoice!

Father, only through the power of the Holy Spirit can I experience joy in trials. Help me to see them as opportunities to grow in my faith and become mature. I ask in Jesus' name. Amen.

Plan for Winter

"Go to the ant, you sluggard, consider its ways and be wise! It has no commander, no overseer or ruler, yet it stores its provisions in summer and gathers its food at harvest." Proverbs 6:6-8

Why study one of the tiniest creatures on earth? To learn a lesson about developing a surplus—a lesson sorely needed in a day when so many people are living hand to mouth. They never have savings because they consume everything they make. They don't understand that these are the harvest years of their lives. Winter is coming when there will be no more opportunity to earn at their current level.

In the budget workshops conducted annually at our church, we have found the main goal of many of the people attending is just to pay their bills that month. They have no long-range vision at all for their finances. Yet when asked how many believe Social Security will be there for them at age 65, not a single hand goes up. So what exactly do they plan to be living on when they have no savings? It is absolutely crucial to have margin; to have money left over at the end of each month.

Is your number one goal to be debt free? Eliminate your debts and you will free up that money to invest for your future. Always remember, the funds you consume now cannot be recovered later. You've not only lost the money you've spent, but you've lost the earning potential that money had if it were invested instead.

The more long term your perspective, the better financial decisions you will make for future needs. Yes, God can provide even if you do nothing, but Scripture provides a very balanced view in that as much as we are able, we are to put aside for ourselves what we can in the summer of our life so that we will be cared for in the winter. Just like the wise little ants.

Father, give me a long-term perspective when it comes to managing money. Let me not squander these years of my harvest. I ask in Jesus' name. Amen.

What Does the Bible Say About Retirement?

"The LORD said to Moses, 'This applies to the Levites: Men twenty-five years old or more shall come to take part in the work at the Tent of Meeting, but at the age of fifty, they must retire from their regular service and work no longer. They may assist their brothers in performing their duties at the Tent of Meeting, but they themselves must not do the work.'" Numbers 8:23-26.

Before you say, "Whoopee! The Bible says I can retire when I'm 50!" remember to consider the context of the verse. This was instruction for the assignment of the Levites in their responsibilities of the tabernacle service, not a directive for everyone. Also notice, they didn't completely retire; they could continue to assist the younger men if they chose. I have the suspicion that those who did lived longer! It's a well documented fact that men who retire to a life of inactivity have a 500 percent increase in the likelihood of an earlier death. Now there's a reason to keep working!

Interestingly, this is the only reference in Scripture regarding retirement. In fact, in ancient Hebrew language there is no word for retirement. The concept does not exist. God never intended for us to be put on a shelf to atrophy as we get older. He still has important work for us to do. We won't be doing the same thing at age 70 that we did at age 30, but we are to be active in contributing useful service somewhere. You will have a lifetime of marketable abilities, skills, and knowledge to offer in your golden years.

God created us for work, and it is in work that we find fulfillment and satisfaction. People who find themselves with nothing to do but recreate become bored and unhappy. Don't place a time limit on what you're able to do in your life.

Father, you know the length of my days and the works you have planned for me. Continue to give me the strength so I can serve you in some capacity as long as I have breath. I ask in Jesus' name. Amen.

Paying Taxes

" 'Show me the coin used for paying the tax.' They brought him a denarius, and he asked them, 'Whose portrait is this? And whose inscription?' 'Caesar's,' they replied. Then he said to them, 'Give to Caesar what is Caesar's, and to God what is God's.' " Matthew 22:19-21

Our society really does abhor paying taxes; April 15 represents one of the most dreaded days on the calendar. People hated paying taxes in Jesus' time; Solomon's subjects were taxed to death centuries before that. It seems taxes have always been with us, and our feelings towards them haven't changed much. Even when the Pharisees came to Jesus with their tax question with the motive of entrapping him, they were probably also hoping he would come up with a loophole. They went away disappointed on both counts.

Christ's answer showed that as dual citizens, we are to live our lives honoring both God and our government. Because taxes are inevitable, what we need most is not more deductions, but an attitude adjustment. Part of the reason for our detestation is that we get little perceived benefit from paying them, and what we do see many times in our opinion is waste.

True, there is waste, and if it bothers you so much, get involved in becoming part of the solution by working to change your representation in Congress. On the other hand, we do enjoy military protection, interstate highways, national parks, and community services, to name just a few of the worthy endeavors our taxes pay for. Paying your fair share is actually good stewardship. Our part is to be faithful and obey what we're obligated to do; the government is also accountable to God for how they fulfill their part of this sacred trust.

Try to look at it this way: Paying taxes proves you have an income sufficient enough to owe taxes! So be of good cheer this day. You don't have to throw a party, but at least count your blessings.

Father, at times I struggle with the issue of paying taxes. Help me to look on the positive side, and be grateful for the government under which I am a citizen. In Jesus' name. Amen.

Tax Planning

*"This is also why you pay taxes, for the authorities are God's servants,
who give their full time to governing. Give everyone what you owe
him: If you owe taxes, pay taxes; if revenue, then revenue; if respect,
then respect; if honor, then honor." Romans 13:6-7*

The apostle Paul had no problem with his attitude towards taxes; in
this verse he is trying to encourage the Christians in Rome to feel
the same. I'm sure it wasn't always to their liking how the government
was using their money, just as it isn't to ours, but Paul says that doesn't
matter. His point is that people in government have given their lives to
public service. Even if they don't acknowledge God, they are still working for him, and they ultimately answer to him for the stewardship of
their position.

We shouldn't have to pay more taxes than we rightfully owe, and
I'm all for tax deductions if they make sense. We've all been brainwashed into believing we should carry a mortgage for the interest
deduction it earns us. But is it smart to pay a bank tens of thousands of
dollars every year just to avoid the modest amount that would go to
the government?

There's no such thing as a free tax deduction. When you hear of
people with large incomes who pay little or no taxes, you can be sure
they are spending plenty of money in other areas to get that tax break.
Never make a financial decision based on whether or not it's tax
deductible! The fact is that if you're in the 27 percent tax bracket, you
need to spend 73 cents someplace that will give you that deduction. We
seem to think it's okay as long as it's not going to Uncle Sam, but it's
hurting us financially.

If you really want to pay less taxes, there's one sure way to do so:
Earn less money! I realize that's not going to be a popular option. But
please review your tax planning and see if what you're currently doing
is wise. Make peace with paying your taxes.

*Father, I need your wisdom in my tax planning. I understand that the government is
your servant and if I cheat on taxes I'm really cheating you. In Jesus' name. Amen.*

Be Content with Your Pay

"Then some soldiers asked him, 'And what should we do?' He replied,
'Don't exhort money and don't accuse people falsely—be content with
your pay.'" Luke 3:14

The crowds that thronged to John the Baptist in the Judean wilderness to repent and be baptized represented all walks of life. Tax collectors and soldiers were among those who came seeking forgiveness, and they asked good questions. They realized their occupations would have potential conflict with their new lives and they wanted to know, "What should we do?"

John didn't tell them to quit and find a new line of work. He told them basically the same thing: Don't collect any more money than they were required to (tax collectors were notorious for defrauding people to line their own pockets) and to be content with what they earned. Both professions had the ability to wield the abuse of power, and that is what John addressed. He didn't condemn the jobs themselves, but the unethical practices associated with them.

The world needs soldiers and tax collectors (yes, we do!) just as the world needs teachers, waitresses, electricians, business owners, truck drivers, butcher, bakers, and candlestick makers. Whatever your job may be, the fact that you're getting paid to do it proves there's a need in our society for it.

Every vocation has a level of income that will determine your lifestyle. It's when an engineer strives to achieve a CEO's lifestyle on an engineer's income, or a teacher wants to live like a doctor that gets people into trouble with living beyond their means. If we look around us and see others making more money than we are, we can lose focus and become discontent. We forget it is God who decides what our gifts and abilities are and where we can best contribute.

As we settle into our chosen field, we are to enjoy our labor and be content with our pay—whatever that amount might be.

Father, thank you for the skills and abilities you've given me. Help me to use them
for your glory, and to live within the income provided by them. In Jesus' name.
Amen.

Blessing without Sorrow

"The blessing of the Lord brings wealth, and he adds no trouble to it."
Proverbs 10:22

Our wealth is a gift from the hand of God and it is intended to be a blessing to us. If we have balance in our lives, if we are not over-working to the detriment of our families and our health, if our priori-ties are in order, then we experience that blessing in the form of a happy home life, contentment, and kids who know and respect who we are.

But if we choose to pursue wealth to the extent that our lives get out of balance—evidenced by working long hours, holding down two jobs, always trying to earn more income—then the Lord may lift his hand of blessing from us. We begin to experience a strained marriage, angry kids, a chilly atmosphere in our home, and deteriorating health. This is because we've taken matters into our own hands and basically told God by our actions that we don't believe he's providing well enough for us. It's a form of discontent.

"Wealth with blessing" doesn't leave us exhausted at the end of each workday from our frantic efforts of earning a living, too tired to play with our children or have any kind of family life. If your job demands that much from you, you need to seek new employment. Trust God to direct you to work that will fulfill you without emptying your tank every day. There are times when a special project at work does demand extra hours, but that should be the exception, not the routine.

The constant race to get ahead or "arrive" really does nothing but frustrate us and rob us of our peace. It can lead us down a path where we're engaging in questionable business deals that end up going bad, or taking unnecessary risks that bring trouble and sorrow upon ourselves. Surrender the source of your income to the Lord and watch how he provides. He does want to bless you.

Father, I recognize your providential care for me and my family. I want to keep my life balanced between work, family, and the purpose you have called me to. I pray in Jesus' name. Amen.

April

More than Enough

"Then Moses gave an order and they sent this word throughout the camp: 'No man or woman is to make anything else as an offering for the sanctuary.' And so the people were restrained from bringing more, because what they already had was more than enough to do all the work." Exodus 36:6-7

Have you ever had the experience of sitting in church and hearing your pastor announce that they weren't going to take an offering that week, because the people had already given so much it wasn't necessary? That's exactly what happened in the Sinai wilderness. After Moses told the Israelites to bring offerings, they brought so much he had to give another order telling them to stop!

How different from what churches have to go through now with building programs. In our generation, when a church announces an expansion, people groan and many leave. They either want nothing to do with a larger church or they don't want to contribute to it.

This is what happened with my home church. We were bursting at the seams and God was clearly leading us to build. He provided 35 acres we were able to purchase, and in faith people pledged to pay off the land and raise the funds required to build. It was to be a three-year program.

Then, people who had made pledges disappeared. People who pledged didn't give what they had said they would. Three years turned into four, as all the plans were scaled back to accommodate the reduced amount available to work with. Finally, we had our beautiful new campus, but we were already beginning to outgrow it only four months later!

My prayer is that next time, the hearts of the people will be moved, as they were in Moses' day, to bring their offerings with willing hearts, excited about what God is doing among us, and that we will have more than enough.

Father, help me to see it's not about buildings and programs, but reaching people who matter to you. Give me a willing, generous spirit to contribute to the building of your kingdom. For Jesus' sake. Amen.

Contentment Is Priceless

"Keep your lives free from the love of money and be content with what you have, because God has said, 'Never will I leave you; never will I forsake you.'" Hebrews 13:5

This is one of several places in Scripture that tells us to keep free from the love of money (see also Luke 12:15; 1 Timothy 6:9) but it adds this precious promise from God: "Never will I leave you; never will I forsake you." This is the same promise he gave to Israel as Joshua was about to lead them into the Promised Land. It brought peace and comfort to them as they faced the unknown, and it should to us as well.

We can experience contentment because if we have the Lord, we need nothing else. When we think of "what we have," we look in the wrong places. We look at our bank account, the house we live in, the kind of car we drive, our electronic toys, our furniture, our possessions. We may also look at our children and our health—and if it's all good, then we may be content. But we can lose any of these things in an instant (remember Job?) and to base our contentment on them is to build on a shaky foundation.

The Lord's presence, on the other hand, is a reality that can never be taken from us. It can't be purchased, bartered, exchanged, or sold. In a materialistic society, things that are unseen are not valued, until it's perceived we don't have them. Do you remember what your life was like before you came to know the Lord? Could any amount of money persuade you to go back to that?

If you have everything except the Lord, you have nothing. If you have nothing except the Lord, you have everything. That's the reason Christians can be content.

O Lord, my heart cries out to you in thankfulness for all you've done for me, for everything you mean to me. Thank you for your promise to never leave me or forsake me. No matter where I find myself today, in whatever situation, you are here. I pray in Jesus' holy name. Amen.

What About Insurance?

"The prudent see danger and take refuge, but the simple keep going and suffer for it." Proverbs 27:12

To be prudent, according to Webster, is to "exercise sound judgment in practical matters; cautious in conduct; be sensible, not rash." Is purchasing insurance, then, demonstrating wisdom or does it show a lack of faith in God? There are Christians in both camps. Who's right?

It all depends on what the insurance is for. In many states, auto insurance is mandatory, and in some metro areas, given the number of accidents and stolen vehicles, going without would not only be illegal but very foolish. Some insurance policies out there, however, are questionable for anyone.

Anytime we find ourselves spending money on insurance out of fear, we need to ask why. Do we trust an insurance company to protect us from every little loss in life? Insurance can divert you from looking to God to take care of you. That's not an excuse for a man not to have life insurance when he has a family he's supporting. The insurance becomes provision to replace a lost income in the event of his death; it is planning to take care of a potential problem before it occurs. God expects us to be responsible to our household without using insurance to excessive levels. A $5 million policy is not needed for the majority of us!

Sometimes whether or not to purchase insurance requires asking God for his wisdom, especially when the needed insurance is unaffordable. We have gone without health insurance for over a decade now and we are comfortable with that decision; not everyone would be. God will give guidance according to what is best for you, which may be different from what's best for your neighbor.

Insurance, used wisely, can bring peace of mind. If you see danger, take shelter! It's the only prudent thing to do. The alternative is to suffer unnecessary loss and heartache.

Lord, you know all my needs and responsibilities. I will look to you for provision and protection, but show me the areas where you deem it prudent for me to have the kind of help insurance would give. In Jesus' name I pray. Amen.

Avoiding the Insurance Fraud Trap

"The righteousness of the upright will deliver them, but the treacherous will be caught by their own greed." Proverbs 11:6

It's easy to fall into thinking that because we've been paying insurance premiums for a period of time, the company "owes" us that amount back in benefits. This is not how it works. Insurance is there to get us through times when we'd be financially devastated without it. It's not an investment we should expect to profit by.

Even Christians aren't immune to this kind of philosophy. Are we using insurance funds to do things we would never consider doing with our own money? If God truly does own it all, he also owns the resources of the insurance companies. He holds them accountable as to how they manage them, and he holds us, the beneficiaries, accountable as well. If we are dishonest in filing an insurance claim, we're not only cheating the company, we're cheating God. When we fail to tell the whole truth in the event of an accident, we're committing deceit.

Although auto insurance probably has the greatest potential for fraud, medical insurance abuse is right up there with it. Some people will run to the doctor for minor incidents and insist on having every test possible done simply because the insurance will pay for it. They would never do this if it were their own money involved, but because it's covered by the policy, they intend to get full use out of it. It is for such reasons that health care costs are escalating. Insurance is getting to be like credit; what would happen to the cost of health care if there wasn't insurance to fall back on? It's been estimated it might be reduced by half!

Think about it. What can you do personally to cut waste in the system? This affects all of us. Do your part to avoid the subtle trap of insurance fraud.

Father, reveal to me any areas where I may be abusing insurance. I put to death this form of greed, also. In Jesus' name I pray. Amen.

Clearing Away the Hedge

"The way of the sluggard is a hedge of thorns, but the path of the upright is a highway." Proverbs 15:19

Ignoring financial problems doesn't make them go away. Burying your head in the sand and pretending everything is okay will only make things worse in the long run. Whether our behavior is caused by fear, naivety, denial, or just plain old laziness, the longer we wait to handle our problems the more boxed in we get and the fewer options we have open to us.

One couple we counseled went an entire year without making a house payment and didn't seek help until foreclosure proceedings had already begun. There wasn't much we could tell them at that point; they ended up losing their home. God in his mercy arranged for the new owner to rent the house back to them—at $300 a month more than their mortgage payment had been.

Procrastination costs! If only they had contacted the lender when they missed their first payment, and arranged for repayment that was satisfactory for both parties, how differently this whole sad affair would have turned out.

You may be absentminded about your obligations, but your creditors are not. Communicating with them goes a long way in clearing your personal financial maze into a straight road you can follow easily. "I meant to" or "I forgot about it" are excuses that will not cut it. Lenders aren't mind readers. If you're not paying your bills and not responding to their inquiries as to why, how do they know you're not some crook? And they will treat you like one! Better to swallow your pride, muster up your courage, and contact them.

Trust me, they want to hear from you. Explain your situation. They can do a lot to help and ease your mind. Don't let shame, hopelessness, fear, or any other emotion keep you from doing the right thing. Ask for help and begin tearing down that hedge of thorns so you can see clearly again. Don't wait!

Father, deliver me from any paralyzing emotions that interfere with my money dealings. I need the courage to take action, and the strength to follow through. I ask in the name of Jesus. Amen.

Waiting Patiently

"Be still before the LORD and wait patiently for him, do not fret when men succeed in their ways, when they carry out their wicked schemes."
Psalm 37:7

Waiting! It's one of the most difficult things God asks us to do, because it involves doing *nothing*. Funny, when we should do something, we sit on our hands and drag our feet, but when we're itching to make things happen, we're required to be still. Either way we're liable to make a mess if we don't obey.

Patience is especially needed in financial decisions, and not just the big ones. We can become imbibed with buying fever until we can't think straight, but then we hear God's still, small voice telling us to wait. He puts the brakes on our wants because he loves us and wants us to steer clear of deals and desires that would bring trouble upon us. How many of God's people could have been saved from scams if they had only listened and waited?

It's a sad fact that there are shysters out there who target Christians for their schemes because they perceive us to be gullible and trusting. We must take every "can't lose" deal to the Lord for his counsel. He may not give us an immediate answer, but that doesn't give us license to rush into something.

God speaks to us through his Word, circumstances, and other Christians, as well as through prayer. He will principally use your spouse to steer you away from a bad financial choice. Listen to him or her, and speak up when you sense something is not right with an investment, a purchase, a loan, anything. Don't fear being a wet blanket on your partner's desires. God may be using you to prevent them from making a mistake they'll regret.

Never let yourself be coerced into a decision you're not comfortable with or sure about. God doesn't push or pressure. He is patience personified, and he wants us to become like him. Learn to be still.

Father, I repent of my hurry-up ways. I'm willing to let "deals" pass me by as I learn to wait patiently for you. In the name of Jesus I pray. Amen.

Get Educated

"The naïve believes everything, but the prudent man considers his steps." Proverbs 14:15

To be naïve is to be ignorant. This is not the same thing as being stupid. It means to be lacking in knowledge. There's an easy solution to that. If you lack knowledge, get it. Don't let pride or fear or shame get in your way of learning what you need to know to make your financial life run more smoothly.

If you don't know how to balance your checkbook, people at your bank will show you. If you don't understand how to put a budget together, find a book at your library or bookstore. Or inquire at your church to see if someone is trained to sit down with you and explain it. Above all, if you don't understand how credit cards work and how the interest is figured on different transactions, don't use them!

Many financial problems can be avoided entirely with a basic understanding of the principles involved. It is a responsibility you must assume. Don't expect your bank to do your record keeping for you; they make mistakes, too. And don't keep your spouse in the dark about family finances. "You just take care of it, honey," is a cop-out. What happens when Honey suddenly isn't there? Some spouses don't care to know anything about household money matters, however, this can put them in a very compromising position when the time comes for them to deal with issues alone. It is never wise for only one person in the marriage to know what is going on. It's why we insist married couples come in for counseling together. They both need to hear the same information from the same source.

When you don't know any better, you tend to believe what you're told, even when it's not in your best interest. Don't get taken advantage of. Get the information you need and use it. It will keep you from causing financial harm to yourself and others.

Father, I confess that there are things about money I don't understand and haven't bothered to learn. I repent and ask your help in getting me the education I need. I ask in Jesus' name. Amen.

The Sorcerer's Sin

"And when Simon saw that through the laying on of the apostles'
hands the Holy Spirit was given, he offered them money, saying, 'Give
me this power also, that everyone on whom I lay my hands may receive
the Holy Spirit.'" Acts 8:18-19

Simon the sorcerer was a recent convert to Christianity. He was
amazed by the miracles that were taking place; Peter and John were
laying hands on the people to receive the Holy Spirit. As a man who
was used to astonishing crowds with his magic arts, it's understandable
that Simon would desire to participate in this work of God.

However, his motives were impure, as Peter discerned immediately.
He rebuked him scathingly: "Your money perish with you, because you
thought that the gift of God could be purchased with money! You have
no part nor portion in this matter, for your heart is not right in the
sight of God. Repent therefore of this your wickedness, and pray God if
perhaps the thought of your heart may be forgiven you. For I see that
you are poisoned by bitterness and bound by inequity" (Acts 8:20-23).

Simon's response to this reveals he didn't really repent; he was only
concerned about the potential consequences of his sin ("Pray to the
Lord for me, that none of these things which you have spoken may
come upon me" Acts 8:24). It makes one wonder if his conversion held.
Church history later identifies Simon Magus as a heretic. His trying to
bargain with Peter is where the word "simony" originates—the buying
and selling of church officials.

We learn from this that money and spiritual gifts are not to be
associated with each other. Some things are so holy they shouldn't be
mentioned in the same breath as unrighteous mammon. The power of
God is not some magic act we can pay someone to give us. We should
never treat it as a commodity, but with reverence and godly fear.

Father, thank you for reminding me that your grace and power are not for sale.
Thank you that they are available to all who will humble themselves and receive
Christ's sacrifice on their behalf. In Jesus' holy name. Amen.

April 27

The Importance of Rest

"It is vain for you to rise up early, to retire late, to eat the bread of painful labors; for he gives to his beloved even in his sleep." Psalm 127:2

God has given man a drive to provide. It is hard-wired into him, and every man who is tuned into this provision drive will be inclined to work, and work hard. If not brought under the control of the Holy Spirit, this positive quality can quickly turn into a negative as work begins to consume his life. Of all the many consequences of this, one that is often overlooked is the lack of rest. As much as God values work, he also puts a premium on his people getting enough sleep.

It's been said that money can't buy a good night's sleep, and there are plenty of wealthy people who toss and turn at night from worries about work. Their lives are out of balance because the focus of their work is misplaced. When work is only about making money, feelings of frustration and unfulfillment set in, since no matter how hard we work and how much money we make, it won't satisfy us. It is vain to burn the candle at both ends to earn more of it. At the end of our lives we will realize, too late, that it was all a waste of time and effort.

Now, think of this: God ministers to us in our sleep. Our spirit can commune with his in our unconscious state. Haven't you had the experience of "sleeping on" a perplexing problem, and in the morning it all seemed clearer to you? God was at work during those hours while your body and mind rested. Often it's the only time God can speak to us as our whole beings are so taken up with work in our waking hours.

Make the effort to slow down, go to bed at a decent hour, and let the Lord restore you. The work will always be there, even after you're dead and gone.

Thank you, Father, that you meet my needs even when I'm asleep and unaware of your activity. Let my first and last thoughts of every day be of you. In Jesus' name. Amen.

Don't Neglect to Write It Down

"He who ignores discipline comes to poverty and shame, but whoever heeds correction is honored." Proverbs 13:18

Do you know any financial "free spirits"? They're the one who never are certain of their checkbook balance, who send off fifty bucks every now and then to the utility company hoping it will cover their electricity from being turned off, and make daily stops at the ATM to get more cash. Hopefully, you don't live with one of these disorganized souls! Their habits will either amuse you or drive you nuts. They're not bad people; they just have never had the discipline to put their finances into any semblance of order. When you try to help them or offer advice, they flippantly say, "Oh, I have things under control."

Yeah, right. This high-wire act without a net can last only so long before there's a huge fall. Living this way is financial suicide for anyone, no matter how much money they make. Budgets aren't just for people with limited resources, they're for everyone.

One characteristic of successful millionaires is that they know exactly how much money it takes to run their households. They have it written down. "Keeping it in my head" isn't good enough. What would you think of a business that didn't have written records? Well, you are a business. You are a manager for God. "I'm just not a 'numbers' sort of person" is not an excuse to avoid putting together a financial plan on paper. There is something about the discipline of sitting down and putting in writing how much you make, what you owe, and where your money is going. It gives you clarity, it puts the brakes on impulse spending, and money that is managed with a controlled system works harder for you.

It may not sound like your idea of fun, but what really won't be fun is to one day discover that your undisciplined financial habits have left you broke and ashamed. Heed correction; there is freedom in control.

Father, give me discipline to keep good financial records. Help me find a system that will work for me and my particular situation. In Jesus' name. Amen.

The Value of a Human Life

"Why should I fear when evil days come, when wicked deceivers surround me—those who trust in their wealth and boast of their great riches? No man can redeem the life of another or give to God a ransom for him—the ransom for a life is costly, no payment is ever enough—that he should live forever and not see decay." Psalm 49:5-9

All through the ages man has sought a way to prevent or prolong the event that ultimately takes us all—death. From the ancient Egyptians building the pyramids to immortalize the pharaohs, to Ponce de Leon searching for a fountain of youth, to twenty-first century scientists trying to clone humans for replacement organs, we as a race are very uncomfortable with the fact that we will one day depart this earth. Christians have the hope of heaven and being with Jesus forever, but for unbelievers, death will separate them from everything they hold dear: their wealth, their power, their possessions, and their relationships. All the money in the world cannot shield them from this fate.

What if it could? What if we did have to purchase our redemption? The cost would be so high only the extremely wealthy could afford it, and where would that leave the rest of us? But only God himself is able to pay the price, and he paid it by leaving heaven and becoming one of us. With Jesus' death on the cross, God showed us once and for all the value of human life. He was willing to die that we might live.

The blood of Christ! How worthless is all worldly wealth in comparison! Those who boast of riches and material goods really have nothing to boast about. We need not be unsettled by such people as, without Christ, money will achieve them nothing of value in this life or the life to come. Only he can deliver us from sin and death. Only he has paid the price.

Almighty God, I bow down at your feet in humility and wonder that I am so valuable to you, that you would pay the price to redeem me with the life of your son. In Jesus' precious name I pray. Amen.

Do You Have a Price?

"Then Judas Iscariot, one of the Twelve, went to the chief priests to
betray Jesus to them. They were delighted to hear this and promised to
give him money. So he watched for an opportunity to hand him over."
Mark 14:10-11

"Everyone has a price." This epithet is used to insinuate that all of us can be bought, that we are willing to compromise our convictions if the monetary stakes are high enough. Whether it's swallowing gold-fish or cheating on their spouse, we hear the stories of people who began emphatically declaring they would not do the deed, only to hesitate as the offer reached dizzying heights. Eventually they would crack and say yes, for $5 million they would commit adultery. Before we judge these folks, we need to look deep within our own hearts. Do we have a price? What would we be willing to sell our faith for?

Judas had a price. He agreed to betray the Messiah for thirty pieces of silver, the price of a slave (Matthew 26:15). In the KJV, Luke 22:4 says he "covenanted," or bargained with, the priests. There are all kinds of arguments about why Judas betrayed Christ, but it seems from these passages that *money* was the motive! Why else would he bargain? We know that as the keeper of the money bag he helped himself to what was put into it (John 12:6). The love of money had taken root in his heart, until it took over his love for Jesus.

Don't think it couldn't happen to you. Judas left everything to fol-low Christ the same as the others; he lived with him for three years, witnessed miracles, heard all his teaching. But simple greed was all it took to turn him into a thief and a traitor. He allowed Satan a foothold in his life that eventually became wide enough for the whole door to get kicked down.

If we neglect Jesus because our lives are focused on the accumula-tion of money, then we have the same spirit of Satan in us that Judas did. And how frightening is that? Don't bargain your soul for any price.

Father, I will give Satan no place in my life; keep me faithful. By the powerful
name of Christ Jesus I pray. Amen.

Money and Your Marriage

"Then make my joy complete by being like-minded, having the same love, being one in spirit and purpose." Philippians 2:2

It has been determined that 80 percent of the divorces that take place today can point at money as being the chief cause. Even in marriages that are stable, money is frequently the source of anxiety and frustration. It really isn't all that surprising when you consider that not only are men and women completely different in their perspectives about how they view money, but they usually come from completely different backgrounds in how their parents handled money. Add to the mix that most of us have adopted the world's views on money and marriage, and it's no wonder we find ourselves in such a stew.

What's really the source of all the strife? To quote a great line from an old movie: "What we have here is a failure to communicate." Most money problems are really communication problems. Money actually can be a great tool for getting a dialogue going, preferably before the wedding vows are exchanged. Sitting down together and discussing budgets, goals, and long-term plans helps you get to know one another better.

Conflict is inevitable when it comes to money, since all money decisions are basically priority decisions and two people in a marriage are going to have different priorities. God asks us to work through our differences to become like-minded, to be one in spirit and purpose. It's impossible to do in our flesh, but God has given us the Holy Spirit, and with him all things are possible.

When we first married, Len and I were on the opposite ends of the spectrum on money (tightwad vs. spendthrift) but over the years as we submitted to each other, we began to meet in the middle until today we have incredible harmony. Good communication was the key.

Commit today to putting in all the time and effort necessary to become one in your finances. Your marriage is very special and worth any amount of struggle it will take.

Father, I commit to taking the time to learn to communicate about money with my spouse. Help us become one in this area also. I ask in Jesus' name. Amen.

Obey or Be Deceived

"Do not merely listen to the word, and so deceive yourselves. Do what it says." James 1:22

The worst thing about being deceived is that you don't know you're deceived! To be deceived is to be made to believe what is not true. This goes further than just cult brainwashing. James is saying that when we hear the truth (and God's Word is truth) and don't act on it, we're really telling ourselves that we don't believe it. If we did we would change. Every behavior is motivated by a belief. It doesn't matter how much you *know* about something, unless you change the way you think, you won't change.

Smokers are a perfect example. They all know how destructive their habit is, they know all the health risks, but until something happens to change their belief that it couldn't happen to them—such as a lung cancer diagnosis—they will continue to smoke.

In our financial counseling, it usually takes some disaster to motivate people to ask for help. When the pain becomes too great, they seek relief. But unless they act on what we tell them to do, their situation won't improve. We can always tell when someone is going to choose to remain in their particular financial ditch as they say things like, "It's just not practical to pay with cash; besides, I need my credit cards." Or we frequently hear, "There's no way we could tithe! We won't eat if we do." They want to argue. They break their appointment because they didn't bother to track their expenses. They're not "sick" enough. What we told them had no impact because their beliefs didn't change.

On the other hand, we can always tell those who will be victorious. They listen humbly, they respond, they ask great questions. They do everything we advise them to. They come back to their next session excited at what God is doing.

The Lord rewards those who are doers and not merely hearers.

Father, soften my heart to receive the truth I hear. Protect me from deception and help me to walk in the light that I have. I ask in Jesus' name. Amen.

The Year of Release

"At the end of every seven years you must cancel debts. This is how it is to be done. Every creditor shall cancel the loan he has made to his fellow Israelite or brother, because the LORD's time for canceling debts has been proclaimed." Deuteronomy 15:1-2

In an age where people borrow money for periods of thirty to forty years pay back time and often remain in continual debt their entire lives, it is incredible to realize that the Israelites were forbidden to have any debt extended beyond seven years. Every seventh year—the year of release—all debts among fellow Israelites were wiped out. This was to help people recover from any financial reverses they had suffered so they would not sink further and further into debt. It gave everyone a fresh start and kept the poor from getting poorer while the rich got richer.

Other guidelines went along with this, the principle rule being that they could not withhold from lending just because the year of release was approaching. God commanded them to "open your hand wide" to him who had a need, and he promised to bless them as they obeyed.

The Lord obviously wants his people to be free of debt. Borrowing is discouraged in Scripture, but not prohibited, or he wouldn't have made provision for it. We don't have anything like the year of release today (don't you wish?!) but we can still practice it. If you must go into debt, plan on paying it back as quickly as you can. Even a home can be paid off much sooner than the accepted thirty years if you plan right. God will honor your efforts in ways you can't imagine.

Debt is bondage; it is abnormal. Don't accept it as inevitable; it doesn't have to be and shouldn't be! Celebrate your very own "year of release" as soon as you are able.

Father, your laws are good and in my best interest. I will commit to my personal release from the bondage of debt with your help. I will stop debting and look to you to meet my needs. In Jesus' name. Amen.

Lending At Interest

"Do not charge your brother interest, whether on money or food or anything else that may earn interest. You may charge a foreigner interest, but not a brother Israelite, so that the LORD your God may bless you in everything you put your hand to in the land you are entering to possess." Deuteronomy 23:19-20

The Hebrew language uses two different words for "interest" or "usury." *Neshek* is a noun and refers to interest on a debt, while *nashak* is a verb and means "to strike with a sting like a serpent; bite; to oppress with interest on a loan." (*Strong's Dictionary of Bible Words.*) How descriptive! Ask anyone who's ever been on the wrong side of compound interest how they felt about it; this definition is accurate.

God gave the Israelites this law not necessarily to forbid all interest, but to assist the poor. In biblical times no one would borrow money unless they were truly desperate, and to charge interest would truly be in the spirit of kicking someone who's down. They could, however, charge a foreigner interest if they wished.

Christians interpret from this that when they lend money to a fellow believer in need, they are not to profit by it. The body of Christ is a family, just as the Israelites were family, and families help one another. Those outside our "family," unbelievers, we can charge interest if it is fair and not excessive. This applies only between individuals; obviously businesses operate under different regulations.

Most Christians in need will turn to their credit cards at 18 percent when they hit hard times rather than ask family, friends, or their church for help. Yet God's way has always been that his people should take care of their own. The law did not forbid lending so much as it encouraged giving. Jesus encourages us to lend without expecting to get anything back (Luke 6:35).

Look to the spirit of the law: Needy people are objects of God's special concern and he uses us to meet their needs. You never know when that needy person is going to be you.

Father, how far we have drifted from giving each other a hand when we need help. Make me available and use me wherever you can, for Jesus' sake. Amen.

May

Merchants of Misery

"He who increases his wealth by exorbitant interest amasses it for another, who will be kind to the poor." Proverbs 28:8

In our society, the poor pay more for everything, especially financial services. As the large traditional banks moved out of low-income areas, wanting to focus their activities on investment products for the affluent, the need for basic banking services in urban communities has been taken up by check-cashing outlets, pawnshops, payday loan stores, and even car-title pawns.

These "fringe banks" are largely unregulated, and take advantage of people who can't afford a full-service bank's minimum deposit requirements. They get around usury laws by calling their transactions "fees" or "leases" instead of loans. Federal law considers 36 percent APR to be the starting point for "exorbitant," yet interest rates in these second-tier financial stores can be as high as 360 to 720 percent APR! The mafia never charged this much.

These "merchants of misery," as coined by Michael Hudson, often have direct ties to the big full-service banks, who have found a way to still gouge the working poor without having to deal directly with them. Desperate people are forced to pay for these "services" not because they're ignorant of what it's costing them, but because they have no choice. Ultimately, they sink deeper and deeper into debt (it's not unusual for someone to owe several thousand dollars to check cashers) while the corporate loan sharks boast about how they are providing this valuable service of consumer credit to a socio-economic group that would be unable to obtain it otherwise. With "help" like this, who needs hinderance?

The truth is that poverty is profitable. Payday loan fees alone are estimated to approach $2 billion in 2000 by analysts at the U.S. Federal Reserve. Someone is getting rich at the expense of the poor. The Bible declares that profit taken by usury is unjust. God will move to help the disadvantaged someday, and it will be at their exploiter's expense.

Sovereign Father, you see the plight of the poor every day. I pray for mercy on them; shut down those who would take advantage of them and give your blessing on all endeavors that truly serve them. For Jesus' sake. Amen.

May

Grace!

"So they went up to Joseph's steward and spoke to him at the entrance to the house. 'Please, sir,' they said, 'we came down here for the first time to buy food. But at the place where we stopped for the night we opened our sacks, and each of us found his silver—the exact weight—in the mouth of his sack. So we brought it back with us. We have also brought additional silver with us to buy food. We don't know who put our silver in our sacks.' 'It's all right,' he said. 'Don't be afraid. Your God, the god of your father, has given you treasure in your sacks; I received your silver.'" Genesis 43:19-23

Joseph is a type of Christ. His story in Genesis 37–50 is prophetic in that it foreshadows over 100 details of the coming of the Messiah. Here are just a few:

- Beloved of his father
- Hated and rejected by his brothers
- Falsely accused as a criminal
- Received a Gentile bride during his rejection
- Brothers do not recognize him the first time, but second time they do
- Reconciled to his brothers, and they are blessed through him

The incident with the returned silver in the sacks is a picture of God's grace—undeserved favor. Joseph's brothers were guilt-ridden from carrying the emotional burden of what they had done to him many years ago. They were so sensitive every episode increased their fear. They poured out their confession to the steward only to be reassured that all was well. Joseph had arranged for the silver to be returned to them—the very brother they had sold into slavery showed them incredible mercy.

They came with their money to buy food, only to be given food in abundance at no cost. They didn't deserve it. Joseph had his chance for vengeance; he gave them forgiveness instead. He rejected their money but still supplied their need. That's grace!

Father, Joseph's story is such a beautiful picture of what Jesus did for us. Help me to extend grace towards those who need it. In Jesus' name. Amen.

Follow the Leader

"The king contributed from his own possessions for the morning and evening burnt offerings and for the burnt offerings on the Sabbaths, New Moons and appointed feasts as written in the law of the LORD." 2 Chronicles 31:3

Leaders can't and shouldn't expect their followers to do what they're not doing themselves. Hezekiah was Judah's king following the reign of his father, the wicked King Ahaz. In the very first month of his reign he set about restoring worship in the temple. He took control of the priests and sent word to all Israel and Judah inviting them to come to Jerusalem and celebrate the Passover. He was a very take-charge sort of guy.

When presented with strong leadership, people respond. By Hezekiah setting the example, they gave generously in support of the Levites when the order went out to contribute a tithe of everything. So much that this was the result: "Since the people began to bring their contributions to the temple of the LORD, we have had enough to eat and plenty to spare, because the LORD has blessed his people, and this great amount is left over" (2 Chronicles 31:10).

All this took place because one man with authority set about to turn the people's hearts back to God. Where I fellowship, the leaders are taught that they are to be the first to sacrifice when there is a need to be met, and the people will follow suit when they see the obedience of those over them.

You may not consider yourself a leader, but you have more influence than you know. Are you married? Do you have children? Your family looks to you for a model. Do you have authority over anyone at work? They are watching you. If you want people to behave a certain way, behave that way yourself. If you are in leadership at your church and you want people to be generous, you give first.

People look to leaders for good or evil. Be a leader to emulate in generosity.

Father, it is sobering to realize the influence I have on those around me. Help me live my life so I can say confidently, "Follow me." In the name of Jesus I pray. Amen.

Greed Hurts the Innocent, Too

"A greedy man brings trouble to his family, but he who hates bribes will live." Proverbs 15:27

God has given men the spiritual authority in their homes. They are accountable to him for the leadership and care they provide for their families. A husband's authority stands as a protective shield between his wife and spiritual attack. How tragic, then, when a man succumbs to greed and that protection is lifted! We see this demonstrated in the life of Achan.

His story is in Joshua 7. After the Israelites' victory at Jericho, Achan violated the express command to keep away from any plunder that was to be devoted to the Lord. He took a robe, two hundred shekels of silver, and a fifty shekel wedge of gold and buried them inside his tent. His sin not only led to the defeat of Israel's army at Ai, but it caused his entire family to perish by order of the Lord. All because of his greed. As the head and the example to his family, Achan involved his whole household in his guilt and punishment.

We see examples of this today when men embezzle from their companies and employers. Eventually they are caught and sent to prison, destroying their families in the process. Some women live with the knowledge that their husband's business practices are unethical but, enjoying the extravagant lifestyle it brings, they deaden their consciences and are corrupted as a result.

Greed has sent men leaping out of windows during stock market crashes, leaving behind shattered families with no means of support. Greed has put women and children in dangerous situations involving drugs and guns for the profitability it brings their men. In the church, greed has caused families to miss out on the blessing that comes from tithing, and the work of ministry is stunted from lack of resources.

Greed is a fierce demon spirit that seeks to destroy us and our loved ones. Those who trample it and allow it no seed in their hearts will be richly rewarded.

Father, put a shield around my heart to protect me from the powerful force of greed. Keep the protection in place around my family. I ask in Jesus' name. Amen.

Leaving an Inheritance

"A good man leaves an inheritance for his children's children."
Proverbs 13:22

What comes to mind when you think of your children's inheritance? Hopefully you think of the spiritual legacy you will leave them which is far more important since it will impact them for all eternity. Here Solomon is referring to the physical estate to be passed on to our posterity.

Inheritances were very highly regarded in biblical times. Under the law God gave to Moses, inheritances (particularly land) were to remain in the same tribal family. Pretty simple. We have complicated things tremendously in our day.

If you are so unfortunate as to die without a will, your heirs are in a real pickle. The state will divide up your estate according to how they see fit. Even if you do have a will, your heirs will be dealing with courts as the will goes through probate. This costs money—lots of money. Attorney's fees, taxes, accountant's fees, and court costs can siphon off up to 70 percent of your estate. There is a better way.

If you truly want your worldly goods to go where you wish them to, you need a revocable living trust. You remain in control of your property, and upon your death you control when and how much your beneficiaries will receive. There is no probate; it is a private document. Wills can be contested, tying up your assets for years; trusts are extremely difficult to challenge. If your estate is worth less than $1 million there are no estate taxes due. If you're worth more than that, you don't need advice from me!

These are the highlights of a living trust. What's the downside? Well, they're more expensive than a will, and you will definitely need an attorney who specializes in them. This is not something for rich people only; the less you have, the more probate hurts! Unless you plan on giving it all away before you die, a great deal of your money will be lost without this important document in place.

Father, I need your wisdom is preparing for my death. Even in my passing from this world, I want to be a good steward in providing for my own and for your kingdom work. In Jesus' name. Amen.

A Good Name

"A good name is more desirable than great riches; to be esteemed is better than silver or gold." Proverbs 22:1

What's in a name? In Bible times, a person's name was extremely significant. Parents would name their children to make a statement (Jabez—"pain"), to memorialize an event (Moses—"drawn out"), to describe a physical attribute (Esau—"hairy"), to make a wish or a prophecy about the child's future (Solomon—"peace") or even to make an inside joke (Isaac—"He [God] is laughing [now]"). Having a good name was everything. A person and their name were so intimately linked that to "cut off the name" of someone amounted to the same thing as killing them.

Today when we say someone has "a good name" we are referring to their integrity, their character, and their reputation. Once it is damaged, it is not easily restored. A reputation has more value than wealth or possessions. You may only think about your reputation among the people with whom you associate, but in our society there is a means for "checking you out" that people with whom you wish to do business put a great deal of stock in. It's called your credit report.

This report is not used only when you apply for a loan. If you're inquiring about coverage to an insurance company, they will check your credit before they give you a quote. Employers will look it over before making a hire. Landlords check credit reports of potential tenants. Utility companies use it to determine if they will request a deposit before providing service.

If you have a low credit score, you will pay more for loans and any service involving a longer-term relationship. It may not be fair, but that's how it works. Credit reports are believed to be an accurate representation of a person's character. Are they responsible in paying their bills on time?

Having a good name is more important now than ever as far as your financial life is concerned. How do you establish one? We'll look at that tomorrow.

Father, I do want my name to stand for integrity, character, and a good reputation as I represent Christ. I pray in His name that is above all names. Amen.

Establishing a Good Name

"A good name is better than fine perfume..." Ecclesiastes 7:1

If you want to make your financial life much easier, you will give some time and attention to your credit report. If your credit "stinks," you will pay the highest interest rates on all loans, be required to put down large deposits on services, pay higher insurance premiums, and be considered high-risk as a tenant. It may even cost you a job. A credit rating carries that much weight.

Good credit qualifies you for those 0 percent car loans, 5 percent or less credit cards, no deposits on utilities, the cheapest insurance rates, and it can even get your bank fees waived. It smoothes the way for any business transactions you care to make. So what are inquirers looking for? This is what helps:

- Pay all bills on time
- Maintain two to four credit cards, no more
- Close all unused credit or store cards
- Keep balances well below limits
- Pay more than the minimum payment
- Establish long-term history (12 to 18 months)

This is what hurts:

- Too many cards or no cards
- High non-mortgage debt
- Delinquent accounts
- Frequent job or address changes
- Charge-offs
- Bankruptcy

Everyone should order their credit report to check for errors. Mistakes do happen. Legitimate black marks take time to remove—for negative items, seven years; bankruptcies, ten years. Value your good credit. Protect it. A good name will serve you well.

Father, help me to keep my credit history clear to reflect my responsibility and integrity, and be my defender if events happen beyond my control that would affect it. I ask in Jesus' name. Amen.

Far Above Rubies

"A wife of noble character who can find? She is worth far more than rubies." Proverbs 31:10

Christian wives have mixed reactions to the Proverbs 31 woman. On one hand she is venerated and looked to as a role model, and on the other she is resented for being everything they feel they're not. She wasn't a real person anyway, but a composite of ideal qualities in a wife presented in the form of an acrostic poem. Over the next several days I want to explore all the ways she contributes financially to her household, starting with her very worth to her husband and children, her community, and even to all the generations who will follow her.

Women today question their worth. If they're not bringing in a paycheck, they may feel guilty, and when someone asks, "What do you do?" their self-esteem falls through the floor as they mumble, "I'm just a housewife." Strike that word from your vocabulary! You're not married to a house (although some days it may feel like it.)

God knew his women would struggle with this issue, so he says right up front what they are worth: "Far more than rubies." Rubies are rare, and in large size, the costliest of jewels. Most of what passes for rubies today are lab-created—meaning fake. "Who can find?" A good wife is priceless. Let's face it, ladies, if we were to be paid the going rate for all the different tasks we handle on a daily basis, who could afford us?

What about the intangibles? Can you purchase well-adjusted kids? Can you put a price tag on spiritual influence? What about the beauty and creativity a woman puts into her home? What's the wage scale on love and companionship?

Our problem is that we look to the world's value system, where life is viewed in materialistic terms. Far better to look to God. His opinion is the only one that counts, and he says our worth is beyond price. It is "far above rubies"!

Father, let all your women take this scripture to heart. We are so brainwashed by society telling us we can't be fulfilled caring for our homes and families. Help us see our true worth. In Jesus' name. Amen.

No Lack of Gain

"Her husband has full confidence in her and lacks nothing of value. She brings him good, not harm, all the days of her life." Proverbs 31:11-12

Whether a man ends up with a nest egg or a goose egg often depends on the chick he marries." So goes an old sexist saying, but it's the truth. A wife's degree of influence on her husband is awesome. It is usually the wife who sets the standard of a family's lifestyle, starting with the house and the neighborhood she chooses to live in. If she is content to live within his income, they can prosper. If she is not, she can put the family deeply into debt with her extravagance. She can push her husband into a vocation for which he is not suited in an attempt to bring in more income, causing him to be frustrated and unfulfilled. This is not "doing him good."

The wife of noble character is disciplined in her spending habits; her husband trusts her with the family finances and isn't anxiously wondering what she's doing. She is frugal and prudent and is not wasteful of their assets, but makes the most of them. She is a careful shopper and takes the time to make meals from scratch rather than use expensive convenience foods. Her presence full time in the home eliminates many child-care expenses. She clips coupons!

The Proverbs 31 woman manages everything in her home carefully and economically, freeing her husband to provide in the marketplace without having any concern over the domestic affairs because his wife has it all covered. She is truly a helpmeet to him. The NKJV puts it this way: "The heart of her husband safely trusts her, so he will have no lack of gain." A wife doesn't have to have a paycheck to add to her family's wealth.

Take on the financial challenge and see how far you can make those dollars go. Manage in such a way as to bring good to your family all the days of your life.

Father, I recognize the important role I play in the stewardship of my family's finances. Show me ways I can do better, as I submit to living on the amount of income you allow us to have. In Jesus' name. Amen.

Willing Worker

"She seeks wool and flax and works with eager hands." Proverbs 31:13

Women of ancient times had a lot more work to do in their homes than women today. They didn't have the J.C. Penney catalog; they had to seek out the raw materials—wool and flax for linen—and go through the process of spinning and weaving before they could make them into the coverings they needed. It was all a part of running the household for them. They had drudge work, just as we do, but our Proverbs 31 woman did these things eagerly and willingly. Our attitude determines how we go about our work. If we feel like unpaid maids, we're not going to enjoy caring for our homes.

Have you ever thought about how important your housekeeping is, the value of what you do? It's the irony of housework that nobody notices it unless it's neglected. I know women who hold down jobs and their homes are disaster areas. There's only so much energy available in the human body every 24 hours, and something has to give. It's usually the house. The homemaker who is there has the time and energy for all the things that need doing (unless there are small children on the scene!). The financial benefits are, of course, that you don't have to pay someone to do it for you. Things that are well-maintained last longer and save you money as they don't have to be replaced as often. A clean, sanitary home cuts down on illnesses. Carpets that are vacuumed daily stay cleaner longer. All these things save money over time.

Take pride in your home and strive for excellence in the management you give to it! The service you are providing your family is so valuable! Even the highest paying jobs have dirty work that no one likes to do. Remember that often the most important work in the world is that which is performed with only fulfillment and praise as the pay.

Father God, give me any attitude adjustment I need so I can go about my work willingly. Thank you that you see and appreciate all I do. In Jesus' name. Amen.

An Enterprising Spirit

"She is like the merchant ships, bringing her food from afar. She gets up while it is still dark; she provides food for her family and portions for her servant girls." Proverbs 31:14-15

Merchant ships of the ancient Middle East sailed around the Mediterranean Sea, stopping at each port to sell and trade their cargo for other goods. The Proverbs 31 woman would head out to market every day with her own goods to barter—homegrown food, handmade garments, and baked goods. This was usually accomplished in the early morning hours before the heat of the day. She was a shrewd shopper, bargaining to get the best deal possible on the highest quality goods available.

We can practice her habit today by knowing where the freshest produce is sold and making the effort to go get it; by having our own organic garden; by sharing with neighbors. We get all the lemons and oranges in season we can use off our neighbors' trees. They're happy to have them picked and we get free fruit. Do you bake the world's greatest chocolate chip cookies? See if you can trade with a friend who makes her own bread. Use your talents in the kitchen to save money.

Flea markets, craft fairs, and yard sales are modern day equivalents of the bazaars of olden times, and they are a good source of bargains. Rising early allows us to get more done; it gives us time to plan and organize so we are efficient in running our errands, which also saves on gas.

You and I may not have human servants, but we have dishwashers, microwaves, automatic washing machines, and dryers at our service. If we have children who are old enough, we can delegate and train them to do chores.

Being well-organized keeps us from wasting our resources. Bills get paid on time. Life runs more smoothly for everyone. The wife is the key to a well-managed home. If she doesn't do it, who will?

Father, thank you for my home. Thank you for all your provision—the food, the modern appliances, clothes, everything we need to live. Continue to help me fulfill my role in a way that is pleasing to you. For Jesus' sake. Amen.

A Head for Business

"She considers a field and buys it; out of her earnings she plants a vineyard." Proverbs 31:16

We never read about the Proverbs 31 woman holding down a job, but in this verse we see she is active as a real estate investor. Two different properties were involved here. A field in Israel was basically a lot which would be cleared of debris, then a wall would be built around it before it would be tilled and planted with a grain crop. This would not only help feed her family, but provide them with another stream of income.

Notice that she "considers" the field first. This wasn't a rash deal; she carefully figured in the cost of the property versus the expected gain from it before she made the purchase. Undoubtedly her husband was involved, as the transaction would have been carried out under his oversight.

Where did she get the money to do this? As we will see, she made and sold garments, and with her profit from that endeavor, combined with her habits of saving and thrift, she was able to make this investment without going into debt. Those same earnings allowed her to buy vines to plant a vineyard.

In the Bible, vineyards were a symbol of peace, security, and prosperity. To have your own personal vineyard made you a person of some esteem. They were a lot of work, but provided the family with grapes, raisins, wine—and another source of revenue. These were wise investments that enhanced her family's finances.

In our day we aren't as agriculturally bent as she was, but we can still invest in real estate through owning rental properties. Wisely purchased, the tenants will cover all the expenses and we can make a profit. Women can be involved in many business investments without having to leave the home. If you have ambitions in that direction, pray and ask God to show you opportunities. Then proceed with wisdom and discretion, with your husband's blessing, of course. I wish you the greatest success.

Father, thank you for the example of the Proverbs 31 woman. Make me aware of any business ventures I could put my hand to. In Jesus' name. Amen.

Stewardship of the Body

"She sets about her work vigorously, and her arms are strong for her tasks." Proverbs 31:17

We have already seen that the Proverbs 31 woman is a hard worker. She's also an early riser; she's industrious and organized. How does she do it? I think her secret is her good health habits. Keeping yourself in top physical condition gives you energy. Her lifestyle would have consisted of lots of exercise and fresh air, given that she didn't have our electric appliances and motored transportation but had to do everything with her own hands and feet.

Her diet would have been whole, natural foods with no chemicals added, nothing wrapped in plastic loaded with sugar and fat, and pure water to drink. Still, good health doesn't come automatically. She put effort into taking care of herself. We have to work even harder at it today than she did, what with our sedentary ways and all the bad food out there. But taking care of our "temples" will absolutely save us money.

First, make water your drink of choice. It's what your body needs most; chronic dehydration caused by coffee and soda leads to a plethora of ailments, and can even keep you fat! Water is cheap; if your tap water tastes good, you're all set.

Next, eat whole, natural foods. Lots of fruits and vegetables. Junk food is expensive; you're paying for advertising and packaging and chemicals. Limit your eating out; restaurants are notorious for high fat, high-sugar, and high-sodium content in what they serve, plus it's costly.

Finally, exercise! Walking costs nothing. Do more chores manually and burn calories as you save electricity. Strength training is the key to weight loss and staying vigorous as we age. Get on a program to pump iron. As you begin to do these things, you will notice your medicine cabinet is no longer jammed with "remedies" to fix what's ailing you, because you'll feel good. You can spare yourself so much pain and expense by staying healthy and fit.

Good health is a treasure we don't always appreciate until it's gone.

Father, I do want to treat my body like the temple of the Holy Spirit that it is. Convict me to improve my health. In Jesus' name I pray. Amen.

Taking Inventory

"She sees that her trading is profitable, and her lamp does not go out at night. In her hand she holds the distaff and grasps the spindle with her fingers." Proverbs 31:18-19

We've seen that the Proverbs 31 woman does all things well, and here she examines her work and recognizes the high quality of what she's produced. She takes inventory of all she has and determines she can turn a profit with her product in the marketplace.

This is the start-up phase of her home based business. She carefully looks over her resources to see what the possibilities are and makes her plans. She assesses her talents and the amount of time she has available to her. As in any new venture, getting it off the ground takes a lot more time in the beginning, which is perhaps why she burns the midnight oil.

But it is her habit to keep the lamp lit through the night. In ancient times this showed hospitality, as there were no motels and travelers would stay in people's homes. A lamp lit in the window meant "welcome." It also showed prosperity, as valuable oil was being used continually.

As soon as the sun was down, she would turn to her distaff and spindle to spin the wool and flax into the yarn and thread she needed for her projects. Late evening, when the regular chores are done for the day and the kids are in bed, is an excellent time to work on our own creative pursuits.

What about you? Can you turn a personal hobby into a professional business? Is there something you enjoy doing as a creative outlet that you could use in your free time to contribute to the family finances? If God has gifted you with any variety of skills, be it business or creative, and if you have the time and the capital to invest, consider what he might have you do. The only limits are those you place on yourself.

Father, I lay this whole matter of my gifts and talents before you, if I should pursue using them to profit my family. I trust you to show me the right timing for any new venture I would like to take on. I pray in Jesus' name. Amen.

May 19

Reach Out and Touch Someone

"She opens her arms to the poor and extends her hands to the needy."
Proverbs 31:20

The Proverbs 31 woman modeled the heart of God as she extended compassion towards the poor. She did this in several ways: as the owner of a field and a vineyard she followed the Lord's directives to leave any loose sheaves after the harvest for "the alien, the fatherless, and the widow" (Deuteronomy 24:19) to glean. At the vineyard, she left the remaining grapes for the poor.

She was generous; she gave as much as her means would allow. She didn't hoard her wealth, but gave out of a willing heart. By allowing herself to be used by the Lord to show mercy and concern for the less fortunate, he in turn honors her and all she does.

Perhaps you don't have her resources, but you can still lend a helping hand. Volunteers are desperately needed everywhere to help the homeless, the infirm, and the disadvantaged, especially now with so many women working outside their homes who don't have the time. A woman in my church started a ministry to the homeless by knitting blankets to pass out to them in the colder weather. I joined her with my crocheted afghans, and in a few years "Covering the Homeless" had expanded to serve over 400 people living on the streets of Phoenix with dozens of volunteers helping. All it costs me is the yarn required for the afghans and my time, which is insignificant compared to the amount of satisfaction and fulfillment I receive from doing it.

Giving lightens our load in more ways than one; it lifts our spirits knowing we're doing good for someone whom everyone else seems to have forgotten about. Extend your hands in outreach to the poor and you find them being filled with benefits by God himself. It is in caring for "the least of these" that we truly touch the heart of Jesus.

Father, I want to be involved with serving the poor. Open my eyes and heart to the opportunities around me, and give me the courage to step out and take some risks. For Jesus' sake. Amen.

Worthy Woman Wardrobe

"When it snows, she has no fear for her household; for all of them are clothed in scarlet. She makes coverings for her bed; she is clothed in fine linen and purple. Her husband is respected at the city gate, where he takes his seat among the elders of the land." Proverbs 31:21-23

The Proverbs 31 woman was prepared. She would have had to make these garments for her family long before winter arrived at her door. They were most likely made of wool, since that fabric took well to scarlet dye, and would have been luxurious and costly. They didn't have closets jammed with clothes the way we do now; they had a few pieces of high quality that were made to last a long time. I decided awhile back I preferred quality to quantity in my closet, allowing me to have nicer clothes but fewer of them.

We see in this verse she also made coverings, or tapestries, for her bed which would have included cushions, pillows, drapes, rugs, and sheets. She is the resident decorator in her home, making it warm and beautiful. It doesn't take a lot of money to make a home inviting and comfortable; we've all been in homes that were done by professional interior designers for thousands of dollars that felt sterile and cold. Just be sure your home reflects *you*, your personality and tastes.

The last thing she does is clothe herself—and what clothing! Fine linen and purple were what the nobility wore. It suggests riches and rank. She had class, and it showed. A wife dressing like a slob—or too suggestively—can have a negative effect on a husband's professional standing. Good grooming and modesty on her part can help further his career. We live in a world that still judges by appearances, but the truth is how you appear to others reflects on how you feel about yourself. Remember that we represent Christ!

Father, thank you for taking an interest in how I look. Help me to look quality as economically as possible, so I will be a good testimony of your excellent care of your children. In Jesus' name. Amen.

Home Based Business

"She makes linen garments and sells them, and supplies the merchants with sashes. She is clothed with strength and dignity; and she can laugh at the days to come." Proverbs 31:24-25

The Proverbs 31 woman ran her own business, but she did it in the context of her home. She wasn't neglecting her family; they came first. We also know she was very professional; the word "supplies" suggests dependability. The merchants could count on her to deliver the goods on time, and we've noted that it was top quality.

Her "thing" was sewing; what is yours? Often home based businesses are born from a vision conceived over a favorite activity, or a hidden talent has suddenly surfaced. If you decide to go for it, do some research first. Is there a market for what you'll be doing? Who will your competition be? What are the going rates; how much can you charge for your product or service? Do you need to be licensed? Must you collect sales taxes? How will you advertise?

In other words, develop a business plan before you get into it neck deep and find out there's more to it than you realized. Find out everything first! No matter how excited you may be about your great new venture, it's not worth it if it's taking more from you than it's bringing in—whether it's money, time, or energy.

Be careful that your side business doesn't turn into the main event that turns your household upside down, disrupting everyone's schedule. We see from this scripture that the Proverbs 31 woman was serene; she was facing the future without worry. Her business wasn't a source of stress to her; she didn't take on more than she could handle. We need to learn this lesson today, as we overextend ourselves in the misguided belief that being frantically busy is a virtue. It isn't!

Not everyone is cut out to run a business, and that's okay. It's just one available option. But do develop your skills and talents; you never know what the future may bring.

Father, you have given me abilities and I don't want to "bury" them. If this is the right time to use them for financial gain, please open the door for me. I ask in Jesus' name. Amen.

Watch Woman

*"She speaks with wisdom, and faithful instruction is on her tongue.
She watches over the affairs of her household, and does not eat the
bread of idleness." Proverbs 31:26-27*

A mother's influence in the home cannot be bought for any amount of money. One of the greatest modern tragedies is that for millions of kids, someone other than mom is nurturing them. It costs $5,000 per child annually for care in an average center; a top quality one or hiring a live-in nanny costs two to four times as much. It doesn't matter how impeccable their credentials or how much they care, they will never have the connection you do with your child. No one is qualified to watch over the ways of your home like you are.

To know and to be aware of everything that is going on, to have your finger on the pulse of every family member, their emotional temperature, their habits and problems, what they're learning and doing, and the values they're picking up is not a part-time job. What happens to society when mothers abdicate this responsibility?

I think all of us would agree that the United States is in a moral decline. Over half of all marriages end in divorce. Single-parent households are epidemic now, and many of these families live in poverty. Without family support, more kids drop out of school, limiting their opportunities to low paying jobs for unskilled labor. What is the cost to our country?

There are no easy solutions to our nation's problems, but you can make a difference in your own family. If you have a choice, choose to be a full-time presence in your home. Teach your kids by word and example the values you want them to have. Many mothers have chosen to homeschool their children and are giving them a very good education.

Happily, the tide seems to be turning as more people are realizing the cost of not being home is too high a price to pay. Mothers in the home are doing their part to make the world a better place for all of us.

Father, I know that just physically being in my home isn't enough. Help me to impart godly values. I ask in Jesus' name. Amen.

Rich Rewards

"Her children arise and call her blessed; her husband also, and he praises her: 'Many women do noble things, but you surpass them all.' Charm is deceptive, and beauty is fleeting; but a woman who fears the LORD is to be praised. Give her the reward she has earned, and let her works bring her praise at the city gate." Proverbs 31:28-31

This beautiful tribute to God's ideal of womanhood should get our attention in a culture where homemaking is not highly prized. It's true that we don't receive a paycheck for our domestic duties, but monetary compensation is only for this world. Our eyes should be fixed beyond this life and on what our efforts will mean in eternity. The acclamation will come if we are faithful to our calling.

The raising of children, and all the tasks that go along with it, often seem to be thankless. It can be overwhelming and exhausting, and we all have days when we wonder if it's worth it. The fact that the Proverbs 31 woman's children "arise" in this verse suggests that they are grown when they pronounce her blessed.

Notice also the compliment her husband lavishes on her. Husbands, encourage your wives! If she feels she gets no appreciation at home, she may want to get outside employment just to get some positive reinforcement for something she does. Being built up by those closest to us gives us honor and dignity and motivation to keep going.

For anyone who thinks "women's work" is without recognition or prestige, we see in this final verse that our woman of noble character is being honored publicly for the life she has lived. It's only in a life is poured out in service to others that we find our true purpose. Never, ever look to a paycheck to validate what you do! God doesn't base his rewards on a monetary scale. The Bible speaks of crowns (1 Corinthians 9:25) and an inheritance that is imperishable (1 Peter 1:4).

Rich rewards, indeed.

Father, help me to look beyond the seeming trivialities of my daily life and see the eternal significance of what I do. Thank you that my value cannot be measured by mere money that perishes. In Jesus' name. Amen.

Character Doesn't Require Money

"And now, my daughter, don't be afraid. I will do for you all you ask. All my fellow townsmen know that you are a woman of noble character." Ruth 3:11

The only woman in all of Scripture to be described in the exact terms Proverbs 31:10 uses (a woman of noble character) is Ruth. As we look at her life, we see that in many ways she is a stark contrast to Proverb 31's heroine. She was a widow; she was poor; she had no skills or talents we're told about; she wasn't even an Israelite, but a pagan Moabitess. It's interesting that God chose women of such opposite station to illustrate what he values most, and that's our character.

Ruth was a peasant, a despised foreigner; so impoverished she was forced to glean in the barley fields so she and her mother-in-law Naomi could eat; a person seemingly of no consequence. The only thing she had going for her was her reputation.

When Boaz, the owner of the field where Ruth was gleaning, noticed her and inquired who she was, she had his immediate respect and concern. The whole town was talking about her devotion and loyalty to a woman whose whole world had been shattered by the deaths of her husband and sons. She impressed Boaz with her work ethic and he made sure she wasn't bothered and that there were plenty of sheaves left for her to gather. As a near relative of Naomi, Boaz could act as the kinsmen-redeemer for Ruth, which he does. By marrying Ruth, he rescues her from poverty and through their son she becomes the great-grandmother of King David and part of the messianic line.

Ruth's story has a happy ending, but do you think God would have used her the way he did if she didn't have such outstanding character qualities? People of excellent character seldom stay down and out for long; they have a way of rising to the top. Worth isn't measured by what's in our wallets. We don't need money to have the qualities of faith, loyalty, humility, and graciousness that Ruth exhibited.

Father, thank you that what you value most in our lives can't be purchased. Make me a person of outstanding character. For Jesus' sake, Amen.

Money Talks

"Two men owed money to a certain moneylender. One owed him five hundred denarii, and the other fifty. Neither of them had the money to pay him back, so he canceled the debts of both. Now which of them will love him more?" Luke 7:41-42

As you read through the Gospels, notice how often Jesus used money and possessions to illustrate the truths he was teaching. In fact, he talked more about money than he did about heaven or hell. Why do you suppose this is?

Well, for one thing, God knows money will always get our attention. It's something everyone can relate to because everyone has to deal with it in one way or another. It's been estimated that 80 percent of our waking hours are spent thinking about money and money-related issues. (For people who dream about money, that statistic would be higher!) Jesus was a master at knowing his audience. The above passage was spoken to a money-hungry Pharisee. You can be sure he was listening, because he got the point Jesus was making about love and forgiveness. Two-thirds of the parables Jesus told relate in some way to money.

The proper handling of money is a life skill everyone needs. How important is it? If we don't have a grip on our finances, every other area of our life will be out of balance. Our enemy knows this, and he uses money to push our buttons. He can use its lack to try to get us to blame God and he can use its abundance to turn our hearts away from God. Money has us coming and going all the time.

Jesus used money to make his point so many times because the pursuit of it is something we need to be converted from, before we can fully convert to Christ. See how many of his teachings on money are evangelistic in context.

Money does speak. The question is—who are we going to listen to?

Father, I'm becoming more aware of the hold money has on life in general, and I don't want to be controlled by it. I surrender completely to you, holding nothing back, so that I no longer listen to the voice of money calling me. For Jesus' sake. Amen.

Dealing with Banks

"If you lend money to one of my people among you who is needy, do not be like a moneylender; charge him no interest." Exodus 22:25

Banks are in business to make money. Hopefully that's not a revelation to you, or you may already be in financial hot water. Banks exist not always to serve you, but to make a profit. As my husband tells people who are debt-prone, "Banks are not your friends."

Of course it depends on the bank but those that charge $1.50 or more through ATM machines to access your own funds are to be avoided. You can evade service fees if you keep an extravagant amount of money on deposit (which of course the bank is profiting by), but you most likely won't be earning much interest on that money.

Banks make most of their money through lending, obviously, and it would seem the only people they wish to lend to are those who don't need the money. They are the ones who get the best deals and the best rates. Many banks still have fiscal sense and scruples about lending to people who will have considerable hardship once they begin to repay, and refuse home loans accordingly. Enter the mortgage lenders.

When it comes to home mortgages, the recent trend has been for lenders to get you to borrow the maximum you qualify for, which is utter foolishness. The percentage of gross annual income allowable for housing has crept up over the years, from 25 percent to 33-36 percent. What it means is more money for the companies and more pressure for you. Remember that everyone who has been foreclosed on "qualified" for their mortgage when they took it out. Lenders aren't doing anyone a favor in granting these loans. Loan officers are basically salesmen. Their product is debt.

Do we need banks? Yes, to handle the mechanics of money. Good banks do exist, but you need to do your homework and shop around for one that will provide you with the best service. Establishing a relationship with a bank where you feel valued can be a great resource.

Father, lead me to a financial institution that will assist me well in my stewardship. I ask in Jesus' name. Amen.

Cleansing the Temple

"Jesus entered the temple area and drove out all who were buying and selling there. He overturned the tables of the moneychangers and the benches of those selling doves. 'It is written,' he said to them, "My house will be called a house of prayer," but you are making it a "den of robbers"'" (Matthew 21:12-13).

This scripture is so fascinating because it gives us a glimpse of the Lord Jesus we've never seen before. Christ having a temper tantrum? We need to see this was a deliberate act. He didn't suddenly "lose it." This temple trade had been going on in Jerusalem his entire earthly life. It actually provided a valuable service for the people coming from far distances who needed animals for sacrifice, though of course the priests were profiting by it and the prices were over inflated. But the time had now come, with the coming of the Messiah, for Israel to be purified of everything that defiled their worship of God.

The vendors were set up in the Court of the Gentiles, the only place in the temple area non-Jews could go for prayer. It encompassed several acres and was also used as a shortcut between the city and the Mount of Olives. All this was interfering with the Gentiles' ability to worship God, as it had become a noisy, smelly marketplace. And God had had enough.

At the heart of it all was idolatry, the worship of mammon opposed to the worship of the one true God. The religious leaders cared more about financial gain than they did the sanctity of the temple area and God's provision for the Gentiles. They hated Jesus because he was a threat to their entire way of life.

What about us? If we take Jesus' teachings seriously, as we should, doesn't what he says about money shake us up? Either Jesus is Lord of our lives or he is not. Will you let him cleanse your temple, drive out all competition to him, and make your heart a holy dwelling fit for the King of kings?

Almighty God, I repent of any mammon spirit. Come in with your whip and remove it. Purify me so I am a clean vessel for you. In Jesus' name. Amen.

The Call of Matthew

"As Jesus went on from there, he saw a man named Matthew sitting at the tax collector's booth. 'Follow me,' he told him, and Matthew got up and followed him." Matthew 9:9

Matthew was minding his business collecting taxes for the Roman government at his tollbooth alongside the highway when Jesus came by. We're not told if Matthew had met Jesus previously, or even if he knew who he was. All we're told is that when Jesus said, "Follow me," Matthew got up and followed him.

It was the same act of obedience displayed by the four fishermen who had answered that same call, but consider Matthew's position. He had a lucrative job, as tax collectors were allowed to extract all the money they could and pocket the difference. All he had to do was sit at his office and levy taxes on the merchandise being transported on that road. It wasn't an easy job to come by, but he had landed it and it was his for life.

Until he met Jesus. Until he got up and walked away from a position that he would never be able to get back, ever. Peter, Andrew, James, and John could return to their fishing nets if this adventure didn't work out; Matthew didn't have that option. For him, there was no turning back.

Have you ever been in the position where Jesus called you away from your vocation to go with him? We understood a little of what Matthew must have felt. When we left Wisconsin for Arizona we went from Len's secure union job to self-employment in a place where we had never been before and where we knew no one. Was it frightening? Not really; it was exhilarating! We knew the Lord was directing us and was with us, and that's all that mattered. Obviously, things worked out for us.

They did for Matthew, too. If you ever have to choose between a job and Jesus, choose the one you can never lose.

Father, there's not a word of praise in Scripture for these men who left everything to follow you. We're not supposed to look at them, but at Christ who bids us come. In his name. Amen.

Beware of Bad Advice

"Blessed is the man who does not walk in the counsel of the wicked or stand in the way of sinners or sit in the seat of mockers." Psalm 1:1

Conforming to the world's way of conduct has three stages. Walking in the counsel of the wicked is listening to their viewpoints. Standing in the way of sinners is behaving as they do. Sitting in the seat of mockers is to fully agree with them. See the progression?

Walk—we're just passing by on our way when we hear something that interests us. *Stand*—we stop to participate in what we've heard. *Sit*—we settle in and embrace the ideas. So we had better be sure that what we're paying attention to is the truth!

When it comes to finances, there's an awful lot of bad advice out there. One school of thought says don't pay off debt. Ever. Just keep refinancing and leveraging and use Other People's Money to do whatever you want. Couples are counseled to not get married until they have a prenuptial agreement drawn up. Car salesmen encourage leases so you will have a new car to drive every two years. Mortgage brokers push you to borrow as much as you can qualify for on a house. Seminars teach borrowing on your home's equity to make investments. They can make it sound so right, so attractive.

No matter how great it sounds, always measure the advice you get by Scripture. Learn to discern. Listen to the still, small voice of the Holy Spirit. What do you feel he's telling you about this? If the contemplated deal causes greed to rise up in you, that is a warning right there. If your spouse hates the idea, don't do it.

Also look at the track record of the people giving you advice. What are their lives like? Just because someone is a Christian doesn't mean they know what they're talking about. Take your direction only from those who follow God's Word.

Father, guide me in straight paths and keep me from the counsel of the ungodly. Give me discernment so I will know when I hear things that are contrary to your Word. I ask in Jesus' name. Amen.

Should I Consolidate My Debt?

"There is a way which seems right to a man, but in the end it leads to death." Proverbs 14:12

A question we frequently get asked in counseling is, "Should I get a debt consolidation loan?" It's a sincere inquiry coming from people who have racked up debt on several credit cards, bank loans, payday loans—you name it—and are looking for some relief. What a consolidation loan does is take all the debt and roll it into one lump sum, which is then financed over a longer period of time, thus reducing the monthly payment. Sounds like wisdom, doesn't it? Here's why it's a bad idea.

First of all, spreading it out over a longer period also means you will end up paying much, much more over the long haul than if you had just set about paying them off one by one. But the biggest reason to avoid them is that they are treating only a symptom, not the problem itself.

The problem is overspending. People use the freed-up money to continue to live beyond their means. Because they can't control their spending, they are soon running up new debt on the credit cards again, which they will have to make payments on in addition to the consolidation loan repayment. They are worse off than before. So off they go in search of a new source of credit, in a cycle that ends in financial death—bankruptcy. Debt consolidation teaches you nothing. It solves nothing. It just makes it easier for you to incur more debt.

So what is the solution? You must bite the bullet and deal with paying back the debts you now have. You must stop using credit, today. You'll never get out of the hole you're in if you keep digging yourself deeper. There is a way, a right way. I'll show you tomorrow.

Father, teach me to not seek quick fix solutions that don't really fix anything. Help me to deal with the root cause of my debting problem. Give me the discipline to do what I know I must do. I ask in Jesus' name. Amen.

Eliminating Debt

"For these commands are a lamp, this teaching is a light, and the corrections of discipline are the way to life." Proverbs 6:23

Are you sick of debt? Have you made the decision to quit borrowing money? You've cut up your credit cards? Then you are ready. This is a method that is taught by both Christian and secular counselors because it works. It won't be fun (at first); in fact, it will be painful. It's supposed to be. You don't ever want to do this again. These are the steps to follow:

- Make a list of all you owe, beginning with the smallest balance.
- Note the minimum payments and the interest rates.
- Contact your creditors and negotiate for the best rates you can.
- Transfer balances to get a lower rate as long as you're not being charged to do it, and cancel the old accounts.
- Figure out how much extra money you have available each month to apply to debt reduction. Even if it's only $10, add it to the minimum payment of the smallest balance. Let's say the minimum payment is $25; you would send $35 a month and pay the minimums on all the others.
- When the smallest debt is gone, take the $35 and add it to the minimum of the next smallest; let's say that total is $75.
- When that one is paid off, apply $75 to the next minimum payment—maybe making it a total of $150. Send in $150 until that debt is retired and add $150 to debt #4.

You get the idea. Keep doing this until all of it is gone and you're left with just your mortgage. By now you have acquired the discipline it takes to live within your means. All that money that used to go out in debt repayment is now available for giving opportunities and for savings. Praise God!

Father, how I long to be out of debt! Give me the patience and discipline it will take to stick to this plan. Thank you for a path to follow. In Jesus' name. Amen.

Eliminating Debt, Part 2

"In his heart man plans his course, but the Lord determines his steps."
Proverbs 16:9

Once you are free of consumer debt, you may choose to go all the way and eliminate your mortgage debt as well. You may get arguments from people who say you shouldn't give up your tax deduction, but they have a math disability. I have lived for years without a house payment and have not yet missed the tax deduction. I do very much enjoy knowing that the roof over my head is paid for, however.

There are several ways of going about paying your home off early. You can do one or all of these options:

- Round up your payment. If your payment is $756, for instance, pay $800 and apply the difference to principal.
- Make bulk "principal only" payments. We would save up $1,000 and have it applied directly off the mortgage.
- Switch to a biweekly mortgage. Your payment will be every two weeks, and will add another full monthly payment each year.
- Get a 15 year mortgage instead of a 30 year, which forces you to make higher payments. If you can't discipline yourself to make bulk "principal only" payments, this is a good way to go.
- Take advantage of lower rates by refinancing if the interest rate is at least 2 points less than what you currently have. Do it only if you are staying in your home for the next five to seven years. You must weigh the costs of the refinance against what you'll be saving each month.

A word of caution: Do not pay off your mortgage (or any other debt, for that matter) at the expense of not having savings. No matter how badly you want to be free of debt, it's savings that will keep you out of debt in the future. That said, there's nothing like owning your own home free and clear. You can experience that feeling sooner if you plan for it.

Father, as I make a plan to pay off my mortgage early, I do so knowing that you are ultimately in control. Guide my steps I pray. In Jesus' name. Amen.

June

Protecting Your Freedom

"Stand firm, then, and do not let yourselves be burdened again by a yoke of slavery." Galatians 5:1

A lot of us know how to get out of debt. We've done it many times. And therein lies the problem; we don't know how to *stay out* of debt. We get relief at last and then our bad habits take over and we find ourselves making payments again. Maybe we've deluded ourselves into thinking we can handle it this time (no, we can't); or we don't really believe it's possible to function in our society without debt. We let ourselves get seduced and sold into slavery again. It's a truly vicious cycle. How to break out of it?

If you are newly debt free, there are things you must do immediately. You must contact the credit card companies and tell them to close your accounts, and *put it in writing*. Otherwise they may not; and when your new card arrives they're hoping you'll be tempted to use it. Don't expose yourself to the temptation! You must shred all offers for cards that arrive in your mailbox. You can't charge up debt if the credit isn't available to you.

Choose to have the presence of no alternative. This means you don't give yourself any other options. The discipline you developed getting out of debt should serve you well here. A key is advance decision making. You decide what you're going to do ahead of time and then you do it. A major oversight in being debt free is once you've achieved your goal, then what? The game is over, there's nothing to reach for, so you go back to being in debt because on one level it's comfortable and familiar.

What you need now is a new goal, one involving putting compound interest to work for you instead of against you. You've paid all that money to creditors successfully, now you can pay yourself the same way. Instead of filling a hole, you begin to build a mountain. Which endeavor sounds more appealing?

Dear Lord, I will stay on my knees and seek you at this time when I feel weak and vulnerable. Give me the resolve to stay clear of debt. I ask in Jesus' name. Amen.

June

God Knows Our Heart

"The Pharisees, who loved money, heard all this and were sneering at Jesus. He said to them, 'You are the ones who justify yourselves in the eyes of men, but God knows your hearts. What is highly valued among men is detestable in God's sight.'" Luke 16:14

It should never come as a surprise when the wicked and ungodly sneer at Jesus. He is an affront to their lifestyles; his authority a wound to their pride. But the Pharisees were considered by their peers to be the godliest of men, and they reacted to Christ the same way. Why?

Their religion was all about obeying the rules and following the letter of the law. It was merely a matter of externals, and Jesus saw right through it. At heart, they were idolaters. They loved money more than they loved God.

Is that true of us? Do we cloak a love of money beneath our Christianity? We can feel self-righteous because we tithe on all our income. So did the Pharisees. Obviously tithing is not the cure for the mammon lust that plagues us. It is too limiting. If all God requires is 10 percent, we give up to that point and hug the remaining 90 percent to our greedy selves and feel we've fulfilled our duty.

I believe in tithing as a Christian discipline. But if we draw the line at 10 percent and don't give beyond that, we have missed the radical teaching of the New Testament. It is true we are no longer living under the law of Moses; now we are expected to obey the higher law of Christ.

It's what flows out of our hearts that God takes into account. The Pharisees thought they were right with God since they were receiving the praise of men. How wrong they were. Their works were detestable in God's eyes because they served no purpose other than to exalt themselves. They had no concern for the poor, only for their own prosperity. God forbid the same should be said of us.

Father, what do you see when you look at my heart? Reveal to me what is there and by your power purify it so that it is acceptable and pleasing to you. For Jesus' sake. Amen.

Why God Commanded the Tithe

"I give to the Levites all the tithes in Israel as their inheritance in return for the work they do while serving at the Tent of Meeting."
Numbers 18:21

No subject, it would seem, can arouse more hostility in the body of Christ than tithing. People have been known to get angry and leave a church the moment the pastor dares to preach a sermon on it. He is accused of "bringing in the law" by folks who are not all that anxious to give in the first place. By shouting "legalism!" they seek to provide their way of escape. The problem is not with tithing itself, but the way we understand its purpose and practice. We have so distorted and abused it that until we fully comprehend why God commanded it to the Israelites in the first place, it will continue to trip us up.

We must get away from the idea that everything in the Old Testament is under the law. It's not. The spiritual heroes of Hebrews 11 all did what they did by faith—some before the law was given, some after. We need to separate the tithe from the offerings Israel was required to give. Of these, only the sin and guilt offerings were mandatory; the others were a voluntary act of worship. The Levites were to be the recipients of the tithe. They did all the work of the ministry—presented offerings, led worship, had all the upkeep of the tabernacle, and were the mediators between God and the people. The tithe was the Lord's way of providing for them. Because everything they did was in service to God and the people, it was only right that the people support what they did.

It is the same way in the body of Christ today. Everything our pastors do is in service to God and to us. It is full-time work. Our tithes should go to support them and the ministry of the church. That is God's plan.

Lord God, your purposes for the tithe are holy and right. Move on the hearts of your people to give so that your work in the world may not be hindered. I ask in Jesus' name. Amen.

June 5

Celebration!

"Be sure to set aside a tenth of all that your fields produce each year.
Eat the tithe of your grain, new wine and oil, and the firstborn of your
herds and flocks in the presence of the LORD your God at the place he
will choose as a dwelling for his Name, so that you may learn to revere
the LORD your God always. But if that place is too distant and you have
been blessed by the LORD your God and cannot carry your tithe (because
the place where the LORD will choose to put his Name is so far away),
then exchange your tithe for silver, and take the silver with you and
go to the place where the LORD your God will choose. Use the silver to
buy whatever you like: cattle, sheep, wine or other fermented drink, or
anything you wish. Then you and your household shall eat there in
the presence of the LORD your God and rejoice. And do not neglect the
Levites living in your towns, for they have no allotment or inheritance
of their own." Deuteronomy 14:22-27

A second use of the tithe was called the festival tithe, which was used to finance the travel and food expenses of worshippers coming to Jerusalem for the annual festivals. Partying on God's money? Are you kidding?! Read the passage again slowly to take in the enjoyment God expects from his people in doing this. He wanted them to celebrate his gracious provision; he had blessed their fields and flocks and they were to praise him for a plentiful harvest. No work was to be done on these days; they were to worship the Lord in joyful festivity—an all-expense paid holiday. Our God is a generous God!

Notice that he makes sure the Levites are not forgotten; provision for them is written into the tithe. His promises of material blessing came with a condition. They were to obey his decrees and commands. An important part of that obedience was in how they treated the poor and needy.

This leads us to the third use of the tithe that we will look at tomorrow.

Father God, teach me to live my life in an attitude of joyous worship and celebration as I look to you to provide everything I need. In the name of Jesus. Amen.

June

The Heart of the Tithe

"At the end of three years, bring all the tithes of that year's produce and store it in your own towns, so that the Levites (who have no allotment or inheritance of their own) and the aliens, the fatherless, and the widows who live in your towns may come and eat and be satisfied, and so that the LORD your God may bless you in all the works of your hands." Deuteronomy 14:28-29

In the regulations regarding the tithe a provision was also made for people who did not have the normal means of earning a living. Every third year the tithe was to be stored locally and used specifically to help feed foreigners, orphans, and widows in addition to the Levites. Foreigners in Israel would own no land, and orphans and widows were defenseless and unable to care for themselves. God's compassion and concern for the weak and needy is evident throughout all the practices and legislation established for the Hebrews. He keeps reminding them how dependent these groups of people were on the tithes that were to be collected. Do you see the theme emerging here?

The tithe has at its heart a spirit of generosity, joyfulness, and provision. At least that is what God intended for it. Do you see how putting the tithe "under the law" kills that gracious spirit?

There was no penalty for not tithing. What kind of a law doesn't have a punishment for breaking it? Tithing was, and is today, a *voluntary* act. It is an act God promised to bless if we will do it. The "punishment" is in the missed blessing when we fail to obey and keep God's part for ourselves. We effectively tie his hands from accomplishing the good works he wants to do for a desperate world that needs to know his love.

Let's return to the heart of the tithe. Let's do it because we love God and we love his people.

Gracious Father, open my eyes to see tithing in its proper place in my life—not as a legal obligation but as a privilege given with joy to meet the needs of my church and people everywhere who need you. In Jesus' name. Amen.

June

Presuming on the Future

"Now listen, you who say, 'Today or tomorrow we will go to this or that city, spend a year there, carry on business and make money.' Why, you do not even know what will happen tomorrow. What is your life? You are a mist that appears for a little while and then vanishes. Instead, you ought to say, 'If it is the Lord's will, we will live and do this or that.' As it is, you boast and brag. All such boasting is evil." James 4:13-16

James is not condemning making plans, just leaving the Lord out of our plans. A lot of financial scrapes could be avoided if we would first make our plans through prayer and direction from God. One of the spiritual dangers of debt is that it *always* presumes upon the future. Any money borrowed has a presumption of repayment. Borrowing is based on a false assumption that tomorrow will be better than today.

Retailers understand this mind-set very well. "90 days same as cash!" "No payments until New Year's!" If they can get you to start thinking along the lines of, "Yes, I'll have received my raise by then" or "I can pay for it with my income tax refund," they have a much easier sale. Why are they so eager to sell you with this method? Because they get their money right away from a finance company. And the reason the finance companies are willing to wait to get their money is because 70 percent of all these deferred payment deals do not get paid within the grace period, but end up being financed at 22 percent with prepayment penalties. And oh, by the way, the interest starts from the date of *purchase,* not at the end of the grace period. That's what it said in the fine print you didn't bother to read because you presumed you would pay for it by the deadline.

At the heart of presumption is arrogance. We get cocky, forgetting that life is brief and unpredictable. Include God in your plans. He knows the future.

Father, keep me from presumptuous sins. Humble me, and let every plan I make be in awareness of your sovereignty. In Jesus' name. Amen.

What Level of Lifestyle Does God Want Me to Have?

"Make it your ambition to lead a quiet life, to mind your own business and to work with your hands, just as we told you, so that your daily life may win the respect of outsiders and so that you will not be dependent on anybody." 1 Thessalonians 4:11-12

Every detail of your life matters to God. He cares about where you live, what you drive, and how you spend your money. If you desire to walk in obedience to him, you have probably asked yourself how you are to live. You know that you're not to live a life of vulgar consumption; yet you're not comfortable with the extreme practices of the ascetics. Is there a middle ground? Where is it? This simple formula can help you find it:

Total income	$_____
Less tithe	$_____
Less taxes	$_____
Less 10 percent savings	$_____
Balance left to fund lifestyle	$_____

Your income is determined by your vocation. Your vocation is determined by how God has gifted you. If you're in your early earning years, of course you're not going to stay at that entry level job your entire life, but the formula still works. In fact, if you follow it from your youth, you will have guaranteed financial success.

Remember that the tithe is only the starting point for giving, and you can always save more than 10 percent. It's debt repayment that throws everything out of whack. Long-term debt really should have no place in our planning or our thinking.

Bringing your finances in line with this diagram may have to be your goal for now. Compare this with your current budget. Where do you stand? Lay it out before the Lord and ask him to show you what needs to change.

This is a radical way to live in society today. Unbelievers will notice, and it will be part of your Christian witness.

Heavenly Father, I choose to have my lifestyle line up with your will. Work with me to bring it about so I can have financial peace and be pleasing to you. In Jesus' name, Amen.

June

Atonement Money

"Then the LORD said to Moses, 'When you take a census of the Israelites to count them, each one must pay the LORD a ransom for his life at the time he is counted. Then no plague will come on them when you number them. Each one who crosses over to those already counted is to give a half shekel, according to the sanctuary shekel, which weighs twenty gerahs. This half shekel is an offering to the LORD. The rich are not to give more than a half shekel and the poor are not to give less when you make the offering to the Lord to atone for your lives. Receive the atonement money from the Israelites and use it for the service of the Tent of Meeting. It will be a memorial for the Israelites before the LORD, making atonement for your lives.'" Exodus 30:11-16

Every Hebrew male twenty years or older was required to pay an annual "tax" to the priests of a half shekel for use in the service of the tabernacle. This tax was referred to as a ransom or atonement. In the Old Testament all atonement is associated with sacrifice. The idea is to pay a price for one's life. Each Israelite paid the same affordable amount; the poor were not to be left out. Everyone had the same access to God through the sacrifices offered by the priests.

This atonement money represented a payment for sin as it was used to purchase the sacrificial animals. The sacrifice of an animal atoned for the sins of the Israelites and turned aside God's wrath. Jesus' sacrifice on the cross eliminated the need for the death of animals in substitution, as he paid the price once and for all, giving his holy, sinless life on our behalf.

We no longer have to pay a temple tax, but every time we give God our money we are acknowledging that our lives are from him and are to be governed by him. We are already redeemed by Jesus' blood. Hallelujah!

Lord God, thank you that it was not with perishable things such as silver and gold that I was redeemed, but by the precious blood of the perfect lamb, your son Jesus Christ. In his wonderful name I pray. Amen.

The Temple Tax

"After Jesus and his disciples arrived in Capernaum, the collectors of the two-drachma tax came to Peter and asked, 'Doesn't your teacher pay the temple tax?' 'Yes, he does,' he replied. When Peter came into the house, Jesus was the first to speak. 'What do you think, Simon?' he asked. 'From whom do the kings of the earth collect duty and taxes— from their own sons or from others?' 'From others,' Peter answered. 'Then the sons are exempt,' Jesus said to him. 'But so that we may not offend them, go to the lake and throw out your line. Take the first fish you catch; open its mouth and you will find a four-drachma coin. Take it and give it to them for my tax and yours.'" Matthew 17:24-27

We get so caught up in the miracle of money inside a fish that we miss the meaning of this little account Matthew includes in his Gospel. He probably found it humorous that Jesus was being chased down by the local tax collector.

So why hadn't Jesus paid the temple tax? Peter went to speak to him about it. Jesus anticipated what he was about to say and cut him off. He reminded Peter that kings collect taxes only from their citizens, not their sons. Jesus, the Son of God, owed no temple tax. The temple belonged to him!

The original purpose of the tax was atonement money for sinful man. Jesus was sinless. The fact that he used the plural "sons" implies that Peter and the other disciples were also exempt from this obligation. Nevertheless, he directed Peter where to find a coin to pay it with.

The word used in this verse for "offend" is *skandalizo*, from which we get our English word *scandalize*. Jesus did not wish to cause a ruckus with the authorities by asserting his right to not pay the tax. "Here's where to find the exact amount needed. Take it and pay the tax if it makes them happy."

Sometimes keeping a good relationship with others takes precedence over our assertion of our "rights." It may cost us money, but God is our supply—even if he has to use a fish.

Father, the resources you have available to meet my needs amazes me. Release me to have the attitude of Jesus towards money. I pray in his name. Amen.

Paying for College

"The laborer's appetite works for him; his hunger drives him on."
Proverbs 16:26

Nowadays when anyone talks about the expense of raising a child, the cost of a college education is automatically assumed. I think we need to really question this. To me, a college education is an option, not a necessity. Incredible financial burdens are placed on well-meaning parents who believe they've failed their kids if they don't pay for their tuition at an institution of high learning. They will leverage their own futures in order to make it happen.

Every child is unique, of course, and for some parents, paying their way would be a worthy investment in their potential—*if* the money is available. I just think we need to move away from this idea that it is a parental *obligation*. Every family needs to decide, preferably when the kids are still small, as to what they plan to do, and let the children know their decision so they have time to financially prepare. People who have worked their own way through college claim they appreciate their education that much more. It also gained them valuable work experience, and they often have more job opportunities than those who waited until after graduation to seek employment.

Going to college is a big decision that requires much prayer. What would God have you do? What I don't believe he wants is for his people to be strapped with huge student loan debts for years to come. This seems to be the norm today, as a college degree is considered a "must." It isn't. Not everyone is college material. It just shows how materialistic we've become and how much we have bought into the world's mindset.

Surrender your whole life to God and he will use it for the greatest good, whether you can afford college or not. He's not limited by your lack of education, only by your unavailability.

Father, I seek your direction for my life—if I should go to school, where, how I will pay for it. I trust you to always guide me in the paths that are best for me. In Jesus' name, Amen.

June

Skilled Workers

"Do you see a man skilled in his work? He will serve before kings; he will not serve before obscure men." Proverbs 22:29

It has always been true that money follows the talent. The people who are the very best at what they do command the most dollars. It certainly is true in sports, which is why an athlete gets so upset if another player in the same position makes even a few hundred thousand dollars more. It's perceived that the highest-paid player is the best.

Having talent is one thing, but sometimes what's overlooked in a person's package of skills is the ability to get along with others. And this *is* a skill. All the talent in the world won't matter if you don't relate well to people. This should encourage us; we're not all geniuses and can do nothing to change that fact, but we can all improve at building relationships.

People skills translate into better jobs at better pay and they are vital in running a business. In my husband's industry he knows many people who are excellent at what they do workmanship wise, but are unsuccessful because they communicate poorly. People will not hire them again, no matter how high quality the work. Honestly, now, did you choose your doctor because you like and trust him or her, or because they graduated at the top of their class in medical school?

This leads me to another point: It really doesn't matter where you receive your training. There are many lawyers without Harvard degrees who are better than those with them. If you have the seeds of greatness in you, you will be sought after and found, however obscure a place you may be in. President and General U.S. Grant sold firewood on the streets of St. Louis before Lincoln discovered his abilities and made him head of the Union Army.

Interacting well with people is a work skill anyone can cultivate. Everything else being equal, it is this attribute that will raise us up to "serve before kings."

Father, thank you for the talents you've given me. I may not be the most skilled in my field, but I do want to be a worker who is valuable in intangibles. I ask in Jesus' name. Amen.

13

Own Or Rent?

"Prepare your work outside, and make it ready for yourself in the field; afterwards, then, build your house." Proverbs 24:27

A financial mistake newlyweds make is to jump too quickly into a house that is beyond their means. Sometimes this desire is fueled by well-intentioned relatives who urge them to not "throw money out the window on rent." Couples are deceived into believing that as long as they have the minimum down payment, they can afford a home. Nothing could be further from the truth.

Even if the mortgage payment is close to what rents are going for in your area, you still need to take into consideration the extra expenses that home ownership entails—property taxes, insurance, maintenance, utilities, and repairs. If you're going to have less than 20 percent equity in your home, you also have to buy private mortgage insurance to protect the lender.

A brand new house is appealing, but they are even more costly. There are no curtains; not even a garage door opener! Older homes can have all sorts of hidden problems. Are you prepared? Do not set your heart on home ownership before fully understanding what you're getting yourself into, and even then, be ready for surprises!

Our first home was a charming old house that was easily affordable for us, but we hadn't owned it a month before we were informed the insurance company was dropping us because the electrical wiring was unsafe. We found another company who would cover us, under the stipulation that the wiring would be upgraded. We didn't have the thousands of dollars it would take, so Len determined to do it himself. Because of that project, he found his vocation in the electrical field today.

The moral of the story is: God will provide according to his will when we trust him. If you are to buy a house, God has the right one set aside for you. But it is his timing, not ours. It's okay to rent while you wait and save. You will then own a home that is within your budget, surprises and all.

Father, help me to be patient while I save to purchase a home. Make me willing to wait for your best for me. In Jesus' name. Amen.

Denying God

"For my thoughts are not your thoughts, neither are your ways my ways," declares the LORD. "As the heavens are higher than the earth, so are my ways higher than your ways and my thoughts than your thoughts." Isaiah 55:8-9

One of the spiritual dangers we risk when we incur debt is that we are denying God an opportunity to work. He longs to display his power and provincial care in our lives, but in our haste to borrow and "have it now," we don't give him a chance. We put a lender in his rightful place. Who needs God to provide for us if someone will loan us the money we need? Debt is blasphemous in this regard.

The Lord has used lack of insurance to bless us, believe it or not. When our first child was born, it took 37 hours of labor to bring him into the world, and had we had medical coverage a totally unnecessary Cesarean section would have been performed. Because we did not, the doctor was patient and allowed him to be born naturally.

More recently God performed what we consider to be a miracle on our daughter. With three children, the odds of any of them needing orthodontia work is quite high. We watched their mouths develop a little anxiously. Both boys were fine but Kristin's teeth were definitely headed in the wrong directions. We dutifully took her in for consultations and were advised to wait a couple years before we did anything. Len made a joke that perhaps God would straighten her teeth; need I say that's exactly what he did? She has a perfect smile today.

It's not always the finances we need that the Lord will provide, but sometimes he removes situations requiring those funds in unexpected, undeniable ways. Too often we are not willing to wait for him to act, but barge ahead and take on debt he never intended for us to have. It's time we start taking God's promises to his children seriously and stop living as orphans.

Father, I don't always understand what you're doing in my finances. Help me to see that your ways are always best. In Jesus' name. Amen.

Are There Advantages to Being Poor?

"A man's riches may ransom his life, but a poor man hears no threat."
Proverbs 13:8

In our wealth-worshipping culture, people of even moderate means consider being poor a fate worse than death. The notion of there being any advantage to that condition seems ludicrous. Yet there is. The rich have worries and concerns the poor never have to even consider.

The rich surround themselves and their possessions with elaborate security systems in an effort to protect what's theirs; the poor have little to lose. The rich tend to think their money will shelter them from all calamity; the poor know they are dependent on the grace of God. The rich can have an exaggerated sense of their own importance; the poor are humble and don't make outrageous demands. The poor know the difference between luxuries and necessities. They understand how much they need each other, while the rich isolate themselves away from those who would impose on them.

In Bible days, being poor was considered to be a sign of God's displeasure. To the contrary, Scripture is filled with references as to God's special love and concern for them. He is on their side; Israel's entire government was set up with a view to help and provide for them. The beatitudes in Luke's Gospel account pay special honor to the weak, the hungry, and the dejected.

The poor don't have the deceitfulness of wealth to come between them and the gospel. They are freer to respond to it for the good news that it is and not perceive it as a threat, as the rich might. Some of the most devout people you will meet live in poverty, and they trust God in ways the rich will never experience. In the Middle Ages people understood very well that wealth interfered with their relationship to God, and the monastery movement began.

We don't have to be poor to have these qualities of the poor, but it is a rare person who has wealth who can hold it as lightly as God calls us to.

Father, the poor do have a special advantage over the rest of us who consider ourselves "well-off". Do not allow my prosperity to ever come between my relationship with you. In Jesus' name. Amen.

A Wife's Discontent

"The wise woman builds her house, but with her own hands the foolish one tears hers down." Proverbs 14:1

The influence of a woman in her home is an awesome thing. We have the power, ladies, to create a home built on love, peacefulness, contentment, and tranquility, or we can choose to take a wrecking ball to it and shatter the lives of everyone around us.

One of the most subtle ways we tear down our homes is through discontent. All sorts of problems can result if we are not willing to live within our husband's income. Obviously a wife with a spending habit can run up credit card debt and create financial strain and sometimes the husband is not even aware of the bills.

Some women don't overspend, but by their remarks they let their husbands know he is not doing enough as a provider. "I wish I didn't have to drive this old car," "I wish we could afford new carpeting"— you get the picture. A man's need to please his wife is very strong, and her comments could send him to working extra hours or taking a second job to try to keep her happy. Now he's away from home more, the kids miss him, and the wife begins to nag him about being gone so much. Some men will insist she go to work just to get her off his back. If she does, the children now lose the presence of a full-time mom, and everyone is under time and energy pressures. Spending goes up beyond what the second income brings in, and they begin to struggle financially even more. All because of discontent!

Submission for wives includes living within the budget. We are also to express our contentment verbally and often, telling our husband that we are happy with what he provides. Guys do need to hear this!

Contentment is an attitude not dependent on outward circumstances. It doesn't demand more. Let's be wise and build a house that will last.

Father, you have blessed me with a home and a family and we have all that we need. I want to learn to be content. Break the spirit of covetousness in me for Jesus' sake. Amen.

A Biblical History of Money

"For the generations to come every male among you who is eight days old must be circumcised, including those born in your household or bought with money from a foreigner—those who are not your offspring." Genesis 17:12

These words spoken by God to Abraham are the very first mention of money in the Bible. I thought it would be interesting to do a little research on the origins of money throughout the Scriptures. In the Old Testament, the word translated "money" is synonymous with silver. It was valued by weight; as a precious metal, its worth depended on the economy. At the time of King Josiah's reign in Judah, around 650 B.C., the Lydians were the first to make actual coinage.

The Romans gave us the word "money" around 390 B.C. They kept their wealth in the temple of Jupiter. When the cackling of the geese that lived around the temple alerted them to a surprise attack by the Gauls, they built a shrine in thanks to their goddess of warning. This goddess was named Moneta, which became the derivation of "money" and "mint."

In Jesus' day, silver was still in use as coins. Judas betrayed him for thirty silver coins. The Greeks had several words for our English word money. *Chrema*—as used in Acts 4:37, 8:18,20, and 24:26—could mean either wealth, price, money, or riches. *Philarguia* appears only in 1 Timothy 6:10 and refers to avarice or love of money. The most common word used—*argurion*—denotes a piece of money, such as a silver shekel or drachma. *Chalkos,* found in Mark 6:8 and 12:41, referred to copper or brass money. The widow's two mites were the smallest coins made.

Although the materials used to make money have changed through the ages, one thing has not and never will change, and that is humankind's desire to acquire it. The mammon spirit behind it will not rest. It has and always will seek to master us. Its power can be broken only by surrender to the lordship of Jesus Christ.

Father God, how frightening that throughout history people have been willing to go to their deaths to keep, gain, or hoard money. Help me to possess it without being possessed by it. For Jesus' sake. Amen.

The Spending Disease

"I denied myself nothing my eyes desired; I refused my heart no pleasure." Ecclesiastes 2:10

Solomon knew how to spend. He was rich, of course, and could afford it. He notes in Ecclesiastes 2:9 that "in all this my wisdom stayed with me." For Solomon this was a grand experiment to find fulfillment. He concludes in the end that he did not, but a lot of folks in our day keep trying anyway.

Some people are addicted to spending. Like an alcoholic who can't stop at one drink, they seem incapable of leaving a store with empty hands. The act of buying something gives them a lift when they're feeling down. They just crave the shopping experience. It doesn't take very long, however, and the "high" wears off and they have to do it again.

It's interesting to observe people in malls. Most are wandering aimlessly, without any real purpose. Malls are designed to seduce us into spending. No one really looks at it as a serious problem. Shopping is, after all, an accepted behavior. We all have to do it. Except that compulsive spending is a huge problem for more and more people. It doesn't help when our culture encourages it.

If you relate to any of this at all, understand that your problem is *spiritual*. When we overspend, shop compulsively, or abuse credit cards, we are trying to satisfy a spiritual need with consumption on a material level. Because "things" will never meet our spiritual needs, no amount of stuff will fill that hole in our souls that only Jesus Christ can fill.

Surrender your life to him. That's your first step. He will meet you where you are. Acknowledge that you have a problem and that you are powerless to change on your own. If that sounds like a 12 step program, it is. It's called Debtors Anonymous. Look them up. Talk to your pastor; get some counseling. Ask for help! You've tried to change your behavior on your own and it hasn't worked. Why struggle alone? God has made us to need each other.

Father, I admit I've been trying to meet my soul needs with shopping. I want to turn from that and turn to you, the true lover of my soul. In Jesus' name. Amen.

June

No More "Two"

"For this reason a man will leave his father and mother and be united to his wife, and the two will become one flesh. So they are no longer two, but one." Mark 10:7-8

God intends marriage to be permanent. When you marry, you and your spouse become a single unit. In fact, the word "one" used in Mark 10:8 has the same meaning as in Mark 12:29: "Hear, O Israel, the Lord our God, the Lord is *one*" (emphasis added).

When we marry, our finances become one as well. In an era when both men and women have been working in the marketplace, it has been common for couples to have "his" and "her" bank accounts. This encourages an independent spirit and is very unhealthy for a marriage. Some couples claim it makes it easier, but what they really mean is that it enables them to avoid the communication on finances that must take place.

It also promotes a lack of trust. One spouse is able to hide expenses from the other. They are free to do their own thing like they did when they were single. They are saying to their spouse in so many words, "This is *my* money, and I'm keeping it that way."

We are to think in terms of "our" money. It doesn't matter who earned it, because we are a unit, a team. Does it matter which player scored the touchdown, as long as the team scored?

A "me" attitude will destroy your relationship. Husbands should not control the checkbook with an iron hand and keep their wives from having any input on the budget. She should have the same resources—checkbook, debit card, cash—as he does, and she should not be kept in the dark as to investments, insurance policies, and estate plans. Everything needs to be known—all credit card accounts, loans, and financial obligations.

It takes effort to understand each other's views. We are to be one—one mind, in harmony and full agreement—even with our money. No more "two."

Father, search my heart for any wrong attitudes I have towards sharing finances with my spouse. Help me to think in terms of "ours" from now on. I ask in Jesus' name. Amen.

The Economy of the Early Church

"There were no needy persons among them. For from time to time those who owned lands or houses sold them, brought the money from the sales and put it at the apostles' feet, and it was distributed to anyone as he had need. Joseph, a Levite from Cyprus, who the apostles called Barnabus (which means Son of Encouragement) sold a field he owned and brought the money and put it at the apostles' feet." Acts 4:34-37

Barnabus is upheld as the testimony to the divine power that took over the young church in Jerusalem following Pentecost. The Holy Spirit moved on the believers to give generously, freely, and with great joy whenever they became aware of a need. They gave up their possessions and their "right" to privacy; everything was for the good of the community. No one thought to go off and enjoy their prosperity in glorious isolation.

In our day we get very suspicious of anything approaching this model; "communes" are closely associated with cults. We think of communism: the totalitarian governments that advocate the elimination of private property and create systems in which goods are owned and shared by all. No wonder we get so nervous when we read of the early church.

But there's a huge difference between them and the Marxist regimes. What the believers in Judea did was totally *voluntary*. No one was forcing them to turn over their possessions. They continued to own private property; they continued in their employments.

Is it possible to live like that today? I believe that if we truly see our local church as our true, eternal family, it would do much to pry our hearts away from our individualism, our excessive possessions, and our culture addiction. We are not committed to the church; we are more interested in our own comfort, being entertained, and having financial security.

The early church understood their oneness with Christ and each other. Their sharing stands as an example as to what can be done by a group of people wholly given to him.

Father, I feel conviction over my self-indulgent lifestyle. Make me more aware of the needs of my spiritual brothers and sisters. I ask in Jesus' name. Amen.

Greed, Lies, and Hypocrisy

"Now a man named Ananias, together with his wife Sapphira, also sold a piece of property. With his wife's full knowledge he kept back part of the money for himself, but brought the rest and put it at the apostles' feet." Acts 5:1-2

What was the sin of Ananias and Sapphira that led to their both dropping dead on the spot? It actually involved three sinful attitudes. The first was their seeking of praise for an act of generosity. They had seen others lay money at the apostles' feet after selling property, and they wanted recognition themselves.

Their next offense was deceit. They wanted it to be believed that they gave the full amount their property sold for when in reality they did not. Now, there was nothing inherently wrong in not giving all of it, as Peter reminded Ananias, "Didn't it belong to you before it was sold? And after it sold, wasn't the money at your disposal?" (Acts 5:4). No one was required to turn over all their money or possessions. This wasn't extortion on the part of the church. Ananias could have simply said, "Here are some of the proceeds from a property I sold," and it would have been perfectly appropriate and acceptable. So he wasn't the hilarious giver that Barnabus was. That was okay.

What might have happened is that they originally intended to give the full amount, but then Satan came in, whispering his suggestions: "Hey, why not just give *most* of the money? Keep some for yourself. No one will ever know." Whether the temptation may have originated with Ananias or Sapphira we don't know; what is clear is that they conspired together, and the third sin of greed took over. They both believed Satan's lie that their sin would not be exposed, and it cost them their lives.

Just because judgment isn't immediate today doesn't mean we can play the Holy Spirit for a fool. What makes anyone think they can hide their financial dealings from an all-knowing, all powerful God?

Everything we do in the dark is visible to the One who is all light.

Father, I know there is no hiding anything from you. You see my heart; let that knowledge strike holy fear into me. I ask in Jesus' name. Amen.

June

Buying on Impulse

"It is not good to have zeal without knowledge, nor to be hasty and miss the way." Proverbs 19:2

Which sex has the bigger impulse buying problem—men or women? According to most financial planners, it's men. And they do mean bigger, literally. While women will buy clothes and cosmetics on impulse, men buy cars, boats, and vacation homes. The consequences of some of these big-ticket purchases can last for years. How many people do you know who are trying to sell their time-share? The sales presentations for these are high pressure and they make sure you don't have the opportunity to think it over. The "great deal" is only good if you buy today. If you know you have low sales resistance, don't go near those things!

Men will also outspend women at the grocery store. It's been proven that 10 to 12 percent more food is purchased when men do the buying. Women tend to follow a list; men wander the aisles and throw everything that looks good into the cart. If you want to save money on food, leave the guys at home!

List-making helps curb impulse spending, and not just at the market. I keep three lists: My "A" list is for things I need right away, the "B" list is for things I know I'll need coming up; writing them down alerts me if I see the items on sale or if it's convenient to pick them up while I'm out. The "C" list is for things I see that I might like to buy. I make a note of them and the date. If after a month I still want them, I'll consider buying them. Usually after 30 days I've lost interest. It's been a good system for me.

Come up with your own method that will work for you. The point is to break that habit of indiscriminately buying everything we see. Because, let's face it, in our consumer-oriented society there will *always* be things we think we want. We need a battle plan if we're going to win the war.

Father, help me to build self-control into my life. Instead of shopping I will spend that time in prayer. In Jesus' name. Amen.

Paper or Plastic?

*"Do not have two differing weights in your bag—one heavy, one light.
Do not have two differing measures in your house—one large, one
small. You must have accurate and honest weights and measures, so
that you may live long in the land the LORD your God is giving you."*
Deuteronomy 25:13-15

Once upon a time money exchanged hands in the form of silver and gold weighed out on a scale. Coins came along in the sixth century. As trade between nations became more complicated, bills of exchange were developed by merchants, becoming the forerunners of today's checking account. These innovations began to transform the very concept of money, as private money in the form of credit instruments began to serve as means of payment.

The Chinese used small base-metal coins that were known as *cash*, the Tamil word for money. Paper money was known to exist there in the late thirteenth century. It wasn't issued in America, however, until the outbreak of the Civil War. People then began to use this ready, liquid money for most transactions.

It wasn't until the late 1970s that credit cards began to hit their stride. By the early 1980s, consumer credit had become the lifeblood of the economy. Clever marketing and appeals to our inherently greedy natures was all it took. It's a slick scheme deliberately designed to distance us from our money. It's not exactly dishonest, but it *is* deceptive.

As a result, money is no longer very real to us, because we rarely handle it physically. We write checks. We swipe plastic cards through little computer terminals. Money is nothing more than electronic blips. Yes, it certainly is more convenient this way; money is more easily transferable. Yet the unreality of it all is why we have such a debt problem. We don't *feel* as if we're spending money.

If you want to truly experience spending, pay cash for everything. I guarantee your impulse purchases will stop. If you think it's too inconvenient, well, we could be weighing out bits of metal on a scale.

Father, as I use cash to pay for my purchases, help me to be more aware of what I'm doing. Open my eyes to the deceitfulness of plastic cards and computer keystrokes. In Jesus' name. Amen.

June

Building Sales Resistance

"The wisdom of the prudent is to give thought to their ways, but the folly of fools is deception." Proverbs 14:8

How skilled are you at dodging sales pitches? We all need some armor of protection against the constant bombardment for our dollars. What follows is a potpourri of ideas to help you forge that armor:

- Develop your spiritual life. Begin to weld personal disciplines, holy habits that will make you sensitive to what you're being exposed to. Fasting, tithing, maintaining a pure thought life—all help in keeping sensual ads from having a pull on you.
- Cultivate contentment and learn to enjoy the possessions you already have.
- Practice praying for your needs and about your needs.
- Avoid sales and coupons on items you wouldn't otherwise buy. You can go broke "saving" money!
- Always check with your spouse before making a large purchase. It is not the item but the lack of input that upsets your partner. Often in a marriage, one of you is very resilient towards being sold and the other is a pushover. Shopping together for big ticket items creates balance.
- Expect that salespeople are going to overrate their products. It's our task to search out the negatives.
- Learn to negotiate on price; you would be surprised at the good deals you can get if you only ask. The keys to negotiation are not talking too much and being willing to walk away. Paying cash helps, too.
- Don't let salespeople scare you. Learn their techniques and use them right back at them.

" 'It's no good, it's no good!' " says the buyer; then off he goes and boasts about his purchase" (Proverbs 20:14).

Lord, give me discernment in my spending decisions. Help me to understand my motivations in buying the things I do, and keep me from unwise purchases. In the name of Jesus I pray. Amen.

Mixed Marriages

"Do not be yoked together with unbelievers." 2 Corinthians 6:14

Obviously we are asking for trouble if we deliberately marry a non Christian. The problems won't be limited to Sunday mornings when your spouse wants to sleep in and you want to go to church. How will you handle your finances? Stewardship is an alien concept to unbelievers. Many wives find themselves in the position of not being able to participate in giving due to their husband's lack of faith.

This is a struggle even in Christian marriages, where one spouse wants to tithe and the other does not. These situations require a lot of prayer and direction from the Lord as to what he would have you do. I would say, though, that God cares more about your marriage than he does about your money.

There are other "unequal yokes" to consider before you marry. Do you come from dramatically different economic backgrounds? Watch out. If it's the man who comes from money, his new wife from the poor side of the tracks could be made to feel like a "gold digger." If it's the woman who comes into the marriage from wealth, her parents may find it difficult to resist supporting her in the way she's been accustomed, thus usurping her husband's authority and provision.

Even if you're both in the same tax bracket, are you financially compatible? Does one of you owe thousands of dollars in student loans, credit cards, or consumer debts? That can become a serious point of resentment for the non-owing spouse. Is one of you fiscally challenged? That is, you know nothing about money and don't care to learn?

All of these can be overcome if you both are willing to submit to the Holy Spirit and to each other, but don't go into marriage with the view that you'll be able to change the other. Only God can do that. Beyond your marriage, do not go into a partnership of any sort with an unbeliever. Your views on money will be too different and you will have contention in everything you attempt.

What fellowship can light have with darkness?

Father, I heed your warnings about unequal yokes. I will avoid unholy alliances in my finances. In Jesus' name. Amen.

Praying for Money

"This is the confidence we have in approaching God: that if we ask anything according to his will, he hears us. And if we know that he hears us—whatever we ask—we know that we have what we asked of him." 1 John 5:14-15

There are principles we can follow for praying for money, but first we must understand that financial blessings aren't God's first priority for us. It is materialism, after all, that pulls us away from God. He desires for us to live simple lifestyles. Really being blessed is having peace, joy, and righteousness. That said, there are times when we need to ask God for financial help. If we are Christians walking in purity and holiness before the Lord, we are free to come boldly before the throne of grace (Hebrews 4:16). Meditate on these verses:

- Psalm 66:18
- Psalm 139:3-4
- Psalm 19:2
- Psalm 24:3-4
- Psalm 15

Be very clear that you're praying for a need and that you're not already spending God's provision on your wants! Your request must fulfill the clear word of Scripture; it is to be his will, not yours. The will of God for our lives is our holiness (1 Thessalonians 4:3). Are we following biblical principles in our giving? God can bless us with more if we're being faithful to the tithe (Malachi 3:10). Finally, will obtaining this money bring glory to God, or will it taint his name and reputation? God cannot lie; he will not do anything contrary to Scripture.

If you have determined it is God's will for you to have this money, make your request giving him full liberty to bring it about any way he chooses. His supply will often come from other people who know nothing about your need. Be open to receive however it happens. Ask in faith, and watch him move on your behalf.

Dear Lord, examine me and know all my ways. I will put myself in a place where I have no will of my own in this matter; please reveal your will to me. In Jesus' name I ask. Amen.

Calling All Couch Potatoes

"For even when we were with you, we gave you this rule: 'If a man will not work, he shall not eat.'" 2 Thessalonians 3:10

Paul had written to the Thessalonians before, encouraging them to work. Apparently his message didn't sink in, since he had to tell them again in stronger language in his second epistle. There were misunderstandings that had arisen from his teaching on the Lord's return. Some felt it was so near that they quit working to wait for Christ to appear and expected the church to take care of them! Paul was swift to correct this erroneous thinking, even ordering the church to withdraw fellowship from those who persisted in this behavior.

The Bible comes down very hard on laziness. Clearly this verse doesn't apply to those who are unable to work, but for those who are able-bodied, God expects us to earn our keep. Work seems to have fallen out of favor since the hard-driving 1980s. Now the trend is to become financially independent and retire at age 35.

We are raising a generation of young people who seem to think work is optional. Over half the population of the United States between the ages of 18-25 still live at home with mom and dad. Many have college degrees. "There are no good jobs out there," they claim. A lot of them really just don't know how to work.

This is wrong. Young people out of high school should not be allowed to freeload. They need to learn to work and acquire job experience. Otherwise, they will be handicapped their entire lives. In Paul's day, the Greeks and Romans despised manual labor and had slaves to do it. The Jews considered work to be proof of good character and trained their children to learn a trade.

The Puritan work ethic had this belief at its core: "Idle hands are the devil's workshop." This is what was happening in Thessalonica; people were becoming busybodies and stirring up strife and division. Paul's cure was work. It is ours, too.

Lord, purge me of any tendencies I have towards laziness. Give me meaningful, fulfilling work to do every day that will bring glory to you and serve your people. I ask in Christ's name. Amen.

Honor the Elders

"The elders who direct the affairs of the church well are worthy of double honor, especially those whose work is preaching and teaching. For the Scripture says, 'Do not muzzle the ox while it is treading out the grain,' and 'the worker deserves his wages.'" 1 Timothy 5:17-18

The word "elder" is interchangeable with the word "overseer" in the New Testament. They were responsible for directing the affairs of the local congregation, but they also preached, taught, shepherded the people, and guarded against error. It was a position of enormous responsibility. Paul is telling Timothy here that the men who were fulfilling their duties excellently were worthy of double honor: respect and financial support.

He quotes both Moses (Deuteronomy 25:4) and Christ (Luke 10:7) to provide proof for the principle of adequate pay for those who labor in ministry. To "muzzle an ox" kept the animal from eating while it worked. If God was so concerned for an animal, how much more for those who preach and teach his word full time! One way we show our love for our pastors is by our openhandedness towards them. I once attended a large church where the congregation took a special offering and gave the senior pastor a brand-new Jeep for his birthday! Now that's generosity!

Are we afraid we will encourage greed in them if we pay them well? The church has been scandalized in its recent history by leaders who abused their power for financial gain, but God has dealt rather decisively with them. We are not to hold back our support because of an errant few. If you don't trust the leadership in your church with your giving, you are not in the right church.

Getting paid to do ministry can be a sticky subject, but we do have the precedent of the Scriptures to guide us. "The worker deserves his wages" comes directly from the lips of Jesus.

Father, thank you for the leadership in my church. They do work of eternal importance and they toil many hours in it. Let us, their flock, be gracious and generous towards them, supporting them both in prayer and finances. In Jesus' name. Amen.

Is Debt Ever Okay?

"For the Lord your God will bless you as he has promised, and you will lend to many nations but will borrow from none. You will rule over many nations but none will rule over you." Deuteronomy 15:6

There is not one positive reference to debt in the Bible. That alone should serve as a warning. To be in debt is to give someone power over you. Yet debt is not a sin, or God would not have made rules concerning it. It can sometimes be used with wisdom, but we must be fully aware of what we're entering into.

Some people simply cannot handle credit. They take on debt just because it's available. Debt is wrong when you borrow knowing you won't be able to repay. People fret about "establishing credit," but the truth is, the longer you can go without using credit, the less likely you will need it.

Of the five kinds of debt—credit card, consumer, mortgage, business, and investment—the first two should be avoided at all costs. These are used simply to inflate our lifestyles. Buying a home is investing in an appreciating asset (usually) and as long as you can afford it, can be the most prudent thing to do. On business and investment debts the rate of return must be greater than the cost (after taxes).

In all debt, it is crucial to not only have spiritual peace about entering into it, but to be in perfect unity with your spouse concerning it. If either of you is unsure, don't do it. This is a no-exceptions rule that can keep you out of financial scrapes.

So, is debt ever okay? It depends. What is the debt for? Could you sell an asset first? Is this a need that can be met in no other way? Does it make economic sense to take on this debt? And is it serving a godly purpose? If it is, it won't destroy you. God will see to that.

Father, sometimes I get so confused on debt; when it's right, when it's wrong. Guide me in all the decisions I have to make regarding it. In Jesus' name I pray. Amen.

God Said It Was Good

"A river watering the garden flowed from Eden; from there it was separated into four headwaters. The name of the first is Pishon; it winds through the entire land of Havilah, where there is gold. (The gold of that land is good; aromatic resin and onyx are also there.)" Genesis 2:10-12

Gold appears in the first book of the Bible, the last book of the Bible, and over 400 places in between. Throughout the creation process God declares his work to be good—and here in this verse the eternal symbol of wealth is also proclaimed good.

What is it about gold? Why does it so strongly attract people to the point of obsession? Obviously God holds it in high esteem as it was the metal he deemed worthy to construct the articles for worship.

While Moses was on the mountain receiving instructions, the Israelites were in the valley making a gold calf. The fact they used gold wasn't the problem (they could have made it out of mud) but that they were worshipping something other than God. When Moses discovered their sin, he had one of his famous temper tantrums, destroyed the calf and made them drink its residue.

That is one way to make gold disappear; otherwise, it is the most enduring element on earth. Almost all of the gold ever mined is still in existence today. It is imperishable and you can make it into anything you wish. It is so dense, a cubic foot weights half a ton, yet it is as soft as putty. Gold is beautiful; its radiance entrances us; it endures as a standard of value; it commands more respect than any other substance in history. "Good as gold," "worth its weight in gold" are the ultimate compliments we can pay to anything.

Gold was presented as a gift to the young Messiah. Our eternal home will be made of it. Perhaps that's the attraction. By seeking gold, we are unknowingly pursuing the everlasting life we all long for.

Lord, I've never really thought about it before, but gold was your idea. It has high value, but Jesus has more. It is to him alone I bow down. In his precious name. Amen.

July

The City of Gold

"Then I saw a new heaven and a new earth, for the first heaven and the first earth had passed away, and there was no longer any sea. I saw the Holy City, the New Jerusalem, coming down out of heaven from God, prepared as a bride beautifully dressed for her husband... the wall was made of jasper, and the city of pure gold, as pure as glass... the twelve gates were twelve pearls, each gate made of a single pearl. The great street of the city was of pure gold, like transparent glass." Revelation 21:1-2,18,21

This is a description of our eternal home. Try to picture it. The most opulent cathedrals ever built don't approach what God has prepared for those he loves. In heaven gold is everywhere—1400 miles in every direction; walls over 200 feet thick, all pure gold.

If you ever get discouraged by your present surroundings, remember where you're going! We can get so caught up in decorating our homes and fretting about the lack of funds to do it, that we forget how temporal and unimportant it really is.

A scene at the end of the film *Schindler's List* shows Oskar Schindler saying good-bye to the Jews whose lives he saved. He looks at them, looks at his gold ring, and is struck with the realization he could have saved more. "One more person," he sobs. "And this car; why did I keep the car? Twenty people..." He breaks down, overcome by grief.

There will be no tears in heaven, but I wonder if we will feel shame at how selfish we were in not using our wealth to help reach lost people. As we stand on the streets of gold, will we regret we didn't do more? All the wealth of the universe will be ours when we reach our final destination. Does it really matter what we have now in light of that?

Heavenly Father, I am overwhelmed by your glory. How I long to see you face to face! Help me to use what you've given me to bring more souls into your everlasting kingdom. In Jesus' name. Amen.

July

The Mind of Christ

*"For who has known the mind of the Lord that he may instruct him?
But we have the mind of Christ." 1 Corinthians 2:16*

As Christians, we share in the life of Christ and as we are attuned to the Holy Spirit, we also have his mind. And he is brilliant! Even as a boy of twelve he amazed the teachers in the temple courts with his understanding and his answers (Luke 2:46-47). What does he think about money? What is his attitude towards it? We need to know if we are to be like him. A careful reading of the Gospels reveals that he had strong criticisms against wealth:

- "Woe to you that are rich!" (Luke 6:24).
- "Watch out! Be on your guard against all kinds of greed" (Luke 12:15).

He taught that one of the best things we can do with money is give it away:

- "Lend, expecting nothing in return" (Luke 6:35).
- "If you want to be perfect, go, sell your possessions and give to the poor" (Matthew 19-21).

Jesus knew this is what it would take to free us of greed. He reminds us that he is Lord of all we have. He himself had an almost careless, carefree attitude towards money and possessions and he calls us to that same unconcern. The Father will provide all we need. Christ challenges us to seek first the kingdom of God. That's what his ministry was all about: "Repent, for the kingdom of heaven is near" (Matthew 4:17). When the kingdom is first in our hearts, all else will fall into its proper place.

As his disciples, let's learn from Jesus how to live our lives as he would have us live them, and so "manifest the mind of Christ."

Heavenly Father, your word tells me that you have given me the mind of Christ. Bring me to a fuller revelation of what that means as I live in obedience to your commands. I ask in the name of Jesus. Amen.

Vacations

"Which of you, if his son asks for bread, will give him a stone? Or if he asks for a fish, will give him a snake? If you, then, though you are evil, know how to give good gifts to your children, how much more will your father in heaven give good gifts to those who ask him!"
Matthew 7:9-11

Have you ever viewed God as some kind of cosmic killjoy, sitting in heaven ready to clobber us if he sees us having fun? If so, you need to read the Bible more. From Israel's joyous feasts and celebrations, to Jesus' attendance at weddings and parties, to the wedding supper of the Lamb (Revelation 19:9), it is clear that God wants us to experience recreation.

As Christians we sometimes are hesitant to allow God to be the Lord of our downtime. We have an uneasy feeling that we're displeasing him at worst, or that he just isn't interested at best. But God is intensely interested in every detail of our lives, and if we have a need to get away from it all, we can bring that request to him without guilt.

God directed the Israelites to take off one *year* out of every seven! Most of us can't afford to do that; usually we feel we can't afford to take the vacation we'd really like to take—Disney World with our kids, for instance. I would challenge you to present your request to the Lord and see what happens.

Through a totally unbelievable set of circumstances, we were able to go to Orlando for a week with our kids and my parents for a fraction of what such a trip would normally cost. You'd be amazed at what God can arrange if you just ask. People have been lent the use of beach houses, recreational vehicles, even time-shares. He has plenty of resources available to you.

Involve him in your vacation plans. God is good!

Father, thank you for your care and concern in every area of my life, including my recreation. I will trust you to provide opportunities for my family to do the things we've always wanted but thought we could never afford. I ask in Jesus' name. Amen.

Let Freedom Ring

"It is for freedom that Christ has set us free." Galatians 5:1

You were born to be free. Because of what Christ did on the cross, sin's power over you is broken. Satan is committed to keeping you from understanding your freedom. If he can deceive you with his lies, you will effectively still be in bondage.

Financial bondage takes many forms: greed, fear of not having enough, overspending, compulsive gambling, shopping addictions—any money behavior that makes you feel out of control. The center of all spiritual bondage is in our minds.

It is also in our minds that we have strongholds (2 Corinthians 10:4) of thought patterns and habits, established when we lived independently of God. When we became a Christian, these strongholds remained. We need to destroy them by choosing to believe the truth. Satan attacks us primarily through our thoughts; if he can control our thoughts, he can control our behavior. He wants us to prefer material and temporal things over the spiritual and eternal, and he'll use any activity that pulls us in that direction to tempt us.

The power of temptation depends on the strength of the strongholds. If you are getting your emotional needs met by spending money, you will find it difficult to stop shopping because your mind has been programmed to believe that shopping makes you feel better. But in Jesus we have the resources to conquer our temptations. We are to "take our thoughts captive to the obedience of Christ" (2 Corinthians 2:10) as soon as they enter our minds by evaluating how it lines up with Scripture. If they are not congruent with God's truth, we're to dismiss them.

Controlling our environment will help curb some behaviors. But above all we need to focus our thoughts on Christ. How long do you think Satan will keep tempting us if we run to Jesus every time? That defeats his whole purpose!

We already have victory! Christ obtained it for us. Claim your deliverance and let freedom ring!

Father, thank you that Satan is a defeated foe, and that he has no authority over those who are in Christ. Help me to affirm this truth in my life. I pray in Jesus' name. Amen.

Honest Weights, Accurate Measures

"Honest scales and balances are from the Lord; all the weights in the bag are of his making." Proverbs 16:11

My God is so BIG! So strong and so mighty; there's nothing my God cannot do." We teach kids that song in Sunday school, but there *is* one thing God can't do: he cannot lie. The Lord hates dishonesty; sprinkled throughout Proverbs are verses condemning it:

- "Differing weights and differing measures—the Lord detests them both" (Proverbs 20:10).
- "The Lord detests differing weights, and dishonest scales do not please him" (Proverbs 20:23).
- "The Lord abhors dishonest scales, but accurate weights are his delight" (Proverbs 11:1).

In Leviticus 19:35, God tells the Israelites to use honest measurements for "I am the LORD your God." They were his representatives to the pagan nations surrounding them, and there was to be no injustice in business transactions. Silver was weighed on scales balanced against a stone weight, and merchants carried stones of different sizes with them for this purpose. It was a simple matter for them to put false labels on the stones. Cheating was common as there was no regulation of standards; everyone was on the "honor system."

It worked as well then as it would today. The prophets Amos, Micah, and Hosea would all later condemn the Israelites for their failure in dealing justly with one another as it was in violation of the commandment to "love one's neighbor as oneself" (Leviticus 19:18).

Our dishonest scales take the form of padded expense accounts, underestimating income to the IRS, remaining silent when we receive too much change, switching price tags, overbilling for work performed, using shoddy materials but charging the premium price—all unacceptable behavior for those who claim to know God.

He is integrity incarnate. Let's imitate our Father.

Lord God, you take even the smallest act of dishonesty very seriously. I want to be known as a person of integrity in all my business dealings. I pray in Jesus' name. Amen.

July

Spoiled Rotten

"Hear this word, you cows of Bashan on Mount Samaria, you women who oppress the poor and crush the needy and say to your husbands, 'Bring us some drinks!'" Amos 4:1

Yes, you read that right. God referred to these women as cows. While it most certainly is an insult in our day, it may have been a backhanded form of flattery to them. In that time period the region of Bashan was renowned for its cattle. It had prime grasslands on which to raise fat, sleek, well-fed cows, the best in all of Canaan. These cows were pampered and indulged and it was this aspect that God was comparing with the upper-class women.

During this time in Israel's history, the prosperity brought about by the reign of Jeroboam II enlarged the wealth of the already economically elite. They increased their properties by throwing the landed peasants off their ancestral lands. The rich became richer, the poor became poorer, and many were sold into slavery. Israel's social structure was falling apart.

Oblivious to the suffering of the poor around them, the wealthy women lived in luxury. They were spoiled and had come to expect special treatment as a form of entitlement. It isn't difficult to think of some contemporary examples (no names, please) but what about us?

Are we living only for our own pleasure? Is our chief concern getting *our* needs and greeds met? Even if you don't consider yourself upper-class, the fact you have the spare time to read makes you a person of some privilege in this world. There's nothing wrong with relaxation or having nice things, but when we begin to demand them as our due, we had better check our value system.

Do our luxuries and leisure come at the expense of the poor? Are we wasting our resources on tanning beds, Botox injections, or other vanity pursuits? There is a world going to hell beyond the manicured grounds of those world-class spas. Do we care enough to do anything about it? Or are we just selfish cows?

Father, I am privileged. Don't allow these blessings to become a snare and a trap to me, but give me a burden for those who are less fortunate For Jesus' sake. Amen.

July

Gehazi's Greed

"A faithful man will abound with blessings, but he who hastens to be rich will not go unpunished." Proverbs 28:20

The Bible is filled with true stories about what happened to real people who let their greed get the best of them. Gehazi's story can be found in 2 Kings 5:20-26.

Naaman, the commander of the Syrian army, was suffering from leprosy. His wife had a young Israelite servant girl who informed her mistress that there was a prophet in Samaria who could heal her husband. Naaman went to Elisha bearing gold, silver, and clothing, expecting to buy Elisha's services.

Naaman had to swallow his pride first, but he did receive his healing, and in gratitude tried to give Elisha the wealth he had brought for that purpose. The man of God refused to accept anything from him. What Naaman had received could not be purchased, and Elisha would not be paid for being God's instrument of divine grace.

Elisha's servant Gehazi, however, had no such scruples. When he saw his master turn down Naaman's offer, he decided to run after him and get something for himself. After he caught up to the entourage, he lied to the Syrians, saying Elisha had sent him to get a talent of silver and two changes of garments for some visitors that had arrived.

Naaman generously gave him two talents of silver and had a pair of his servants lug it back to where Gehazi could hide it. When Elisha asked him where he went, he lied again: "Your servant did not go anywhere." But Elisha wasn't fooled. "Is this the time to receive money or clothing …? Therefore the leprosy of Naaman shall cling to you and your descendants forever" (2 Kings 5:26-27). The last we hear of Gehazi, he leaves Elisha's presence leprous, white as snow. It was a fate worse than death; he would be cut off from others for the rest of his life.

At least he had his silver to comfort him.

Father, I understand how greed can ruin a person's life and I ask your help in crucifying any spirit of greed that is within me. In Jesus' name I pray. Amen.

Women Who Ministered to Jesus

"After this, Jesus traveled about from one town and village to another, proclaiming the good news of the kingdom of God. The Twelve were with him, and also some women who had been cured of evil spirits and diseases: Mary (called Magdalene) from whom seven demons had come out; Joanna the wife of Cuza, the manager of Herod's household; Susanna, and many others. These women were helping to support them out of their own means." Luke 8:1-3

Once Jesus left his carpenter's trade to be an itinerate preacher, his livelihood depended not on miracles, but upon the hospitality of those he ministered to. A group of women who traveled with him and the disciples supported his ministry with their own money. Their names don't appear in the Gospels that often, but they played a crucial role in the spread of the good news of the kingdom of God.

In Jewish culture, women were not supposed to learn from rabbis. By allowing them to come along on his preaching tours, Jesus lifted the role of women from servitude and degradation to one of service and equality. He had healed these women of infirmities and demon possession, Mary Magdalene in particular, and out of their gratitude they used their wealth to benefit God's work.

They were the behind-the-scenes contributors to the drama of what was happening center stage. What these women did for Jesus is preserved for us in the Scriptures for all time. Their loyalty followed him all the way to the cross, and Mary Magdalene was at the tomb, the first to see the risen Lord.

Their unselfish service and devotion to their Master earned them places of distinction and honor in God's kingdom. The ministry of those in the foreground is made possible by those in the background. No deed done for the sake of the King is too small.

Father, what a special group these women were. Give me a measure of the spirit that was in them, to serve you loyally wherever I am and to make possible the work of the kingdom that still goes forth today. I pray in Jesus' name. Amen.

July

Faith or Presumption?

"Look at the birds of the air; they do not sow or reap or store away in barns, yet your Heavenly Father feeds them. Are you not more valuable than they?" Matthew 6:26

Some people interpret these words of Jesus to mean that they don't have to do anything. God will provide. They will trust him. So they do no financial planning; no budget; no savings. They have no idea how much money is in their checking account. They say they're living on faith, but they're really living on presumption.

Jesus is not telling us we can sit on our sofas and expect to be served supper. Birds don't perch in trees waiting for the worms to come to them. On the contrary; they're up before first light, hunting for their daily sustenance. Scripture makes it clear we are to work, and through our labor God provides for us.

We are not to take liberties with the money God gives us to manage by frivolously doing whatever we please with it. If we don't know where our money is going, we are very poor stewards indeed. This is not a trust issue. Who has more anxiety—the person who is confident they're living within their means or the person who recklessly spends and is never quite sure?

Christ's point is this: Birds don't worry. They seek what they need and are content with what they find. If any creature is on God's dole, it's a bird. Yet look how hard they work! No one builds their nests for them; they painstakingly search out the materials they need, and when the wind and weather destroy their efforts they patiently build again. They may not "earn" their keep, but their living certainly isn't handed to them, either.

Faith trusts, presumption demands. Our faith frees us from worry as we go about the business of life; our presumption has us living rashly, overstepping God's expressed commands. "But my righteous one will live by faith" (Hebrews 10:38).

Lord, I seek to live my life by faith in you; make me aware of any area where I cross the line into presumption. Thank you for your provision and the ability you give me to work for it. In Jesus' name. Amen.

Loaves and Fishes

"When Jesus looked up and saw a great crowd coming toward him, he said to Philip, 'Where shall we buy bread for these people to eat?' He asked this only to test him, for he already had in mind what he was going to do. Philip answered him, 'Eight months wages would not buy enough bread for each one to have a bite!' Another of his disciples, Andrew, Simon Peter's brother, spoke up, 'Here is a boy with five small barley loaves and two small fish, but how far will they go among so many?' John 6:5-13

Jesus gave Philip a test, and he failed miserably. He didn't even get the question right; Jesus asked him *where*, he responded with *how*. "Eight months wages wouldn't be enough!" In other words, "Come on, Jesus! Even if there were a bakery right here, there's no way we could afford to feed all these people!" To Philip, it was a matter of finances.

Andrew was more helpful. He had found a young boy who had the foresight to bring his lunch along that day. But he pointed out the inadequacy of this provision. "What good are five little barley loaves and two skimpy fish?"

The real hero here is a little boy who turned over what he had to Christ. Barley was the bread of the poor. It's not the best, but that didn't matter. What we give to Jesus, no matter how meager, is multiplied in his hands. If we clutch it to ourselves it remains what it is—finite, limited. When we release it to do kingdom work, it can do more than we can possibly imagine.

Never feel that what you have to offer isn't enough to do much good. Impossible situations can't be solved by our own resources anyway. God's math is different from ours. We can't make it compute; we don't have to. We only need to believe.

Father, thank you that you will bless and multiply what I give, whatever the amount. Remind me that you use the weak things of this world to reveal your power. In Jesus' name. Amen.

Casting Your Bread

"Cast your bread upon the waters, for after many days you will find it again. Give portions to seven, yes, to eight, for you do not know what disaster may come upon the land." Ecclesiastes 11:1-2

Diversify! It's the number one rule of investing, before "buy low, sell high." All good portfolio managers make sure that assets are distributed between fixed income investments (CDs, treasury bills, bonds, money market funds), equities such as mutual funds and stocks, and real estate (raw land, commercial holdings, rental properties). It's essential for the preservation of capital, as all markets aren't always performing well at the same time. If the stock market is up, real estate may be down. If interest rates are up, equities could go either way. Diversification is a very wise principle.

But that really is not what this verse is speaking to. It's telling us to give in as many places as we can. "Cast out your bread! Release it!" Don't hug it to yourself and hoard it; it will become moldy and useless. We're to be as generous as possible to as many as possible.

We can do this in a variety of ways. Invest in people. Is there a single mother you could help financially? Invest in your church. God's kingdom work needs funds. Support worthy organizations, locally and internationally. Volunteer your time if you're short on money. What ministries could you get involved in? Don't wait for conditions to be perfect. They never will be. We're to be adventurous; there are no gains without a certain amount of risk.

When we do this, Scripture promises, the good we have done will return to us. Someday we may be the ones in need of assistance, and because we have given liberally, we will have many sources from which to receive blessing back.

So cast your bread upon the waters! Who knows where the current will take it?

Father, give me wisdom in "casting out my bread." Guide me to people and places to invest in. Release me to be generous. I ask in the name of Jesus. Amen.

Sowing and Reaping

"Do not be deceived; God cannot be mocked. A man reaps what he sows." Galatians 6:7

An agrarian culture understands very well the concept of sowing and reaping; their livelihood depends upon it. If you want a harvest in the fall, you must plant in the spring. That's a natural law, and there's no way around it. We can't force or fake a harvest. If we want corn, we plant corn. If we want tomatoes, we plant tomatoes. It's not complicated. So why do we expect one kind of crop when we've sown to something else?

Our financial health is based on principles such as saving, thrift, tithing, and staying out of debt. If we sow to these habits, we can expect to reap peace of mind, security, and contentment. We will not reap these benefits if we are sowing to credit cards, not budgeting, poor investment decisions, and living beyond our means. We are also guilty of trying to break the "law of the farm," as Stephen Covey calls it, when we plant in July and want our crop in September. It doesn't work that way. We don't reap in the same season we sow.

Get-rich-quick schemes try to subvert this and we end up losing our original "seed." One virtue of farmers is that they are patient. They know growth takes time, and the process can't be hurried. You have to keep doing the right things—watering, fertilizing, weeding—while you wait. Crops need to be cultivated and tended during the growing season if you want the harvest to be bountiful.

Our money is the same way. We can't just dump it in a mutual fund and forget about it. We need to pay attention to what the markets are doing, make any necessary adjustments in our budgets, be aware of rising costs for things we use, and be diligent in our savings plan. If we do these things, we will have fruit in the fall.

The law of the farm is a law that cannot be broken. Let's be certain of what we're sowing.

Father, you have made the laws of nature inviolable. I commit to doing what it takes to reap a good harvest. In Jesus' name. Amen.

Don't Go It Alone

"Two are better than one, because they have a good return for their work: If one falls down, his friend can help him up. But pity the man who falls and has no one to help him up! Also, if two lie down together, they will keep warm. But how can one keep warm alone? Though one may be overpowered, two can defend themselves. A cord of three strands is not quickly broken." Ecclesiastes 4:9-12

Single parents make up more and more of the demographics in this country. It is usually the mother who is awarded custody of the children, and she is faced with the task of not only raising her family but supporting them as well. Thanks to liberal "equality" laws, men are no longer required to pay alimony in some cases, and the amount of child support granted is usually insufficient.

Some of these women have few job skills and can't possibly live on minimum wage salaries. They have the expenses of child care, transportation, and housing. Welfare checks won't cover all the bills. It is truly a dilemma.

A potential solution is to team up with another single mother and pool your resources. Rent an apartment together. Split the bills. Perhaps even share a car. One mother could be available for child care if working hours are compatible. This arrangement would also allow for one to take evening classes in vocational training.

It is uncomfortable for many of us to do this; we take pride in our independence. But if it would allow you to stay current on your bills and keep your child out of day care, wouldn't you be willing to try? Find out through your church if there are other single mothers in the same predicament.

You could also be a live-in companion for an elderly person who doesn't need a nursing home, just someone to be there. Your situation isn't hopeless. God can make a way where there seems to be no way.

Father, I have despaired of ever being able to find a way out of my situation. By faith I will trust you to provide a solution. Open my eyes to the help that is around me, and give me the grace to receive it, I ask in Jesus' name. Amen.

When Money Should Mean Nothing

"My brothers, as believers in our glorious Lord Jesus Christ, don't show favoritism. Suppose a man comes into your meeting wearing a gold ring and fine clothes, and a poor man in shabby clothes also comes in. If you show special attention to the man wearing fine clothes and say, 'Here's a good seat for you,' but say to the poor man, 'You stand there' or 'Sit on the floor by my feet,' have you not discriminated among yourselves and become judges with evil thoughts?" James 2:1-4

This exact situation that James described actually happened to Mahatma Gandhi. He had gone to a church to investigate Christianity and because he was humbly dressed, the usher treated him like a third-class citizen. Gandhi left the church that day convinced that Christianity was no better a path than Hinduism because of the acts of one man who failed to realize he was representing Christ to a seeker.

God does not show favoritism, and his children should not either. Our tendency to judge people by how well they are dressed is sinful. It violates the royal law of love. It follows the world view that people who dress well have money and therefore should be respected. In the church I attend we have a casual dress code, and the people who come in wearing suits and dresses stand out as a little different. (It's how we tell who the visitors are!)

All kidding aside, money should not make fellow believers think better of us. We are all sinners saved by grace. Wealthy church members should not be catered to because of their ability to give. So many times a pastor is afraid to deliver a message because he might offend the rich and they would leave the church and take their tithe with them. By the same token, leadership in the church should not be determined by who has the bucks, but by who has the gifting. Money should never be used to assign status to people. In and among the body of Christ, money should mean nothing.

Father, open my eyes to see how I treat people. Do I show favoritism by how much money I think they have? Teach me to look at everyone through the eyes of Jesus. In his name I pray. Amen.

Balaam's Error

"They have left the straight way and wandered off to follow the way of Balaam son of Beor, who loved the wages of wickedness. But he was rebuked for his wrongdoing by a donkey—a beast without speech—who spoke with a man's voice and restrained the prophet's madness." 2 Peter 2:15-16

You remember Balaam. He was the guy who got bawled out by his own donkey. What was his sin? He misused his gift for personal gain. Balak, the king of Moab, came to him concerned that the Israelites were going to annihilate the Moabites the way they did the Amorites. He thought he could be spared if he paid a prophet to put a curse on Israel. So he sent a delegation to Balaam along with "fees of divination." Balaam consulted God and the Lord's response could not be clearer: He was not to curse the people.

But Balaam was greedy for the big bucks he knew were in this deal. He tells Balak's men, "The Lord has refused to let me go with you." So Balak sends the big boys this time: "I will indeed *honor you richly.* Please come and curse this people for me" (Numbers 22:17, emphasis added). Balaam replies that he cannot do anything beyond what God would allow. But then he says he will ask him again. What?! God already said no! He told Balaam to go along with the men, but he was very angry. If it hadn't been for Balaam's donkey, the angel of the Lord would have slain him. Even then Balaam is still bent on getting paid for his "services." He found a way to get some of the Moabite king's money—he gave him some friendly advice on how to entice the Israelites into sin. If he couldn't put a curse on them, their own sin would.

Balaam manipulated his way around being obedient to God's command. Do we try to finagle our way around his clear word to us? Let's obey him not only outwardly, but with our whole hearts.

Father, please teach me instant obedience. Don't allow the love of money to blind me to your clear direction. In Jesus' name I ask. Amen.

True Prosperity

"He is like a tree planted by streams of water, which yields its fruit in season and whose leaf does not wither. Whatever he does prospers."
Psalm 1:3

The "prosperity doctrine" gained popularity in America around the early 1980s and is still preached and taught in some places. What it basically expounds is: God wants to bless us. He wants us to have abundant life and our material prosperity glorifies him. We're King's kids, and we should live like it. The way to financial blessing is to give to the Lord and he will give you a hundredfold return.

Now all that sounds scriptural enough, but it is out of context with the rest of the Bible's teaching on wealth and possessions. Christianity is not a road to riches. When we come to Jesus, we are to give him everything we have, because he is the rightful owner. God does want to give us abundant life—an abundance of Jesus!

We misunderstand the word "prosperity." It means to have success in what we do. If we are raising obedient children, we are "prospering" in our parenting. If we're making a valuable contribution in our work, we are "prospering" in our vocation. It's much more than material success.

One way to test any kind of teaching or doctrine is to examine what kind of fruit it would produce in your life if you were to follow it. Does it challenge you to a closer walk with the Lord or does it appeal to your flesh? Will it spawn a sect of Christians who are self-centered and think God exists to serve them instead of the other way around?

We are to expunge any kind of teaching that leads us away from pure, wholehearted devotion to the Lord and the things he cares about—winning the lost and caring for the needy and oppressed. Possessions have their place in the life of a believer, but it's not *first* place. Let's prosper in our pursuit of God above all.

Father, I repent of all the wrong ideas I've had about "prosperity." Lead me to teachers who will challenge my heart to love you more. In Jesus' name I pray. Amen.

Serve Jesus and Get Rich?

"Peter said to him, 'We have left everything to follow you!' 'I tell you the truth,' Jesus replied, 'no one who has left home or brothers or sisters or mother or father or children or fields for me and the gospel will fail to receive a hundred times as much in this present age (homes, brothers, sisters, mothers, children, and fields—and with them, persecutions) and in the age to come, eternal life.'" Mark 10:28-30

The prosperity doctrine uses this verse to shore up their position that serving God is a means to material gain. They conveniently leave out the part about persecutions, but they stress the "hundredfold return" they say is promised to those who will follow the Lord.

We need to see Jesus' words in its context. He has just had the encounter with the rich young ruler and had offered him treasure in heaven, but the ruler had turned away, preferring to keep his treasure on earth. Peter points out that, indeed, he and the other disciples *had* left everything to follow the Lord. Jesus speaks this promise as an encouragement to these men who had *already* given up their homes and families, not to those who were looking to use God's promises for selfish gain. He's telling them that all things that belong to God also belong to those in Christ. It wasn't meant to be literal—a hundred homes, fields, sisters, etc., in return. He was assuring them that their needs on earth would be amply met and they would be repaid richly in the world to come.

This scripture is not to be used as a blanket promise that anything we give to God (especially money) will be multiplied 100 times and given back to us. Jesus never even mentions money here; he was talking about leaving possessions and relatives.

Beware of any ministry that claims if you send your money to them, the Lord will multiply back what you gave. That's manipulation. We're to give and serve from a pure heart. The blessing is in the giving.

Father, help me to discern the times I'm being manipulated to give. I don't want my offerings to be tainted with any stain of greed. I pray in Jesus' name. Amen.

The Deceitfulness of Wealth

"The one that received the seed that fell among the thorns is the man who hears the word, but the worries of this life and the deceitfulness of wealth choke it, making it unfruitful." Matthew 13:22

The kind of fruit we produce in our Christian walk starts with the condition of the soil in our hearts. If we have good soil, we will have an abundant harvest of righteousness and joy. But if the soil of our hearts is filled with the thorns and brambles of worry and coveting after wealth, they will choke the life of God out of us.

Wealth deceives us into thinking that it is somehow tied in with our self-worth, that our value depends on our income and how much we have. It would have us believe that it is the key to contentment. It would have us measure our success in life by it.

If we govern our lives by these lies, we will be miserable as they go against everything the Bible teaches. God says that money is dangerous because if we desire it and set our hearts on it, we will put ourselves into situations that can destroy us. Money lavished on ourselves can harden our hearts to spiritual things. This is the true deceitfulness of wealth; if we have it, we can start to believe we don't need God anymore.

How many of us are unavailable to God because we are serving money through overwork, our debt load, and the sheer quantities of stuff we have to maintain? These are what choke the Word in our lives and make it unfruitful. We need to pull out of our hearts by the roots the weeds of worry over money and the desire for it, so the Word can prosper and produce a good crop of fruit in our lives. Weeds can't thrive where the grass is thick and healthy. Cultivate your spiritual life and the garden of your soul will be green and flourishing.

Father, come and tend the soil of my heart so I can receive your word eagerly and with joy. Let there be nothing to choke or corrupt the life of Jesus within me. In his name I pray. Amen.

Joseph of Arimathea

"As evening approached, there came a rich man from Arimathea,
named Joseph, who had himself become a disciple of Jesus. Going to
Pilate, he asked for Jesus' body, and Pilate ordered that it be given to
him. Joseph took the body, wrapped it in a clean linen cloth, and
placed it in his own new tomb that he had cut out of the rock."
Matthew 27:57-60

We don't know a lot about the wealthy Joseph of Arimathea, but he is mentioned by all four Gospel writers for the service he performed for Jesus—giving him an honorable burial.

A prominent member of the ruling council of the Sanhedrin, Joseph did a very bold thing. When it was ascertained that Jesus was dead, he went to Pilate and asked for his body. To release the body of one executed for high treason to someone who was not a relative was highly unusual. The remains of criminals often were left unburied. Joseph's actions were to fulfill prophecy: "He was assigned a grave with the wicked, and with the rich in his death" (Isaiah 53:9).

Previously Joseph, along with Nicodemus, another council member, had kept their discipleship to Christ a secret. Now it would seem they no longer cared what anyone thought. Out of the twelve, eleven had run away and one was dead, so these men took it upon themselves to provide for Jesus' burial. They brought seventy-five pounds of myrrh and aloes, such as used in royal burials, and they used fine linen, another costly material, to wrap the body. They used their resources to lavish their love and care on their slain Master.

Joseph played a huge role in the drama of the resurrection. God needs people of means to carry out his purposes. If that's you, make your resources available to him. Only in eternity will you know the difference your wealth made for the kingdom.

Father, thank you for the disciples who use their wealth to serve you. Bless and multiply their assets so they can give even more. I ask in Jesus' name. Amen.

Peace of Mind

"The sleep of a laborer is sweet, whether he eats little or much, but the abundance of a rich man permits him no sleep." Ecclesiastes 5:12

It is ironic that we believe having money will solve all our problems. What it does in reality is create a whole bunch of new ones. Look at the routine of a typical blue-collar worker. He punches the clock in the morning, works, punches out, heads home to dinner, messes around with his kids, and goes to bed. He's asleep in less than two minutes. Not much hassle there. He pays his bills, takes his family to church, goes fishing, and, in short, enjoys a simple lifestyle.

Contrast that with the schedule of a wealthy business owner: up at dawn for the long commute to the office; ringing phones; meetings; deadlines; demands of colleagues, customers, and creditors; deals that need to be closed; problems that won't stay at the office. He gets home late and goes to bed late, but he can't sleep—too much on his mind. Money—making and keeping it—occupies the majority of his thoughts. He's not worried about paying his bills, but he has no peace of mind. Money has brought him luxury and comfort but not freedom from anxiety.

Money can be a cruel taskmaster. To keep on top of it, we can find ourselves doing things we'd rather not, being with people we don't like, and having worries that rob us of our rest. This is the side of wealth many of us don't see. We see the glamour—the big house, the luxury sedan, the prestige—and we are envious. But even if we could have everything we ever wanted, we still would be sad and dissatisfied. How much better to enjoy life where God has placed us and get our fulfillment from our relationship to Jesus Christ. He gives peace of mind freely to all who come to him.

Father, thank you for the peace of mind faith in Christ brings. I pray for those who labor under the burden of riches; lead them to your Son so they may know true abundance. In Jesus' name. Amen.

Everything You Do

"And whatever you do, whether in word or deed, do it all in the name of the Lord Jesus, giving thanks to the Father through him." Colossians 3:17

If we profess the name of Christ, the world is watching us, whether we're aware of it or not. They are especially watching how we handle our money. People may not know how much we give, but they can surely see how we live. Our money is a testimony. If there is no difference in the lifestyle of a believer, no more freedom from financial anxiety, an unbeliever could conclude Christ is of no relevance to practical daily living.

Everything we do should be done with the Lord in mind. It should influence the house we live in, the car we drive, the companies we invest in, and the stores where we shop. If we are in a leadership position at our church, we must be especially careful that we don't cause another believer to stumble. New believers watch mature Christians to discern what appropriate behavior is, and how we spend our money is an area where we can set a good example.

We used to have a Corvette. Because our kids are now older, a sports car would fit our lifestyle again, but we've decided against it. As leaders in our church, we're concerned that it might be too ostentatious and could send the wrong message. There's nothing wrong with driving an expensive car if you can afford it and your conscience before the Lord is clear. Ours would not be.

Always remember, whatever you give money to, you're empowering. If you buy junk food, you encourage those companies to keep making and selling it. If you subscribe to a magazine, you empower the publisher to keep printing it. If you invest in companies that support things you are against, you are helping them to continue. We should care what use our money is being put to once it leaves our hand. Everything we do is a witness to Christ. Let's make it our aim to please him.

Father, help me to examine how and where I'm spending money and if it is honoring to you. I want everything I do to glorify you. In Jesus' name I pray. Amen.

Confidence in God

"The One who calls you is faithful and he will do it." 1 Thessalonians 5:24

Has God ever put a call on your life that required you to make a radical lifestyle change? In 1993 we were living in Wisconsin when out of the blue the Lord called us to move to Phoenix, Arizona. We were well settled at the time. All our extended family was nearby, Len had a secure job with benefits, we had a new house. Our three children, all under eight years old, were happy and healthy. We belonged to a good church. Outwardly we had everything. Inwardly we were empty. Len was working third shift in a dead-end job that didn't require his vocational training skills, and we were being held back in our ministry gifting. We were asking each other, "Is this all there is?"

Then we heard the call. Phoenix? We didn't know a soul there; we'd never been to Arizona. But we said, "Yes, Lord," and put the house up for sale. It took a year to find a buyer, an emotionally trying year. Finally, after we had both surrendered 100 percent to God's perfect will, he released us to go.

Len quit his job and we headed west. We had no income, only proceeds from the sale, but we went about setting up our electrical business. God blessed us in every way possible from the time we left. I can honestly say we never had a single moment's anxiety because we knew he was with us.

But for all this to happen we had to say yes to the Lord first, *before* we knew how it was going to work out. If you find yourself today in a similar situation, I want to encourage you to make that leap of faith. Don't look at your resources or lack thereof. God is faithful; what he calls you to do he will provide and equip you to do. You can have confidence that he will complete what he begins.

Father, thank you that I can place my confidence in you. You can be fully relied on to do what you say. Increase my faith to obey your calls on my life without hesitation. In the name of Jesus I pray. Amen.

Parasites

"Wealth brings many friends, but a poor man's friend deserts him."
Proverbs 19:4

How frequently do we see this occur? Someone becomes successful, and all of a sudden relatives he never knew he had are showing up at his door. The first thing most lottery winners do is get an unlisted phone number. Everybody wants a slice of the pie. Money attracts people like manure attracts flies.

Entertainers discover this truth quickly enough. Many of them come from poor backgrounds and are ill-equipped to handle overnight wealth. They feel so grateful for their new status in life that they want to share the bounty by putting friends and family on their payroll. These "parasites" are more than happy to live off the star's income and often do nothing in return. The entourage grows and as long as the star shines brightly, they all live high in the fast lane. But a celebrity who was once on every magazine cover can quickly become yesterday's news, and once the money pile is depleted, the parasites move on to their next host, leaving the ex-star to deal with his problems alone.

Money has a way of sifting out our true friends, who love us for ourselves and not for what we can do for them. Money blindsides the innocent who strike it rich; it makes the cynical suspicious of anyone who comes around them. Neither is desirable. Only the Lord can bring the necessary balance—to handle riches wisely and protect our boundaries, and to know who to trust and who is only along for the ride.

Jesus also had a way of sifting the wanna-bes from the true disciples. In John 6:35-71 many of his followers deserted him after being unable to accept some of his teachings. Christ let them go; he knew their hearts were not truly committed to him. Simon Peter, speaking for the twelve, declared their loyalty to their Lord and Jesus affirmed that *he* had chosen *them*. Better to have few friends but true friends.

Father, I ask for discernment in choosing the people I allow to be close to me. Give me friends to whom money doesn't matter, whether I have much or little. In Jesus' name. Amen.

Plunder and Spoil

"The Israelites did as Moses instructed and asked the Egyptians for articles of silver and gold and for clothing. The LORD had made the Egyptians favorably disposed toward the people, and they gave them what they asked for; so they plundered the Egyptians." Exodus 12:35-36

The Bible frequently refers to spoils—the loot, the goods, and the plunder taken in battle by the conquerors. The word is first mentioned in Genesis 14, when Abram rescued his nephew Lot from the enemy kings. This was the plunder out of which Abram tithed to Melchizedek, the priest, for the purpose of maintaining the ministry of God's house.

When Moses led the Israelites out of captivity, God commanded they plunder the Egyptians so they would have the resources to construct the tabernacle in the desert. Following King David's many military victories, he took back spoils that were set aside to be used in the building of the temple, which took place under his son Solomon.

Before his death, David had also set up a special treasury to provide for the maintenance of God's house once it was established. Whenever God's people overcame their enemies, the plunder was to be used for God's purposes.

In 2 Kings 6, God gave the spoils of war to restore and refresh the starving Samaritans. Esther was rewarded Haman's estate, worth millions, after his scheme to annihilate the Jews was exposed.

The spoils God supplies his people with today are in the form of battles won through spiritual warfare. These are the riches of joy, hope, peace, wisdom, courage—plunder we can't gain anywhere else except by our trials with our enemy.

The struggles we all experience with money gain us strength as we stay in the fight, for God has promised us victory. We can have total confidence that he will bring good out of our troubles.

Father, thank you for defeating the enemy and awarding us with the goods of battle. Help me to use them to build up the body of Christ. In his name. Amen.

July

Today's "Widows and Orphans"

"Religion that God our Father accepts as pure and faultless is this: to look after orphans and widows in their distress and to keep oneself from being polluted by the world." James 1:27

Widows and orphans have always been among the most defenseless of people due to their inability to support themselves. God ordained specific laws to help care for them and warned rulers not to take advantage of them under penalty of death (Exodus 22:22). The women's liberation movement began to alter the perception that women as the weaker sex should be supported by a husband. The laws began to change, and today women are almost expected to be self-supporting as two-income families have become the norm.

When a marriage ends in divorce, some of these women who are educated and have well-paying jobs are able to manage. It is the homemaker wife who really struggles, especially when she has minor children. At least in the case of death they would be provided for by insurance. To me, these women and their kids are "orphans and widows" also.

Some men are responsible and pay child support, but it is usually never enough. These single-mother families end up in dire financial straits, sometimes losing their home, their car, and their credit. The courts aren't looking out for them, neither is the government. The church needs to wake up!

Churches often do not want to help because they feel it would be condoning divorce. This is a shame. Other churches, however, use their single-mother ministries as an evangelism tool, bringing women and their children to Christ through their provision and concern. The need is great, and churches can help with benevolence funds, financial counseling, child care, handyman and mechanic services, and small groups to provide spiritual support.

Yes, love costs. But Jesus asks us to reach out and care for these abandoned families with his love. How can we refuse?

Father, open my eyes to the needs around me. Show me where I can lend a hand, either with money or my time or my skills. Stir up the church to offer programs that would serve the "widows and orphans" among us. In Jesus' name. Amen.

If You Need Help, Ask

"During the night Paul had a vision of a man of Macedonia standing and begging him, 'Come over to Macedonia and help us.'" Acts 16:9

What keeps needy people from reaching out to get help? They may say things like, "I'm doing fine, really," or "I don't want to be a bother to anyone." Meanwhile, their situation worsens to the point of desperation. Often what gets in their way is their own pride. They may not want anyone to know their financial condition out of shame or guilt. They may fear that if they do ask for help, they may be refused. This fear is misplaced. Christians are eager to give assistance when they know a need exists. But you need to speak up!

Some Christians will say, "God knows my need, and he will provide without me having to ask." That can happen. God often does provide supernaturally by moving on someone's heart without them knowing the reason behind it. However, it is more likely he would want you to humble yourself and request what it is you need. Our church has a food bank and a clothing closet available, but it is surprising how few members avail themselves of this help.

I don't discount the emotions that motivate this behavior, but God would not have them go without when he has equipped others to meet those needs. How can they exercise their gifts and share their resources if people are too timid to ask? They're being denied the opportunity to do good!

I know Len and I would be much busier as financial counselors if everyone who needed assistance and advice would come forward to receive it. From our side, it saddens us that so many would rather crawl along on their own than accept a hand up to walk with support.

Don't think of it as charity or welfare. Think of it as being offered an opportunity to empower yourself, because that's truly what it is. Help is available. All you have to do is ask.

Father, I admit I don't ask for help when I need it. Release me to receive and give me the courage to ask. In Jesus' name I pray. Amen.

Meeting the Needs of Others

"Our desire is not that others might be relieved while you are hard pressed, but that there may be equality. At the present time your plenty will supply what they need, so that in turn their plenty will supply what you need. Then there will be equality, as it is written: 'He who gathered much did not have too much, and he who gathered little did not have too little.'" 2 Corinthians 8:13-15

Giving is a ministry to which all Christians are called. Any study of the early church shows that generosity was one of the hallmark qualities of those new believers. It stood as a witness to the world: "See how they love one another!" exclaimed Tertullian, expressing the amazement of the pagans and fulfilling what Jesus had declared in John 13:35: "By this all men will know that you are my disciples, if you love one another."

By A.D. 250 Christians in Rome were caring for 1500 needy people—the hungry, orphans, widows, victims of shipwreck—anyone who needed assistance. I Clement said, "Let everyone be subject to his neighbor; let the rich man provide for the wants of the poor; and let the poor man bless God, because he hath given him one by whom his needs may be supplied."

In the above passage, Paul was concerned that there be equal distribution among the churches. Can God be pleased by the great gulf that exists between Christians in the wealthy West and the impoverished believers in other parts of the world?

We have many opportunities to give. My church's most recent collection was to help a new church plant in the central city. Our small groups take up collections for families with an urgent financial need, send people on mission trips, and give aid in areas of natural disasters. We can do one-on-one giving as God would lead us.

As Christians we must be about the ministry of giving. It is how we demonstrate the love of God in a tangible way.

Father, what a privilege to contribute to the needs of the saints. Place a generous spirit within me so I can imitate you, the greatest giver of all. In Jesus' name I pray. Amen.

Simplicity

"The light of the body is the eye; if therefore thine eye be single, thy whole body shall be full of light." Matthew 6:22 (KJV)

Simplicity is something everyone seems to be longing for in the new millennium. No one can define what it is exactly as it means something different to everyone. What was Jesus talking about when he referred to a "single eye"?

This term has a double meaning (no pun intended!): It is to have a single purpose in life *and* a generous spirit. Its opposite is to have an "evil eye"—a spirit of covetousness. Christ is telling us that we should look to him and his kingdom with our single eye, living our lives in contentment and unselfishness. That is Christian simplicity.

How can we put it into practice? Often we feel it is our jobs that keep us in the rat race of life, but we need the income from these jobs to support our lifestyles. So round and round we go, like a gerbil on a wheel who doesn't know how to get off. We need to stop running.

We do this by eliminating all unnecessary activities and expenditures. We must quit wasting our time and our money on things that are frivolous. Get rid of everything you don't need or don't want. Strip your possessions down to only what really matters. This alone will simplify your life beyond belief. You may find your house is too large now. Consider downsizing. Free up your resources for the kingdom. Try to live on half of what you earn. If you don't think that's possible, check your budget and see where the money is going. For most people, half their bills constitute debt. Once the debt goes, you're there.

For me, simplicity is the freedom to work for the kingdom without being encumbered by a lot of stuff and obligations. It is to live with Christ at the center.

Father, help me to live in simplicity with my single eye fixed on you. Show me what changes I need to make in my lifestyle to do this. I ask in Jesus' name. Amen.

Small Things

*"Who despises the day of small things? Men will rejoice when they see
the plumb line in the hand of Zerubbabel." Zechariah 4:10*

Zechariah prophesied in the period after the Jews had returned from
exile in Babylon and were working to rebuild the temple.
Zerubbabel was the civil governor in charge of the project. The people
who remembered the temple in its former glory were disheartened by
the insignificance of the new structure, but God did not look down on
their efforts. He saw the finished work.

We can apply this insight to our finances. Do we get discouraged
because the amount of money we are able to save every month is so
minute? Ron Blue tells the story of a retired pastor who came to him
for advice. This man had never earned more than $8,000 a year in his
life. At age 80 he had a net worth of $1,663,000. Do not despise small
things!

Have you ever felt badly about being able to give only a small contribution? If you gave what you could, you should not feel guilty. God
can multiply your small gift. Remember the loaves and fish! We suffer
from the "bigger is better" syndrome in ministry as well. But God sees
our small things as big things.

Tabitha had a ministry of making garments for widows. She probably didn't think it was a big deal, but she was so mourned by those she
served that God had Peter raise her from the dead (Acts 9:40). John the
Baptist counseled those who came to him to do such small acts as
sharing clothing and food with those who had none (Luke 3:11).

Not all of us are in the spotlight, but all of us are called to the ministry of little things that count for much in God's eyes. Only he can
truly evaluate what they are worth. We will be astonished once we're in
heaven and the far-reaching effects of our efforts are revealed.

*Father, teach me to not look down on things I think are too lowly to matter much.
It is not for me to judge what is or is not significant, only to obey. In Jesus' name I
pray. Amen.*

Having Vision

"Where there is no vision, the people perish; but he that keepth the law, happy is he." Proverbs 29:18 (KJV)

The Hebrew word for "vision" used here refers to a dream, as in a revelatory word from God. This is different from goal-setting. Goals should flow out of the vision God gives us. We can't formulate a strategy to get us from point A to point B until we know where we are going!

As we've studied what the Bible has to say about money, God may have been speaking to you about the fruit he would like to develop in your life and finances. What has he revealed to you? Vision is a very personal thing; God will give everyone something unique to them and their situation. You may be at the point right now where all you want is to get out of debt. You haven't the imagination or the money to envision that day, but God does. He sees beyond our limited aspirations for ourselves and he desires us to see it, too.

Get away with him for an extended period of time and let him reveal to you the desires of your heart. He will confirm your dream as you bring it to him in prayer. Then you need to commit to it. Now you are ready to set goals to make it happen. Use the SMART method:

- Keep it *simple*. You should be able to write your goal in one or two sentences.
- Keep it *measurable*. You need to be able to tell how you're progressing.
- Keep it *attainable*. Don't set your goals impossibly high.
- Keep it *realistic*. You can't save $1,000 a month when you earn $1200!
- Keep it on a *time line*. Some goals are monthly, some are yearly.

Setting goals should get you excited. God gives big dreams! It's in remembering what God told you in those mountaintop experiences that will keep you going when you are in the valley of despair and the enemy is whispering you'll never make it. With prayer and perseverance, you will.

Father, reveal the dreams you have for me. I need fresh vision to move with confidence into the unknown future. I ask in Jesus' name. Amen.

Jubilee

"Consecrate the fiftieth year and proclaim liberty throughout the land to all its inhabitants. It shall be a jubilee for you; each one of you is to return to his family property and each to his own clan." Leviticus 25:10

Jubilee in Hebrew means "ram's horn" or "trumpet." Once in an Israelite's lifetime, he was to hear a trumpet sound on the Day of Atonement as liberty was proclaimed. Freedom from debts—all were to be canceled. Freedom from slavery—all slaves were to be set free. All land was to revert back to its original owner. Families would be reunited and able to return to their land debt-free to make a new start.

The year of Jubilee was a Sabbath year, as was the forty-ninth year before it. This meant the land was to be rested; no crops were to be planted for two years in a row. God anticipated the people's anxiety about this and assured them, "I will send you such a blessing in the sixth year that the land will yield enough for three years" (Leviticus 25:21). This promise had a condition: "Follow my decrees and be careful to obey my laws, and you will live safely in the land. Then the land will yield its fruit, and you will eat your fill and live there in safety" (Leviticus 25:18-19).

God made it clear that he was the owner of the land, and the Israelites were his tenants. The land had value only for the number of crops it would produce until the Jubilee. Its use was to feed people; it was not an investment as it is in our day.

There is no evidence that the Israelites ever celebrated the Jubilee. The fiftieth year came and the rich tightened their grip on what they had. The poor were not given the opportunity to reverse their fortunes. Greed overruled justice and equity.

Sound familiar?

Father, your laws are right and are given for our welfare. Help us today to bring about a society that is just and where people have priority over property. I pray in Jesus' name. Amen.

August 1

Deceptive Food

"When you sit to dine with a ruler, note well what is before you, and put a knife to your throat if you are given to gluttony. Do not crave his delicacies, for that food is deceptive." Proverbs 23:1-3

Have you ever been wined and dined in a sumptuous setting? Most of us have never been invited to dinner with heads of state at the White House, but perhaps we've been a guest at a luxury hotel or resort where everything was first class. All the details, from the light fixtures to the carpeting were expensive and luxurious. The food was served on exquisite fine china; the atmosphere was elegant. It was a heady experience.

The Queen of Sheba was dazzled when she traveled to pay a visit to King Solomon. She herself was quite wealthy, yet the scope of Solomon's household left her at a loss for words. Overwhelmed by the splendor, she finally states, "The report I heard in my own country about your achievements and your wisdom is true. But I did not believe these things until I came and saw with my own eyes. Indeed, not even half was told me; in wisdom and wealth you have far exceeded the report I heard" (1 Kings 10:6-7).

There is another half we are not told concerning fabulous wealth, and that is the dark side of the lives of the rich and famous. All that glitters is *not* gold. We see only the glamour and we covet that lifestyle for ourselves. Solomon tells us *don't*. That food is misleading!

He is warning us not to be deceived by a façade. Behind all the lush comforts of what appears to be paradise lies a web of responsibilities, anxieties, temptations, financial entanglements, and pressures. The owner is not free to enjoy his pleasure palace as a guest in a hotel who can simply pay the bill and check out. The rich often feel trapped in a golden cage.

Put a symbolic knife to your throat if you are susceptible to being influenced by displays of opulence. Don't desire deceptive food!

Father, open my spiritual eyes to see the trappings of wealth for what they really are. Make me like Jesus, who could dine with the wealthiest Pharisee and not be ensnared. In his name I pray. Amen.

Money in High Places

"The rich rule over the poor..." Proverbs 22:7

One of the reasons people pursue money is that often with money comes power and influence. Money can put you in control, especially over those who don't have any. The rich are the ones with the real estate, the education, and the connections with others who are rich. They have the ability to grease the wheels of government to turn in their favor. They determine the laws of the land, either by becoming politicians or by dangling their money as a carrot in the faces of those who are.

This is the power of money to corrupt. People are blinded by the promise of wealth and cast aside any scruples of justice and mercy. Where does all this leave the poor? Intimidated, shut out by a wall of red tape, feeling as if they have no rights, and no one to turn to when what rights they do have are violated.

The powers of darkness are drawn to those with wealth, seeking to use them for evil purposes, to abuse their position in manipulating others. James puts it this way: "But you have insulted the poor. Is it not the rich who are exploiting you? Are they not the ones who are dragging you into court? Are they not the ones who are slandering the noble name of him to whom you belong?" (James 2:6-7). If you have wealth, be aware that Satan will attempt to entice you to use it to gain advantage over people.

How do we defeat him? We must remember he is already defeated by the cross; he has no power over us. Then we must renounce all—our wealth, our status, our reputation—into the rightful hands of God. They are not ours to do with as we please; we submit our power to the authority of God's power. We are to use our power to serve, not to be served.

God needs wealthy Christians in high places to administer justice and mercy to the oppressed. People of high character, yielded to the Holy Spirit, who will use their influence to overcome evil with good. The rich will always rule over the poor, but may it be the godly rich.

Father, I pray for Christians in places of authority and influence, that you would protect them from corruption and the devil's wiles. Give them courage to stand against tyranny wherever they encounter it. I ask in Jesus' name. Amen.

The Sin of Indifference

"He who gives to the poor will lack nothing, but he who closes his eyes to them receives many curses." Proverbs 28:27

The story Jesus told of the rich man and Lazarus is considered to be a parable, although it is the only one in which he uses an actual name. It illustrates how seriously God takes the plight of the poor.

Here was a rich man living in opulence. We are told he dressed in purple and fine linen, the clothing of royalty. I'm sure he lived in a mansion and had many servants. There was just one blight on this scene—a beggar named Lazarus who was laid at his gate (Luke 16:20). He may have been brought there by people who believed the rich resident would use his vast resources to care for this suffering soul.

The only attention Lazarus received was from the dogs that came and licked his sores. He was starving and willing to eat whatever leftovers he was offered, and he died still waiting for help that never came.

The rich man died also and as he was being tormented in the fires of hell, he recognized Lazarus far away being comforted by Abraham. He requests that Lazarus come to bring him some relief by dipping his finger in water to cool his tongue. The beggar that he ignored, that he couldn't be bothered with in life, was now supposed to serve him after death?!

Abraham tells him this isn't possible, and reminds him that in his lifetime he received good things. The standard by which he treated others was now being applied to him. The man's crime wasn't that he was rich. His offense was in being so lacking in compassion that while he lived in luxury and waste, a man in rags was dying in his driveway. Jesus deemed that deserving of hellfire. What are the implications of this for us?

Father, open my eyes to the needs of those around me. I don't want to be guilty of living so high that I become immune to the suffering of others. I pray in the name of Jesus. Amen.

August

Only What Is Needed

"The Israelites did what they were told; some gathered much, some little. And when they measured it by the omer, he who gathered much did not have too much, and he who gathered little did not have too little. Each one gathered as much as he needed." Exodus 16:17-18

Imagine the task of feeding over a million people in a desert wilderness! If I had been among the Israelites as they set out from Egypt, I'd be wondering about the food supply for the trip. It took a month for them to start to complain that they were going to starve.

God told Moses he would rain down bread from heaven for them, but it was to be a test. Could they follow instructions? They were to gather only the manna they needed for *one* day, and they were not to keep any of it until the next morning. They had to trust God to meet their needs on a daily basis.

Some of the people demonstrated their doubt and their lack of faith by trying to save leftover manna for breakfast. After waking up to maggots and stink, I'm sure they didn't do that again!

The exception to the "one day's worth only" rule was that they were to gather twice as much food on the day before the Sabbath to avoid working on the day of rest. This day the manna supernaturally did not spoil, although some people went out to look for more anyway. The Lord was getting frustrated. "How long will you refuse to keep my commands and my instructions?" (Exodus 16:28).

This tendency to hoard seems to be encoded in our sinful natures. We cling to more than we need out of fear there will be no more for us in the future. This grieves God to the heart; he wants us to trust him as our good Father who provides for us. He will never let us starve. He is faithful even when we are faithless.

Father, I confess that I feel more comfortable when I have a surplus. Teach me to live in faith and dependence on your supply for my daily needs. I ask in Jesus' name. Amen.

The Unknown Future

"Do not boast about tomorrow, for you do not know what a day may bring forth." Proverbs 27:1

We once took a financial risk that may not seem all that risky to some people, but it sure felt that way to us. We had a buyer for our house in Green Bay and knew that with the proceeds from the sale, we could get the things we needed for our new house in Milwaukee. We wanted the carpeting installed before we actually moved in, so we did one of those "90 days same as cash" deals, counting on the other house to close on the scheduled date. We did the same deal with a refrigerator. Until we had the check, it was rather nerve-wracking owing that money.

The house did close, although we found out later it almost hadn't due to FHA red tape. What a relief to pay that stuff off! We vowed we would never do that again. You just don't know what can happen.

Really, life is what happens to us while we're making other plans. I thought I would continue to work throughout my first pregnancy; instead I was so sick I was laid up from my second month until I delivered. So much for any extra money!

College students will rack up credit card debt, in addition to their student loans, under the impression that once they graduate they'll land a great job and pay it all off. It rarely works that way. Some have to drop out of school to take any job they can just to make ends meet.

"Don't put the cart before the horse" is still great advice. We've counseled people to earn the money first, then purchase what they want—not the other way around. Who knows what tomorrow may bring?

Len started his electrical business without incurring a penny of debt, but we see so many businesses get behind the eight ball with creditors at their start-up that they can never turn a profit.

We are not to boast about tomorrow. We are not to make financial decisions based on what we think or hope may happen. We take the chance of living with years of regret if we do.

Father, only you know what the future holds. Guard my heart against making boastful assumptions with my finances. I ask in Jesus' name. Amen.

Honoring Your Mother and Father

"And he said to them, 'You have a fine way of setting aside the commands of God in order to observe your own traditions! For Moses said, "Honor your father and your mother," and "Anyone who curses his father or mother must be put to death." But you say that if a man says to his father or mother: "Whatever help you might have received from me is Corban" (that is, a gift devoted to God), then you no longer let him do anything for his father or mother.'" Mark 7:9-12

"Honor your father and your mother" is the fifth commandment, the one with the promise: "So that you may live long in the land the LORD your God is giving you" (Exodus 20:12). To *honor* means to prize highly, respect, care for, and obey. The Pharisees had devised a way for a Jewish son to get out of his responsibility to support his parents once the roles were reversed.

By using the word *Corban,* meaning "offering," in a religious vow, the earnings that would have gone to the parents could be dedicated to God, even if the money wasn't to be used for religious purposes. The teachers of the Law held that the oath was binding. Jesus condemned this practice. Children have an obligation to their parents that cannot be set aside by adherence to another command or oath.

Our elderly parents need us—if not financially, they most certainly need us emotionally. They need to know we're there for them and looking out for their best interests. If we are faced with putting them in a care home, they still need our time and our love. We can't turn our backs on the people who brought us into the world and raised us at such great personal sacrifice without disobeying the Lord. Jesus himself made provision for his mother as he was dying on the cross (John 19:26-27).

Honor your mother and father at any cost. Remember what you cost them.

Heavenly Father, thank you for my parents. I will call them today to tell them how much I love and appreciate them. Please bless them and keep them, for Jesus' sake. Amen.

Zacchaeus, the Tax Collector

"But Zacchaeus stood up and said to the Lord, 'Look, Lord! Here and now I give half my possessions to the poor, and if I have cheated anybody out of anything, I will pay back four times the amount.'" Luke 19:8

The conversion of Zacchaeus is extraordinary to our modern methods of evangelism. We're happy to get someone to say the sinner's prayer; we'll work on getting them to tithe later. For some Christians this process of converting their wallets takes years, even decades. Here we see a wealthy man so touched by God he was instantly delivered from the love of money. His genuine repentance produced immediate fruit.

He publicly declared his intentions, thereby making himself accountable. Here's a spiritual lesson: When God tells you to do something, tell someone as soon as possible what you're going to do. It's so easy to get so much distance between ourselves and the emotion of the moment that the Holy Spirit's conviction lifts and we no longer feel compelled to follow through. Others can apply needed pressure to ensure we make good on our promises.

Zacchaeus' dramatic salvation makes some people uncomfortable. They want to go to heaven, but they don't want to yield up their personal estates. They want to keep a foot in each kingdom but Christ says that's impossible. This is why so many Christians don't know spiritual victory—their hearts are divided, their souls diluted by trying to serve two masters.

Zacchaeus should be remembered for more than being that short guy who climbed a tree to see Jesus. He is a wonderful testimony to God's life-changing power of a totally surrendered life.

Father, bring me fully into your kingdom. I know I can't live a double life, and if I even try I'll be miserable. Help me to stop watching Jesus from a "safe" distance; to tear down the barrier of money between myself and intimacy with my Savior. I ask in Christ's name. Amen.

The Problem With Prenups

"Jesus knew their thoughts and said to them, 'Any kingdom divided against itself will be ruined, and a house divided against itself will fall.'" Luke 19:8

Most Christians avoid having a prenuptial agreement when they marry the first time. If they marry a second time, they may be put under pressure by the children of the first marriage to make such an agreement to protect their inheritance. The arguments for keeping the assets separate can be quite convincing.

The problem with having a prenuptial contract is that it gives Satan a place to drive a wedge into your new marriage. A couple cannot really become "one" if they're not willing to merge their material possessions. This would include the refusal of one spouse to add the new spouse's name onto deeds and titles of property owned. You should really even question the wisdom in marrying someone who insists on drawing up a prenuptial as it indicates a lack of trust. How close of a relationship can you have if you don't trust each other?

It's natural for kids to be suspicious of a new stepparent, particularly if their parent has a large estate. But they must not be allowed to interfere with or control the finances of the new union because of selfishness and greed.

When we marry, we are to withhold nothing from each other. A prenup says up front, "I'm keeping what's mine. There is no 'ours.'" This creates a division that can eventually destroy the marriage. We are not to follow the ways of worldly people who do not take vows seriously and do not understand the meaning of the word "commitment." Have you noticed that many couples who do sign prenups end up in divorce court? It seems to be a self-fulfilling prophecy.

Avoid prenups. You will only be inviting trouble to your wedding.

Father, give me the freedom to fully enter into a "one-flesh" relationship with my spouse. Help me to think only in terms of "ours." I ask in Christ's name. Amen.

August

Abigail

"A wife of noble character is her husband's crown, but a disgraceful wife is like decay in his bones." Proverbs 12:4

Abigail's story appears in 1 Samuel 25. She was married to the wealthy Nabal, whose name means "fool" and is described as being "surly and mean in his dealings" (1 Samuel 25:3). We see these characteristics in his treatment of David's men. David had protected Nabal's flocks and requested provision in return. Nabal ungraciously answered them and sent them away empty-handed. David was enraged and came after Nabal with four hundred men, intent on slaying him and all who belonged to him.

The servants told Abigail what had happened, and she immediately took matters into her own hands. She loaded up donkeys with food and sent them to meet David. Then she went herself and bowed before him, offering apologies and assuming the blame. David accepted her gift and praised her for preventing bloodshed in the incident.

Nabal knew none of this until the next morning. When his wife told him what had happened, "his heart failed him and he became like a stone. About ten days later, the Lord struck Nabal and he died" (1 Samuel 25:37-38).

There are times a wife needs to assume responsibility for the family finances when the husband is irrational. It is not "going behind his back." Scripture praises Abigail for her actions, while Nabal is punished with death. A husband's foolishness can bring a family to ruin; a prudent wife has the ability to prevent it, and she should. She can be his "crown" and a credit to him, no matter what his disposition.

Abigail is described as intelligent. Wisdom is needed to know where submission ends and sin begins. A wife should not sign tax returns she knows are fraudulent, and she is not being insubordinate if she refuses to do so. "We must obey God rather than men" (Acts 5:29).

Behind even a bad man can be a good woman.

Father, I ask for your protection from compromising situations. Give me the wisdom and the courage to do what is right and still be respectful and submissive. I ask in Jesus' name. Amen.

The Great Test

> *" 'Does Job fear God for nothing?' Satan replied. 'Have you not put a hedge around him and his household and everything he has? You have blessed the work of his hands, so that his flocks and herds are spread throughout the land. But stretch out your hand and strike everything he has, and he will surely curse you to your face.' " Job 1:9-11*

Job was God's model of a faithful servant. The Lord points him out to the Accuser as one whom he could *not* accuse. Satan questions Job's motives for serving God; he insinuates that Job worships Yahweh only because he's wealthy. Take away the blessings, Satan asserts, and Job would turn away from his faith. So God basically says, "Okay, you're on. We'll see who's right." He allowed Satan to take Job's servants, his livestock, and the lives of his children, all in one day. Can you imagine?

Job's response is to fall on the ground in worship. God wins round one. When Satan comes before him again, God points out that Job still fears him, even after losing all his possessions. Satan isn't impressed yet. He insists that Job will curse God if his own body is struck. God gives his permission, and Job is inflicted with painful boils. This is too much for Mrs. Job. "Curse God and die!" She tells her husband. But incredibly, Job clings to his faith. God wins again.

I wonder, Do I have that kind of faith? Could I lose everything, even my health, and maintain my trust that God is good? God knew Job would pass the test, or he never would have allowed it in the first place.

And are we still clinging to the false belief that our prosperity proves God's favor towards us? The truth is, God is not obligated to bless us when we obey him. He is sovereign and free to act in any way he chooses. He restored back to Job double what he had lost, but we can't presume he will do that in every instance, nor should we expect our devotion to gain us material rewards.

Can we respond like Job? "The LORD gave and the LORD has taken away; may the name of the LORD be praised" (Job 1:21).

Father, let the truth that you are good sink deep into my heart where it can never be shaken. I pray in the name of Jesus. Amen.

Not for Profit

"Unlike so many, we do not peddle the word of God for profit. On the contrary, in Christ we speak before God with sincerity, like men sent from God." 2 Corinthians 2:17

They were around in the apostle Paul's day as well—hucksters who saw a way to make a quick buck by jumping on the latest fad. In our culture if something becomes popular, it won't be long before you will be able to purchase everything from cups to key rings with the new media darling's image on it. It's called merchandising, and it's mostly harmless, if not a waste of money.

When we're talking about the gospel being "merchandised," that's something entirely different. False teachers had infiltrated the church at Corinth, and their only interest was to get money out of the naïve believers there. Christianity was the "hot new thing" they could use to make a profit. They saw Jesus as a means to earn their living by taking offerings in return for speaking. It wouldn't surprise me if they sold "Jesus memorabilia" at a table in the back!

There is nothing wrong with guest speakers offering their books and tapes for sale at places they are invited to minister. They are often sold at or near cost and the author is not getting rich by this practice. It is giving the saints a valuable resource.

Paul, however, was concerned with *sincerity*. The motive of these peddlers was not to see people give their lives to Christ, but to see their own pockets grow heavy. They weren't even believers themselves, they had just learned to present themselves persuasively.

Christianity is still used today by hypocrites who care more about promoting their own agenda than the saving power of God. "By their fruit you will recognize them," says Jesus in Matthew 7:16. The results of their "ministry" will reveal if they were sent by God or not.

Father, help me to discern when I'm hearing wolves in sheep's clothing. I will not knowingly support any false teachers with my finances. I pray in Jesus' name. Amen.

Money Doesn't Make the Man

"Better a poor man whose walk is blameless than a rich man whose ways are perverse." Proverbs 28:6

The Bible makes a strong case against wealth, but if we examine its teachings closely, we see that it is not riches it condemns, but wickedness. The wicked are characterized as greedy, ruthless, violent, arrogant, and oppressive. Sometimes these traits are coupled with having money, but we must not make the assumption that all the rich are corrupt.

Somewhere back in Christianity's history the church got the idea that to be poor was to be godly. Orders of monks rose up who took vows of voluntary poverty and were looked upon by their contemporaries as super-spiritual and holy. This was a far cry from the early Jews who believed wealth was the mark of God's favor on one's life. Today the pendulum has swung the other way again—you are blessed if you are rich.

Proverbs 28:6 sums up Scripture's balanced view of the rich and the poor. It's not your economic station in life that counts, but your character. It provides a counterargument against the worldview of holding someone up in respect and awe just because they have money, while putting down someone who does not.

Money can't buy character, but it can corrupt character. Poverty doesn't guarantee godliness, but it does develop dependence on God. There is a mixture of good and evil in both. The Bible has just as many examples of the righteous rich as it does the wicked rich. God accepts everyone who fears him and does what is right (Acts 10:35).

We are not to stereotype people based on their net worth. People of integrity and compassion can be found in every tax bracket. God doesn't play favorites and we shouldn't, either.

Father, give me your spiritual eyes to look at people's hearts and not at their outward appearances. Make my walk blameless so I will always honor you. I ask in Jesus' name. Amen.

The Joash Chest

"Jehoiada the priest took a chest and bored a hole in its lid. He placed it beside the altar, on the right side as one enters the temple of the LORD. The priests who guarded the entrance put into the chest all the money that was brought up to the temple of the LORD." 2 Kings 12:9

When Joash became king of Judah at age seven, the temple of the Lord had fallen into disrepair from neglect during the reign of Athaliah. With the priest Jehoiada instructing him, Joash instituted many religious reforms. He gave orders to the priests to use the money from the offerings to restore the damage, but years went by and nothing was done. Joash then took matters into his own hands and had a special chest set up to collect all the offerings brought to the temple. This money was used to pay the laborers and purchase the needed materials, and the work was completed.

I attended a church that had a "Joash chest" placed in front of the sanctuary platform. The money collected in it went to the retirement of the church's debt. A specific time was designated every Sunday for anyone who wanted to come up and donate to the Joash chest. The senior pastor would stand beside it and personally thank everyone who contributed. It was a huge church, but it seemed the same people went up every week.

To this day I really don't know what to think about that. I'm still thinking about it. Maybe it was done in that way in Joash's day, but is it appropriate for us? To me, it involved too much personal recognition for those doing the giving. And I wonder, Was that their motive? Couldn't they put a check in the offering plate marked "debt fund"?

When I left that church I was convinced it would never be out of debt. They were always busy building *something* and the participants in the "Joash chest" ritual enjoyed it too much to give it up. Maybe I'm wrong about it, but I felt a check in my spirit that something wasn't right there.

Father, teach us at what times giving should be done anonymously. Help us to avoid exalting those who give and robbing them of their reward from you. In Jesus' name I pray. Amen.

Comparison and Competition

"But he answered one of them, 'Friend, I am not being unfair to you. Didn't you agree to work for a denarius? Take your pay and go. I want to give the man who was hired last the same as I gave you. Don't I have the right to do what I want with my own money? Or are you envious because I am generous?'" Matthew 20:13-15

In this passage, Jesus tells a story of a vineyard owner who hires workers early in the morning, telling them he would pay a denarius for a day's work. This is agreeable to them and they set about the job.

Three hours later, the owner hires more workers and tells them he will pay them whatever is right. He hires again at noon, at 3:00, and at 5:00 in the afternoon. One hour later the day is done and he orders his foreman to pay the men beginning with the one-hour workers. They were amazed to receive a full day's wage; they certainly hadn't earned it. The owner obviously put people before profits; a family needed a denarius a day to live on.

The three-hour workers also received a denarius, and the word spread down the line of laborers who began to eagerly calculate what they would be paid, having worked eight- and twelve-hour shifts. When they were paid one denarius as agreed, they became angry and took their complaint to the owner: "We have borne the burden of the work and the heat of the day, and you make them equal to us!"

The owner reminds them that they received what they had contracted for, then asks a pointed question: "Are you envious because I am generous?" Literally, "is your eye evil?" They were covetous.

The parable of the vineyard workers illustrates our typical response when we see someone else on the receiving end of what we think is undeserved compensation. We grumble and complain, we file a grievance with the boss.

When we are always looking at what others have, we can't enjoy what we have been given. We have a generous Father. Let's not compare and compete with each other.

Lord God, thank you for giving me what I need and not what I deserve. Keep a complaining spirit far from me. For Jesus' sake. Amen.

Wrong Motives

*"When you ask, you do not receive, because you ask with wrong
motives, that you may spend what you get on your pleasures." James 4:3*

Prayer is not rubbing a genie's lamp to get our wishes granted. God
is not Santa Claus. Intellectually we all know this, but sometimes
we behave like we don't. We ask for something that wouldn't be good
for us and God says no. He is not obligated to indulge all our desires,
and it's a good thing he doesn't. He is a loving, protective Father, and
he won't willingly supply us with things that will harm us.

My pastor preached a message many years ago in which he stated
that one of the dangers of credit is that it removes barriers to harmful
items. It allows us access to purchase things that we otherwise could
not due to lack of funds. When God doesn't supply the money, we
whip out the Visa and get it anyway.

If God truly is against using debt, what does he think of our
lifestyles that basically let us do whatever we want as long as we have
credit? Small businesses now use credit cards for start-up funding
rather than commercial bank loans. They no longer have to submit a
sound business plan and fill out a lengthy application; just take the
cash advance and go. Independent filmmakers do the same. *The Blair
Witch Project* was funded by credit cards when traditional financing
couldn't be obtained.

The word James uses for "pleasures" or "lusts" (KJV) conveys the
idea of hedonism. Our chief aim in life is to live for God's glory, not
for our own happiness and gratification. An indulgent attitude towards
ourselves will only hurt us spiritually. We are to crucify our flesh and
its desires (Galatians 5:24), those things that are against God.

When we pray, let us pray with right motives for God's goodwill
towards us.

*Father, thank you that don't answer all my prayers in the affirmative. Thank you
for loving me and wanting only the best for me. Help me live for your glory and not
my own happiness. In Jesus' name. Amen.*

Only the Best

*"If the offering is a burnt offering from the herd, he is to offer a male
without defect. . .when anyone brings a grain offering to the Lord, his
offering is to be of fine flour." Leviticus 1:3, 2:1*

Leviticus is chiefly a book about worship—how the Israelites were to
go about it, the duties of the priests, and the various sacrifices the
Lord required. The holiness of God is emphasized throughout; nothing
unclean or impure was allowed to enter his presence.

Holiness is symbolized by physical perfection, which is why only
animals that were unblemished, with no defects, could be offered. We
are so far removed from the blood sacrificial system, we don't always
realize the implications of this. Basically, the Hebrews were to take
their very best male breeding animals and slaughter them as atonement
for their sin. As anyone who has ever raised animals knows, the ones
you want to cull from your stock are the weak, the imperfect, the
"uglies," if you will. The best animals were the ones you raised to
maturity for breeding to improve the gene pool.

God was telling them they couldn't hold back their best and still be
acceptable to him. They were to trust him to continue to keep their
herds vigorous, despite giving up the animals needed to do just that.
Even in the bloodless offering of grain, the flour had to be the finest
milled.

After their return from exile, God came down hard on the
Israelites for offering blind, lame, and diseased animals on his altar.
This not only defiled the Lord's table but caused the people themselves
to be cursed (Malachi 1:13-14). The man who had an acceptable animal to offer but gave a blemished one instead was called a cheat.

We cheat the Lord when we fail to give him our best and offer our
leftovers instead—things we won't miss and are glad to get rid of anyway. He is to be honored as the great King that he is with the finest we
have.

*Lord God, you are deserving of so much more than I can give. I will not hold back
my best from you, but offer it willingly. For Jesus' sake. Amen.*

Christianity or Commerce?

"A silversmith named Demetrius, who made silver shrines of Artemis, brought in no little business for the craftsmen. He called them together, along with the workmen in related trades, and said: 'Men, you know we receive a good income from this business. And you see and hear how this fellow Paul has convinced and led astray large numbers of the people here in Ephesus and in practically the whole province of Asia. He says that man-made gods are no gods at all.'" Acts 19:24-25

Demetrius' little speech to the tradesmen of Ephesus resulted in a riot. The real reason for all the uproar was not the silver workers' zeal for the goddess Artemis, but for the threat Paul's message posed to their industry of making shrines and images. The temple of Artemis was a tourist attraction like the Eiffel Tower is today. The people who came to view it would purchase miniature silver images of Artemis as souvenirs. Some things never change!

Sales of these little idols were falling off as people turned away from the deities of the Greeks and Romans to worship the one true God. The craftsmen blamed Paul for the downturn of their lucrative business. Anything that touches people's prosperity is going to be opposed with utmost aggression.

Part of the reason Christianity is so vehemently despised by the forces of evil is that it causes people's hearts to move away from the things of the world. The "vice" industry—liquor, tobacco, drugs, gambling, pornography—all suffer loss as people give their lives to Jesus. Certain magazines, music, and movies are no longer part of our lifestyles. We remove our money—the true object of their worship—from their coffers and they hate us for it.

We must be careful that we are not engaged in any type of business, no matter how profitable, that would compromise our walk with Christ. We need to be very clear on which God we are serving.

Father, I pray you strengthen your people against evil powers that would try to keep us in bondage to the goods of this world. I ask in Jesus' name. Amen.

Ill-Gotten Gain

"Ill-gotten treasures are of no value, but righteousness delivers from death." Proverbs 10:2

Two of our bicycles were stolen yesterday. My husband and daughter went for a bite to eat and came out to find the lock cable neatly cut through. I had mixed feelings on hearing about this. We had talked about selling the bikes but didn't think we'd get enough money to justify getting rid of them. Now they're gone and we *really* have nothing. There's a lesson there somewhere.

I think about our thief. The police say these "tweakers" will steal items to sell at pawn shops so they can buy a quick hit of drugs. What a wretched lifestyle! To steal only to get money to consume on a destructive habit. Of course, we don't know for sure his motive for stealing them. They were God's bikes, anyway, so wherever they end up really isn't our concern.

What is our attitude when we've been robbed? In our feelings of violation, we want to take vengeance. What helps me is to remember it's much better to be "thieved" from than to be a thief. God promises to look out for his own who walk in righteousness, and we are to leave retaliation to him. Yes, we are to file a criminal report, but we leave justice in the hands of God.

Our reaction to incidents like this reveal the condition of our heart. Have we truly given all our possessions over to God? If we have, losing them in this way shouldn't really upset us all that much. Nothing touches us except what God allows, even in extreme cases like Job's. We have to trust his purposes behind our setbacks. We need to pray for those who sin against us. Their deeds bring them no gain of value; the wages of sin is death (Romans 6:23). *Our* treasure is in heaven, "where thieves do not break in and steal" (Matthew 6:20).

Father, when I'm the victim of a theft, remind me that the things of this earth are only given to us temporarily to use. I will trust in your justice to make things right. In Jesus' name I pray. Amen.

August

Pearl of Great Price

"Again, the kingdom of heaven is like a merchant looking for fine pearls. When he found one of great value, he went away and sold everything he had and bought it." Matthew 13:45-46

I love pearls. Not strands of them, but individual ones that can be set into a ring or a pendant. I have several, and I acquired them in a unique way. Vacationing with family, we'd always run across pearl-diving booths where you could choose an oyster and they would open it for you to reveal your pearl. After watching my sister-in-law do this for several years, I decided I wouldn't mind one for myself. Len picked out the oyster, and we were stunned at what was inside: a huge, beautiful silver-grey pearl. I felt like I had won the lottery.

That began a tradition to go pearl hunting on special occasions. Len always picked; he'd get a "feeling" about a particular oyster, and he chose some beauties—pearly pink, gunmetal gray, buttery gold. The odds of getting a pearl that isn't an ordinary white are about 2 out of 100 according to the proprietors of these places.

So I understand a little of what the pearl merchant in Jesus' parable felt when he came across one of great value. Your heart beats faster in excitement upon the discovery. You feel elation. You feel blessed! The pearl merchant was willing to sell everything he owned to acquire this one pearl. Did he care about the cost? No! He understood the opportunity. He was anxious to be sure he closed the deal.

And Jesus says that's the value of the kingdom; it is worth giving up everything we have to gain it. It can't be bought with money or good deeds, but it does cost us our wills as we totally surrender them to God.

I love pearls because when I wear them they remind me of the kingdom—God's rule and reign—and the words of my pastor one evening long ago when he urged us all, with tears in his eyes, to "Buy the pearl!"

Father, your kingdom come! Help me to put aside everything that would distract me from pursuing it. In the name of Jesus I pray. Amen.

Practicing Hospitality

*"Offer hospitality to one another without grumbling. Each one should
use whatever gift he has received to serve others, faithfully administering God's grace in its various forms." 1 Peter 4:9-10*

One of our pastor's wives once said how disappointed she was to
find out her spiritual gift was hospitality. She said she felt like she
had won the Miss Congeniality award in a pageant; nice, but not
important. Since then, she has realized otherwise.

One of the first acts following conversion was baptism; next, it
appears to be the practice of hospitality. Lydia opened her home to
Paul, Silas, and Luke after receiving Christ (Acts 16:15). After an earth-
quake rocked his prison, the Philippian jailer believed and took Paul
and Silas into his home (Acts 16:34). Mary, John Mark's mother,
hosted prayer meetings (Acts 12:12).

My church has over 70 small groups that meet in homes, following
the example of Acts 2:26: "They broke bread in their homes and ate
together with glad and sincere hearts." Hospitality builds Christian
community.

Our society is not comfortable going into the home of a "stranger."
When traveling, we'd rather stay in motels. We're not comfortable
inviting people into our homes. We feel we're not set up for entertaining. Hospitality does cost us in time and money, yet we are commanded to do it. It is a ministry; we serve Christ by opening up our
home to others. "Practice hospitality," says Paul (Romans 12:13).

Is keeping our house clean and our kitchen to ourselves more
important than meeting the needs of the body of Christ? We hosted a
small group for four years and yes, the carpet got dirty and the furniture was worn, but the relationships we built were more than worth it.
If you have the gift of hospitality, rejoice! It's anything but unimportant.

*Father, help me get over my selfishness and give me opportunities to practice hospi-
tality. Open my heart to open my home as if Jesus himself were coming—because he
is. In his name I pray. Amen.*

Giving Cheerfully

"Each man should give what he has decided in his heart to give,
not reluctantly or under compulsion, for God loves a cheerful giver."
2 Corinthians 9:7

This verse is frequently cited by people as the reason they don't tithe. They cannot part with 10 percent of their income cheerfully so they keep their level of giving down to where they "feel good" about it. This is dangerous thinking. It leads to living by our feelings, doing whatever our emotions are dictating to us at the moment. What if we treated all the Christian disciplines this way? We prayed only when we were in the mood; went to church only when it was convenient? We would be so spiritually unstable we'd fall away from the Lord completely. That can't be what Paul was talking about.

The Greek word for "cheerful" (*hilaros*) is such a unique word that this is the only place it appears in the New Testament. We get our English word "hilarious" from it, and it conveys the idea of joyful generosity. When our hearts are right, we don't have to be browbeaten into giving.

You have probably had the experience of being subjected to a fund-raising drive for something you really didn't want to donate to. You may have given grudgingly, but it was money you hated to part with. At other times you may have felt forced to give because of what others would say or think if you didn't. That's giving under compulsion.

Paul was motivating the Corinthians to give out of love. This was giving beyond the tithe. He was telling them that God prizes those whose hearts are prompted by joy to give with generosity. When we stand this verse on its head, we are merely looking for loopholes as reasons *not* to give. What does that say about our hearts?

God desires us to give; it draws us closer to him. Where our money goes, our hearts will follow. When we truly love God, we can't help but be cheerful givers.

Father, examine my heart for the motives of why I give. I want to give out of love for all that you have given me. In Jesus' name I pray. Amen.

A Complaining Spirit

"In the desert the whole community grumbled against Moses and Aaron. The Israelites said to them, 'If only we had died by the LORD's hand in Egypt! There we sat around pots of meat and ate all the food we wanted, but you have brought us out into this desert to starve this entire assembly to death.'" Exodus 16:2-3

Exactly one month out of slavery in Egypt and the Israelites had had enough. They directed their complaints to Moses and Aaron, but they were really expressing their discontent to God. They were thirsty, they were hungry, and when the Lord did provide food, they got bored with it. "We never see anything but this manna!" (Numbers 11:6).

God didn't bring his people directly into the land he promised them because he intended to test them first to see what was in their hearts (Deuteronomy 8:2). They failed his testing horribly; they rejected his provision, his leadership, and his laws; and they died in the desert. Only Joshua and Caleb survived of that generation to take possession of Canaan.

Everything that happens to us is also a test. How will we respond to our circumstances? Do we complain about what God has provided? It must amaze the rest of the world that the richest nation on earth is also the most dissatisfied. We never have enough money. If we own a house, we want a bigger house. If we have a car, we want a new car. Our wants never cease.

Do we see this as grumbling against God's provision? Can God not bring us into the fullness of our spiritual inheritance in Christ because of our discontent with what he's already given us? What do we do as parents when our children complain against all we have given them? We get upset and insist they appreciate what they have. In the same way, we tie God's hands when we fail to be grateful. He can't release all that he has for us and we cannot enter his rest.

A complaining spirit leads to death in a desert.

Father, I repent of the times I've grumbled against all you have provided for me. Help me to cultivate a heart of gratitude. For Jesus' sake. Amen.

What's Wrong with Welfare

"The sluggard's craving will be the death of him, because his hands refuse to work." Proverbs 21:25

Our welfare system has gone through a lot of reform in the last few years; it's not as much the free handout it used to be. Still, it's going to be difficult to undo the damage the first thirty years of this experiment has done to our society.

Our problem began in the 1930s when people were seeking relief from the Great Depression. They elected a president who promised to take charge of the economy and put the government in authority. This laid the foundations for federal intervention in all aspects of people's lives. The welfare system is what we get when we turn the role of provider over to the government. It set out with the good intentions of eliminating poverty; instead, it destroyed families by encouraging laziness and immorality. It assured more poverty for the next generation by trapping them into a lifestyle of being unable to do for themselves.

The churches abdicated their mandate to help the needy to federal programs, and that's where people look now to bail them out of their problems—not to God. Without the influence of the church, we spawn people like the unmarried woman I knew who had two children by different fathers and was actively seeking a third pregnancy in order to increase her welfare check.

The American dream, according to Larry Burkett, is the belief that hard work will earn us a better life than the generation before us. Welfare squashes that belief by taking away people's initiative. Why work if you can sit at home and get paid? It creates an entitlement mentality and it is totally unscriptural.

God wants us to take personal responsibility for our lives. If we are able-bodied, we are to work. We are to teach our children to work. Work is a witness to our faith. Welfare takes away more than it gives.

Father, I will look to you, not the government, as my source of help. Give our nation's leaders wisdom as to what to do about the welfare system. I ask in Jesus' name. Amen.

The American Idol

"You shall have no other gods before me." Exodus 20:3

We use the word "idol" very loosely in our day. Celebrities and sports figures are "idolized" and we buy their merchandise and attend their events as a form of worship. It's considered harmless and few of these "idols" have any great staying power; most are cast aside when the next popular personality comes along.

When we think of religious idols, we tend to imagine little statutes or carvings worshipped by primitives somewhere in Africa. The ancient Greeks and Romans had their gods, but we're enlightened and know better than that. We believe we're in no danger of breaking the first commandment.

In truth an idol is *anything* that comes between us and God. As a nation, our idol is money. We treat money as a deity; we look to it for security, it controls our behavior, it determines our morals. We sacrifice relationships on its altars. We kill babies for economic reasons; we put them in day care so we can serve money.

How long will a jealous God put up with it? His judgment may come by striking down our economy, which is faltering as I write this. People are crying out to the government to deliver them from unemployment and taxes when they should be crying out to the Lord to deliver them from their bondage to a false god. The prosperity of the 1990s did nothing to bring us closer to God; instead, we drifted further away.

God means what he says. If we continue to place money ahead of all other considerations, we will experience his discipline. He demands exclusive devotion to himself alone. We are to look to him for our security. The Holy Spirit is to control our behavior, and his word is to govern our lives.

If we don't tear down the American idol, God will do it for us.

Father God, you are Lord! There is nothing on earth that can compare with you. Lead us as a nation back to acknowledging your sovereignty. I ask in Jesus' name. Amen.

The Cost of Being a Disciple

"In the same way, any of you who does not give up everything he has cannot be my disciple." Luke 14:33

Jesus has already counted the cost of discipleship. He tells us what it is and asks us to consider it before we make the decision to follow him. The price tag is high: Everything we have. Not 10 percent, but 100 percent. We are to hold nothing back.

Our evangelism techniques often emphasize the benefits of being a Christian, and these are many and very valid. The danger is in creating disciples who come to Christ *only* to be blessed. These shallow conversions fall away when the new believers experience adversity, then they claim Christianity doesn't work and go back to serving the world and themselves.

Jesus never sugarcoated the gospel. He said things that drove people away (John 6:53-66); he wanted followers who were wholeheartedly committed to the kingdom of God. Money and self-interests were no longer to be served. We try to straddle the fence; we surrender partway and then wonder why we don't experience any power in our lives.

What would really set us apart from the world, and make us stand out as disciples of Jesus Christ, is our choosing to put people before money. Mother Theresa was respected and honored the world over by her willingness to live among the poorest of the poor in the slums of Calcutta. People listened to her testimony and scorned the televangelists with their expensive clothes and gaudy jewelry.

Jesus tells us we can't have it both ways. We cannot keep our pet possessions to ourselves and be his disciples at the same time. Some people will be called to sell everything; some will relinquish all they have only to have it given back to them to manage as stewards. Jesus is our master; he decides. He has purchased us with his own blood. He has the right to set the cost of discipleship.

Father, what Jesus suffered to pay the price for my sin is more than I can afford to give in return, but I do give you what I have—everything. I pray in Christ's name. Amen.

Lydia of Thyatira

*"One of those listening was a woman named Lydia, a dealer in purple
cloth from the city of Thyatira, who was a worshipper of God. The
Lord opened her heart to respond to Paul's message." Acts 16:14*

Paul and his traveling companions were in Philippi, a city with so
few Jews there was no synagogue, so the people met for prayer
along the river banks. While they were gathered there on the Sabbath,
Paul presented to them the gospel of Jesus Christ.

Lydia was a Gentile, a wealthy businesswoman. She was from a
region famous for its purple dye, which had to be gathered drop by
drop from a certain kind of shellfish. Lydia used this very expensive
dye to make purple fabric, probably linen, which she would then sell to
be made into garments. Purple and linen are associated with royalty,
wealth, and the priesthood (Exodus 28).

She was a woman of influence; her entire household believed and
was baptized soon after she became a believer in Christ. She immediately opened her home to the traveling evangelists—Paul, Silas,
Timothy, and Luke. Her house became their base while in Philippi
(Acts 16:40).

The Philippian church that was established there owes much to
Lydia. She used her wealth and prominence to build up the new believers; the fellowship most likely was begun out of her home. She receives
special mention by Luke for her unselfish hospitality. She was an
instrumental part of the church plant Paul began in that part of the
Roman Empire, and her wealth helped advance the kingdom of God.
We are never told of a husband; Lydia is a shining example of what a
single woman can accomplish who gives herself fully to the Lord's purposes. First Corinthians 7:34 reminds us that singles are free to live in
undivided devotion to Christ.

Lydia began as a worshipper of God whose faith in Christ led to
good works. This is what the Lord intends for all of us.

*Father, thank you for telling us in your Word of the people you used to build your
church. Let my life and resources play a part in the history of where I fellowship. I
ask in Jesus' name. Amen.*

Is Investing Scriptural?

"All a man's ways seem innocent to him, but motives are weighed by the LORD." Proverbs 16:2

Some sincere Christians will not invest in the stock market because they believe it constitutes gambling. Whether it is or not depends on how you're going about it. If you are looking to get rich quick on a fast strike based on a "hot tip," then you're not only gambling but you're dealing with a spirit of greed. On the other hand, if you are knowledgeable and are investing in solid companies for long-term growth, you are exercising good stewardship. The difference is the motive.

The question to ask is: Why am I investing? Is it to be able to give more? To meet future family needs? These are legitimate reasons. If your heart is right, you can handle whatever wealth may come from investments. But if you are investing out of greed, ego, or the desire to quit working, then you'd better stop and talk it over with the Lord.

One way to discern your motives is to check your track record of giving. If you are generous now, you will continue to be as your resources increase. If you're saying, "I'll give more when I can afford it," you're only kidding yourself. More money never cured stinginess; in fact, the trait increases right along with your net worth.

Another way of examining yourself is to ask what an acceptable rate of return is for you. If you're not content with the standard 8 to 12 percent, then you're being unrealistic and your investing will be riddled with impatience and poor decisions.

Investing for a tax shelter is questionable. If you're so eager to reduce your taxes, why not just give the money away? And finally, how would you feel if the money were lost? All investments involve *some* risk. The best reason to invest is that you want to multiply the resources God has given you for his use and his glory.

Father, search my heart and reveal my motives for investing. Give me the wisdom to invest wisely and well for your glory. I ask in the name of Jesus. Amen.

When Should I Invest?

"There is a time for everything, and a season for every activity under heaven." Ecclesiastes 3:1

You have examined your heart and you know that your motives for investing are correct. Now you need to determine if you're at that place in your financial life where you can. This is very important; some people are using funds to invest that could be put to much better use in other places.

Before investing, you should eliminate all high interest debt such as credit cards and consumer loans. This alone will give you an immediate return of 12 to 24 percent depending on the interest rates. You should have at least one month's income available in your checking account, an emergency fund of at least three month's income in an interest bearing account, and savings set aside for major purchases, such as a car, upcoming repairs, or anything your normal budget isn't structured to handle. Once you've reached that point, you're ready to invest.

If you're not yet at that point, you're putting money you need out at risk, and you can't afford to do that. It's tempting to use the emergency fund money for tuitions, vacations, wedding expenses, and the like, but it's critical that you don't do this. What will you live on if you lose your job? What if you're hurt and are unable to work for a time? Disability claims take awhile to process. And consider this: If you should die, the insurance company will not pay out benefits until they have a certified death certificate and it can take up to three months to issue one. Don't touch your emergency fund!

Investing should come from "gravy" money after all the other contingencies have been met. Don't worry about missing out on a great deal while you're accumulating in these other areas. If you invest too soon with money you can't spare, a great deal can quickly turn into a horrible *ordeal*. Can you really afford to lose this money?

Before you invest in anything, learn the rules you must play by. We'll look at that topic tomorrow.

Father, you know my needs both now and in the future. Guide me to know when the season is right for me to invest. I ask in Christ's name. Amen.

How Should I Invest?

*"My heart is not proud, O Lord, my eyes are not haughty, I do not
concern myself with great matters or things too wonderful for me."*
Psalm 131:1

You must have a strategy before you are ready to invest. This will
depend on what your goals are. Is the money for retirement?
College? These would fall under the accumulation strategy. You need
investments that will grow your money over time, such as mutual funds,
zero coupon bonds, or real estate holdings. If your goal is to create
income to live on or to live off the interest of your capital, you need a
preservation strategy. In this situation, U.S. Treasury bills and bonds are
typically the investments used as they are considered to be more "safe."

A rule of investing is: The higher the rate of return, the higher the
degree of risk. Depending on your age, you may be comfortable with
more risk, because you have time on your side. Older people do not.
Everyone is different; what's risky to one person may be conservative to
another. It depends on temperament and level of knowledge.

Which leads to the number one rule of investing: If you don't
understand it, stay out of it. This means you know exactly what you're
doing, and you can explain it to your spouse well enough that he or
she understands it, too. If not, you're getting involved in a matter too
great for you. It's best to keep it simple at first.

If you really want simple, do this: Keep it liquid, keep it portable,
and keep it diversified. This would eliminate real estate, which for
some people is an excellent investment. Know yourself and your tolerance level. Some investments can be quite time-consuming. Be sure
your investment makes economic sense. People will "feed" an investment just to have the tax benefits. Is that smart?

Make decisions based on wisdom. Learn all you can. Investing isn't
something you do once and forget about it; you keep managing your
money. You pray and ask for God's guidance. It's all for him anyway,
right?

*Father, I do seek your wisdom in choosing the right investments. Keep me humble
and out of anything that is over my head. I ask in Jesus' name. Amen.*

Inflation

"Now this is what the LORD Almighty says: 'Give careful thought to your ways. You have planted much, but have harvested little. You eat, but never have enough. You drink, but never have your fill. You put on clothes, but are not warm. You earn wages, only to put them in a purse with holes in it.'" Haggai 1:5-6

Haggai is accurately describing the effects of inflation. It erodes the purchasing power of our money, forcing us to earn more just to keep up with the rising costs of goods and services we need. We haven't experienced it much recently but we fear it and it influences our financial decisions.

There's nothing we can do about it except plan for it. We're not to be fearful; we're to be shrewd. Inflation can work for you if you are on the right side of the magic of compounding. In the early 1980s we were earning 17 percent on our money market fund. We never made so much as when we had double-digit inflation! Of course, our mortgage was at 12 percent. That's the downside.

A study was done that shows over the last 700 years the average annual rate of interest charged for loans was about 3 percent greater than the average annual inflation rate. This means that as long as we're on the lending side of the equation, we can beat inflation. We also beat it by spending less than what we make.

Inflation is measured by the Consumer Price Index, which is *not* a cost of living index. It is a list of prices for specific things. Some things listed are luxuries that many of us hardly ever buy. It does not account for consumers changing their buying habits, or the fact that we don't buy a new appliance every year. Your lifestyle has more influence on your finances than inflation does.

God is sovereign and he ultimately controls all governments and economies. Whether we have inflation, recession, or depression, he is Lord. We will trust in him.

Yes, Father, you are Lord! We are not to have irrational fears of what the economy is going to do. You can be trusted at all times. In Jesus' name I pray. Amen.

Time Is Money

"Still other seed fell on good soil, where it produced a crop—a hundred, sixty, or thirty times what was sown." Matthew 13:8

Compound interest has been called the eighth wonder of the world. If you have it working in your favor, you can grow money far beyond the amount you actually start with. Money has time value. A dollar spent today doesn't just take one dollar out of your future. It takes multiple dollars because the money is gone forever and can't be put to work for you. A dollar a day may not seem like much, but that's $30 a month; in 12 months $360. If you invested that $360 and could earn 6 percent, it would take 12 years to double it to $720. That's saving only $1 a day! What if you saved $1200 a year and earned 6 percent? In 12 years you would have $2400. At 10 percent, it would take only 7.2 years.

The Rule of 72 says that any interest rate divided into 72 will always give you the length of time required for an amount to double in value. That's if you never added any more savings into the pot each year. What would happen if you did that year after year?

Suppose you opened a Roth IRA and put in the annual maximum amount allowable for a married couple (currently $6,000) and you could average 8 percent. In nine years your interest earnings would equal your yearly contribution. In twenty years you would end up with $480,000—all tax free. Your $120,000 investment would have earned 147 percent! That is the magic of compounding. Interest earns interest which earns interest, on and on and on.

Compounding involves four variables—the amount available, the amount needed, the time period, and the interest rate. The sooner you begin, the less you need to start with. The higher the interest rate, the later you can get started. But don't wait! Start with whatever amount you can. *Money has time value.* What's in your wallet today is worth far more in the future, if you sow it into good soil.

Father, compound interest is your concept, as illustrated by nature. Reveal to me the nonproductive ways I use money that could be put to greater purposes. I ask in the name of Jesus. Amen.

The Income of the Wicked

"The wages of the righteous bring them life, but the income of the wicked brings them punishment." Proverbs 10:16

A young man was asked why he sold drugs when he didn't use them himself. "If I don't, someone else will. I may as well make the money," was his answer.

It's all about the money, isn't it? People are willing to risk jail time for the lure of an easy buck. Breaking the law holds no fear for them; their chief concern is avoiding getting caught.

It matters how we earn our money, whether we are Christians or not. An income derived from fraud, dishonesty, or illegal activity will ultimately bring down not only the individuals involved, but will hurt all the innocents around them as well. How many families are broken up because a parent has committed a crime?

The "money for nothing" philosophy has so pervaded our society that even decent, upright people get taken in by illegal betting pools, shady investments involving off-shore accounts, and outright tax evasion.

Some occupations, even if perfectly legal, should be avoided by those who profess Christ. Working in a casino, as a bartender, or at a club can compromise our witness and expose us to harmful activities and people of questionable character.

Devastating debt can cause even Christians to do things they never would consider under other circumstances. Embezzling funds from an employer with the intention of paying it back has been the downfall of many. Desperation, not greed, was their motive. They hope the judge will take that into consideration when he hands down the sentence.

Income tainted by sin is unacceptable to God, and he will make his displeasure known. When we earn our wages ethically and nobly, they bring us life. If they are shaded by impropriety, they administer pain.

The Lord sees the source of our income even if no one else does.

Father, I will earn my income with clean hands. Protect me from any compromising opportunities that would damage my testimony for you. In Jesus' name I pray. Amen.

The Good Samaritan

"But a Samaritan, as he traveled, came where the man was; and when he saw him, he took pity on him. He went to him and washed his wounds, pouring on oil and wine. Then he put the man on his own donkey, took him to an inn and took care of him. The next day he took out two silver coins and gave them to the innkeeper. 'Look after him,' he said, 'and when I return, I will reimburse you for any extra expense you may have.'" Luke 10:33.

We are so familiar with the story of the Good Samaritan that we tend to pass over it without really understanding all this man did for a total stranger. Would any of us go as far as he did to help someone in need?

Robbers had attacked a lone traveler, beaten him, and stripped him of his clothes. A priest and a Levite both passed him by, not willing to risk becoming ceremonially unclean if the man were dead. The Samaritan had compassion. He used his valuable oil and wine to clean and disinfect the man's wounds, then put the man on his donkey and walked instead of rode however far it was to the nearest inn. We don't know what his business was that required him to make the trip, but he set his agenda aside to care for the man through the night. In the morning he paid the innkeeper for two months lodging with the promise to pay any additional costs incurred. Wow!

If we were ever confronted with an opportunity to render aid like this, would we have the funds available to do it? Or are we so strapped by debt that we would pass to the other side? Debt limits our ability to do good. Just one more reason to avoid it.

Father, I pray that as I see the needs around me, I would be prepared to show mercy out of my resources. I ask in Jesus' precious name. Amen.

The Right of Support

"If we have sown spiritual seed among you, is it too much if we reap a material harvest from you? If others have this right of support from you, shouldn't we have it all the more? But we did not use this right. On the contrary, we put up with anything rather than hinder the gospel of Christ." 1 Corinthians 9:11-12

The apostle Paul was being questioned in Corinth and elsewhere if he really was an apostle. He makes his defense in 1 Corinthians 9, asserting that he had seen the Lord Jesus, and that his ministry among them had produced good results. He also reminds them of his rights as an apostle—to be provided with food and drink, and to have a wife travel with him as the other apostles did.

Paul laid aside these rights to avoid being accused of preaching the gospel for profit. He worked at making tents to provide for his needs when necessary, not wishing to burden any of the churches where he was ministering.

However, he strongly asserts that God's workers were to be paid for their labors. He gives several illustrations: Soldiers do not serve at their own expense, vineyard workers eat of the grapes, shepherds drink the milk of the flocks they tend. It should be no different for those whose "occupation" is ministry. "The Lord has commanded that those who preach the gospel should receive their living from the gospel" (1 Corinthians 9:14).

Paul voluntarily surrendered his rights out of personal conviction that his only reward should be in offering the gospel free of charge. (1 Corinthians 9:18). He was willing to suffer deprivation to this end, but didn't claim his choice was to be applicable to everyone.

Much confusion occurs in the church over whether or not to accept money for ministry and who should or shouldn't be on the payroll. If we follow Scripture's example, it would seem only in certain cases that someone would be led to labor for no pay.

If we are being paid to minister, we are following biblical precedence.

Father, thank you for the privilege we all have as believers to share the gospel. Bless all those who do so full time and provide for them generously. In Jesus' name. Amen.

Family Responsibilities

"If anyone does not provide for his relatives, and especially for his immediate family, he has denied the faith and is worse than an unbeliever." 1 Timothy 5:8

The Bible states that the first way to put our religion into practice is by caring for our families, including our parents (1 Timothy 5:4) because this pleases God. Such a simple thing; the majority of us do it naturally. Most men are conscientious about being a good provider, at least while the family unit is intact. It is after it breaks down due to divorce that provision can become a problem.

If couples would only realize how much better off they'd be by staying in the marriage! Emotional distance would be easier than dealing with the financial can of worms a marital split opens up. Money that used to support one household now has to support two. Is it any wonder so many fathers aren't sending their child support checks?

In the warehouse where my husband once worked there were four men, all divorced, who shared an apartment together just so they could pay their child support. Their ex-spouses are fortunate; most men marry again and take on another family. The judge will award support amounts accordingly.

For some women, the amount is never enough to cover their expenses when and if it does arrive. There's a lot of indignation out there against deadbeat dads, but I fail to see how putting a man in jail will get his kids the money they need.

Men who abandon their families financially are worse than unbelievers, says Paul. But women with the attitude of "taking him to the cleaners" are part of the problem, too.

God hates divorce (Malachi 2:16) for good reason.

Father, I pray for all those who are struggling in the ruins of a broken marriage, trying to make ends meet. Heal these families, Lord, and put them together again for Jesus' sake. Amen.

september *5*

The Right Course

"Then you will understand what is right and just and fair—every good path. For wisdom will enter your heart, and knowledge will be pleasant to your soul. Discretion will protect you, and understanding will guard you." Proverbs 2:9-11

Something we need to remember about our personal finances is that they are just that—personal to us. We all have different life situations and priorities for our money. What's right for one person may be totally wrong for another. The 10/10/80 plan is our overall guideline, but it doesn't give us the details of where to put our 10 percent savings or how best to live on the remaining 80 percent. For that we need wisdom.

God has not left us to figure it all out on our own. If we know the Lord, he will enable us to choose the right path among the many available to us. We do have to yield to his leading, however, and that can be difficult for those who would rather hold the reins themselves.

When we take our finances into our own hands, we are at the mercy of our limited understanding. But when we seek God's wisdom, we receive protection from making a bad decision that could cripple us for years to come.

I have seen too many houses that never should have been bought, too many cars that never should have been leased, too many businesses that never should have been started—so much financial pain that could have been prevented if the Lord's ways had been sought first.

Why don't we ask our Father? We're afraid he'll say no! We've already made up our minds what we want, and nobody had better try to stop us. We act like spoiled children who want their own way, then we run crying to God when the dream turns into a nightmare and we can't meet our obligations.

There's a better way—the right course of obedience.

Father, I will turn my ear to wisdom and my heart to understanding. Save me from myself and my poor decisions. I will follow your ways. In Jesus' name I pray. Amen.

september

The Rod of Discipline

"Do not withhold discipline from a child; if you punish him with the rod, he will not die. Punish him with the rod and save his soul from death." Proverbs 23:13-14

God requires parents to discipline their children. As our heavenly Father, he does not hesitate to apply the rod when *we* need it; and money is a very effective rod for most of us. It is not used against us out of anger or spite—God isn't like that. It is because of his great love and his desire for us to become mature. These are the same motives we need in disciplining our kids.

We must never forget that we are the parents and we control the funds. Too many people let their kids walk all over them when it comes to money. Doling out twenties every time they want something does nothing to teach them about money. Be very careful about "allowances"; it implies money for nothing. Kids should *earn* any cash they receive from us. We're not paying them to breathe.

The concept of "no work, no pay" should be taught early. It needs to be enforced; this is the way the real world operates. We do them a terrible disservice if we lead them to think otherwise. They should be made to feel the consequences of laziness and they should be responsible for as much as their personal spending as their ages would allow.

It doesn't end when they leave home, either; constantly bailing out a grown child only enables them to continue to depend on your financial support. Some parents can't stand the thought of their child "suffering," so they'll pay the rent, make the car payments, or foot the food bill, but this is not showing love. Love does what is best for someone and yes, love must be tough.

Our goal is to launch well-adjusted, financially savvy young people out into the world who understand that money comes as a result of work. Discipline is a tool to make that happen.

Father, give me the courage to make tough choices with my children in regards to their financial training, and help me to discipline them wisely. I ask in Jesus' name. Amen.

What Good Is the World?

"What good is it for a man to gain the whole world, yet forfeit his soul? Or what can a man give in exchange for his soul?" Mark 8:36-37

Engage yourself in a little fantasy here. What would you do if you suddenly were the only person left on the planet? All the world's goods—houses, cars, airplanes, gold, buildings, parks, malls—all became yours by default. What would you do with it?

It might be fun at first to pick out which house would be your primary residence, and which vehicles you would want to drive. It would be cool to go to Rodeo Drive and get all the clothes you wanted. Think of the jewelry that would now be yours! All the toys—boats, motorcycles, electronic equipment—at your disposal. The most valuable and exquisite art of the world's museums belongs to you now.

Is there a downside to this? Well, you'd get pretty lonely. All that food but no one to share it with. You'd quickly discover what a heavy burden it is to maintain all that stuff. Things left to themselves deteriorate.

What if the price you paid to have all this was your own soul? It would all be yours only as long as you existed on earth. On the time-line of eternity, our lives are a microscopic dot. We will exist there for far longer than we will here. Yet we live our lives as if just the opposite were true.

We accumulate more and more stuff and always want more. How much is enough? Would the whole world fulfill us if that was possible? Peter reminds us that "the elements will be destroyed by fire, all the earth and everything in it will be laid bare" (2 Peter 3:10). Not even the earth will be around for eternity. "Since everything will be destroyed in this way, what kind of people ought you to be? You ought to live holy and godly lives" (2 Peter 3:11).

Material things are transitory. Our soul is eternal. Jesus is telling us to get our priorities straight.

Father, thank you that the things that will last are those that are the most valuable—the souls of human beings. In Jesus' name. Amen.

Voices of the Poor

"If a man shuts his ears to the cry of the poor, he too will cry out and not be answered." Proverbs 21:13

The Bible speaks of curses coming on those who close their eyes to the poor (Proverbs 28:27). Now we are told if we shut our ears to their cries that we will not be helped in *our* time of need. The flipside is that if we do give, we lack nothing. Generosity is the path of blessing.

Do we hear the cries of the poor? What are they saying?

- Their children go to bed hungry, and how devastating it is as a parent to be unable to meet this most basic need.
- They sometimes have to choose between paying rent and buying needed medicine.
- They are often faced with going without heat or going without warm clothing.
- Their children must drop out of school to help support the family, so they do not receive the education that could help release them from poverty.
- They want to work, but they lack transportation to get there.
- They could work more if they weren't sick so much, but they can't afford to go to a doctor for treatment.
- They feel they are being denied their very human rights.

In a world that is so rich, how is this possible? It is because we have closed our ears. We do not wish to know, because it makes us feel guilty and uncomfortable. Or we feel that anything we could do would be so insignificant it wouldn't matter anyway, so we do nothing.

At the same time, we will petition God for that high-paying job, that the real estate deal will close, that our child gets that scholarship. Do you see the dichotomy here? We are deafened by our own selfishness. God tells us in his Word to open our eyes and ears and begin to reach out to those who are oppressed and defenseless.

We have the resources to help. All we lack is the will.

Father, my ears are open now. I'm listening. Show me where I can make a difference. For Jesus' sake. Amen.

Sow Generously!

"Remember this: Whoever sows sparingly will also reap sparingly, and whoever sows generously will also reap generously." 2 Corinthians 9:6

Paul uses the principle of sowing and reaping as an illustration of what happens when we give to God's work. We don't get back in the harvest only the amount of seed we plant; we get back multiplied many times over the seed sown. Think of what a single kernel of corn can produce—an entire ear with many more kernels! There is absolute abundance in the kingdom of God.

Knowing this, Paul urges us to invest in God's work. The more we plant, the bigger the harvest. A farmer who is stingy in the amount of seed sown will not have the bountiful harvest of his neighbor who generously scattered seed.

What Paul asked the Corinthians here was: How zealous are you for the church? Do you care about the needs of your suffering brothers? How badly do you want to see the kingdom advance? And if you say you care, put your money where your mouth is!

The fact is that God's work is stifled when we are stingy in our giving. The Great Commission is still in effect: "Go therefore, and make disciples of all the nations, baptizing them in the name of the Father and of the Son and of the Holy Spirit, teaching them to observe all things that I have commanded you" (Matthew 28:19-20). It takes resources to do this.

No cause, no work is greater than being a part of what God wants to accomplish on earth—to bring all people to acknowledge his Son as Lord and King. For this, we are to gloriously expend ourselves of our time, our money, our very lives.

Sow generously! Show a needy world and our Lord that we care.

Father, you use the laws of nature to show us what happens in the spiritual realm. Prepare the ground to receive the seed we sow, so there may be a hundredfold return. In the name of Jesus I pray. Amen.

september

A Piece of Advice

"Listen to advice and accept instruction, and in the end you will be wise." Proverbs 19:20

Financial counseling is not only for people who are already in trouble with their money. That's how we tend to look at it, but the best counseling is preventative. To seek *counsel* is to consult on a plan of action. If more people did this, there would be less need for other kinds of counseling.

The best time to seek advice is months before a major life change, such as getting married. Engaged couples should have their budget for their first year of marriage worked out before they say "I do." Nothing can shatter that post-honeymoon bliss faster than fights over money. Planning ahead will help keep the peace.

Buying a house is a major financial commitment. People go into a mortgage thinking they can afford it—and finding out too late they can't. One way to know for sure is to begin setting aside the amount of money it will take to cover the difference between the payment you're contemplating and your current obligation. Also set aside in savings what the utilities will be beyond what you pay now, the taxes and insurance, and an extra $100 for maintenance and surprise expenses. Do this for at least six months. If you can pay this amount to a savings account easily, faithfully, every month, then you can start shopping for a house in that price range. If you missed some payments, better you find out now, or you will already be in danger of losing your home.

New babies also need to be carefully planned for, if you have that option! Is Mom planning to still work? What if she can't? What if she doesn't want to? How much will diapers and other necessities add to the budget?

These are life's happy events that will be all the more enjoyable if you have a plan in place before you take them on. As the wise saying goes, an ounce of prevention is worth a pound of cure.

Father, I will seek counsel before I make major changes in my finances. I will submit my will to doing what is wise. In Jesus' name I pray. Amen.

The Towers Have Fallen

"The merchants who sold these things and gained their wealth from her will stand far off, terrified at her torment. They will weep and mourn and cry out: 'Woe! Woe, O great city, dressed in fine linen, purple and scarlet, and glittering with gold, precious stones and pearls! In one hour such great wealth has been brought to ruin!'" Revelation 18:15-17

I was driving my daughter and her friends to school that Tuesday when the friends told me a plane had hit the World Trade Center. Back home, I turned on the TV and watched in disbelief at what was happening. I must admit, the above verse was the first thing to go through my mind. It refers to a future Babylon, of course, not New York City or Washington, D.C., but even one news anchor declared, "Think of it, our two symbols of power and prosperity have been smitten in one hour." A little eerie, isn't it?

People were asking, "Where is God in all this?" Well, God was still on the throne. He controls all events. He allowed this disaster for a purpose. He wants to speak to us through this tragedy. I went to a prayer meeting that morning, and as we wept and asked God for mercy, we discerned that he was calling America back to himself.

We worship money above all else in this country. Our military strength is our great pride. We are trying to remove God's name from our schools, our government, and our history. We are hypocrites, giving lip service to the Lord as we continue to fall farther into immortality. If we don't heed his warnings, worse calamities await us.

That is God's way. He warned Israel again and again through his prophets to no avail. He who did not spare his chosen people to whom he made all his covenant promises will not spare us, either.

What can we do? We can make the Lord our dwelling place (Psalm 90:1). He is our only shelter when the storms of life hit.

"Blessed is the man who makes the LORD his trust, who does not look to the proud, to those who turn aside to false gods." Psalm 40:4

When the Wall Comes Down

"The wealth of the rich is their fortified city; they imagine it an unscalable wall." Proverbs 18:11

Financial 9-11s can strike any of us, at any time. An unexpected job loss, a devastating accident or illness, a tragic death—these are events we can't control and can't always plan for. Nothing can really prepare us for them.

No matter how large of a pile of money we may be sitting on, it can't protect us from the very real calamities of life. Using money to build a fortress of protection around ourselves only lulls us into a false sense of security. It can even have the opposite effect. Depending on how visible our wealth is, it can just make us a bigger target in our litigious society.

What are some of these imaginary walls?

- Money can buy us the best doctors, but it can't buy us health.
- Money can help us acquire the finest education, but it won't give us job security.
- Money can retain the services of the best lawyers, but it won't stop us from being sued.
- Money can buy protection in the form of alarm systems and bodyguards, but it can't buy us safety.
- Money can buy insurance policies, but it can't stop terrorists from flying airplanes into buildings.

In contrast, Proverbs 18:10 states "The name of the LORD is a strong tower; the righteous run to it and are safe." Only in the person of God will we find the security and protection that will bring us through with confidence when our world comes tumbling down. Putting our wealth in his place is an illusion and an act of misplaced trust.

Money is so limited. God never meant for it to be our savior. If money could save us, he wouldn't have sent his Son.

Father, thank you that you are my fortress, my stronghold, and my deliverer; my shield in whom I can take refuge. I put my trust in you. In Jesus' name. Amen.

september **13**

The Cost of Repentance

"Many of those who believed now came and openly confessed their evil deeds. A number who had practiced sorcery brought their scrolls together and burned them publicly. When they calculated the value of the scrolls, the total came to fifty thousand drachmas." Acts 19:18-19

When the new believers at Ephesus burned their books and scrolls, it wasn't only because they were trying to suppress or delete something they considered objectionable, the definition of censorship. They were destroying their ties to their old way of life which was anti-God. To keep these items around would hinder them in their new faith and even lead them back into sin.

The monetary value of these books would take ten laborers twenty years to earn. We can almost hear the voice of Judas: "Why weren't these sold and the money given to the poor?" (John 12:5). Destruction of harmful or sinful things keeps others from being harmed or influenced by them. We are not to sell items that could lead others astray, no matter how much they're worth.

You may reason there's no harm in selling that old pornography collection if you give the money to God. But in his eyes this would be a great offense; it is a tainted offering. We are not to profit from evil; we are not to cause any one to stumble into sin (1 Corinthians 10:32). We should not even consider donating such items to get a tax deduction!

God set the precedent when he told the Israelites, "The images of their gods you are to burn in the fire. Do not covet the silver or gold on them, and do not take it for yourselves, or you will be ensnared by it, for it is detestable to the LORD your God. Do not bring a detestable thing into your house or you, like it, will be set apart for destruction. Utterly abhor and detest it, for it is set apart for destruction" (Deuteronomy 7:25-26). Zero tolerance!

Repentance can cost plenty.

Father, I will dispose of anything in my life that is offensive to you, no matter what the cost. I will hate what you hate. For Jesus' sake. Amen.

Indulgences

*"Listen, my son, and be wise, and keep your heart on the right path.
Do not join those who drink too much wine or gorge themselves on
meat, for drunkards and gluttons become poor, and drowsiness clothes
them in rags." Proverbs 23:19-21*

Our youth is when we discover money's ability to buy us a good time. Before the advent of credit cards, we were limited in how much we could indulge ourselves by the amount of cash we had in our pocket. Today, the sky is as high as the credit limit. The average college student graduates with $18,000 in credit card debt. They have already spent almost a year's salary on food, drink, clothing, and entertainment before even embarking on their career.

Social pressure contributes to this. The desire to go along with the crowd and be included in the fun is a temptation hard to resist, and credit cards make it possible. The power of plastic money is heady stuff for a young person. They will sometimes treat all their friends to meals to act like a big shot and to be popular.

This lifestyle catches up to them. They have to work so many hours to pay the bills, their studies suffer. Grades fall; scholarships may not be renewed. Some students are forced to drop out. Opportunities are lost as education gives way to full-time work just to pay off the credit cards.

All this can be the result of choosing the wrong friends to hang out with. Some kids can't handle being scorned for paying cash and practicing frugality so they will get credit cards to prove they're as "with it" as everyone else.

The road to ruin is paved with plastic cards that we pretend give us power when, in reality, they put us into financial prison. Are we willing to travel that path just because "everybody else does it"? Jesus said, "For wide is the gate and broad is the road that leads to destruction, and many enter through it" (Matthew 7:13).

Choose the narrow road of solvency.

Father, protect me from being influenced by the wrong friends. Give me the backbone to stand up for my convictions, no matter what anyone else is doing. I ask in Jesus' name. Amen.

God Is in the Details

"Then the word of the Lord came to Elijah: 'Leave here, turn eastward and hide in the Kerith Ravine, east of the Jordan. You will drink from the brook, and I have ordered ravens to feed you there.'" 1 Kings 17:2-4

Elijah was God's prophet at a time when wickedness ruled Israel. As judgment, God sent a drought for three years on the land, and famine was widespread. But not for his servant Elijah!

Look at how God cared for this man. He told him exactly where to go to find the provision he needed, and then miraculously supplied it. He kept the brook from drying up and commanded ravens to bring Elijah bread and meat. Elijah was well fed in the desert while the people in the towns were going hungry.

God is not limited by circumstances. No matter how desperate the situation looks, he has pledged himself to meet our needs. He even knows our preferences. I read a story about a needy family who had no food in the house and was praying for God's intervention. The mother had a real yearning for Oreo cookies, but she said nothing in her prayer because she felt it was too selfish a request when what they needed was nutritious food. Later that day a bag of groceries was delivered to them with—you guessed it—a big package of Oreos in it. The woman cried at the goodness of the Lord to supply her with even her favorite treat.

Have you ever experienced God giving you detailed instructions of what you should do? He speaks to all his children, and the more time we spend with him, the better we will know his voice. When hard times come, we can have confidence that he will tell us exactly what his personal instructions are for us. We can trust and obey, no matter how strange those orders may seem!

We serve a truly personal and awesome God.

Father, forgive me for ever limiting you in what you can do. You are truly in all the details of my life, and I praise you. In Jesus' name. Amen.

What's in It for Them?

"The plans of the righteous are just, but the advice of the wicked is deceitful." Proverbs 12:5

You can't turn on the TV any given Saturday morning without seeing them: infomercials for investments. Whether it's real estate, how to work the stock market, or direct sales plans, they're all presented as sure-fire, no-risk, no money down, guaranteed income for little or no work. What's wrong with this picture?

The people who pitch these are so enthusiastic. They have a veneer of trust that makes what they say credible to their gullible viewers. They show off their big homes, their fleet of luxury cars, their boats, and their extravagant lifestyles with the promise that you, too, can live like this. They spend half an hour telling you basically nothing, but if you want to know their secrets, you can—for only four easy payments of $29.99.

Live seminars are pricier. People will ante up thousands to hear a speaker promote a book or tape series in hopes of duplicating their success. Some of these are legitimate, but more than likely this person got rich from conducting seminars and selling books and tapes, not by following their own program.

We have to be discerning about who we listen to today. There are so many choices and places for our money, we can be completely confused. Many financial advisors are basically salespeople who want you to buy their particular investment product so they can earn a commission. They make money whether you do or not.

What's in it for them? This is a question we need to ask any time we're confronted with someone promoting a "great deal." Why are they sharing it with us? Pay attention to any red flags the Lord waves in your mind as you consider getting involved. Don't lose money you can't afford to lose because you ignored his warnings.

The Lord will reveal and protect us from deceitful financial schemes if we will but ask him. After all, it's his money.

Father, block my path and wall me in so that I cannot find my way to seminars and programs that would lead me astray. I ask in Jesus' name. Amen.

All Grace, All Things, All Times

"And God is able to make all grace abound to you, so that in all things at all times, having all that you need, you will abound in every good work." 2 Corinthians 9:8

There are four "alls" in this verse. Paul is pouring it on so we will realize the abundance we have in God. Our supply is in no way diminished by our giving. On the contrary, God sees to it that we receive more so we can continue to give.

If not for God's grace, we would be in no position to give. It all begins with him. He is the source. "Now he who supplies seed to the sower and bread for food will also supply and increase your store of seed and will enlarge the harvest of your righteousness" (2 Corinthians 9:10). It's been said that God doesn't need our money, but that he chooses to partner with us in his work so we may be blessed through it.

Think about it: An all-powerful God who owns the entire universe has decided to use sinful human beings to accomplish the work he wants done. Why not use angels? They're always obedient and certainly more efficient and they don't have all our hang-ups about money and giving. But angels haven't experienced redemption. Only forgiven people are able to respond to the love of God by giving of themselves in expression of thanks (2 Corinthians 9:12).

God planned the good works he would do long before we were even born (Ephesians 2:10). It was for this purpose we were created. When we cooperate with God in participating in acts of giving, we fulfill our mission.

Hudson Taylor said, "God's work done God's way will never lack God's support." The Holy Spirit moves on the hearts of yielded Christians to give where there is a need. No ministry should have to beg or resort to worldly fund-raising tactics if God is behind it.

We give out of gratitude to God, the first and greatest giver.

Father, thank you for your never-ending supply of grace for me. Thank you for the difference it makes in my life; that it releases me to give. In Jesus' name. Amen.

Refiner's Fire

"The crucible for silver and the furnace for gold, but the Lord tests the heart." Proverbs 17:3

Precious metals go through an intense process to remove all their impurities and unwanted materials. It involves very high temperatures to turn the metal into liquid so the dross can be skimmed off. Only in this way can the metal be made pure.

It is the Lord's desire to refine his people as well. He puts us into the crucible or furnace, not because he wants us to suffer, but because there is no other way to remove all our imperfections and to change us to be like Jesus.

He uses "silver and gold"—the wealth of this world—as a means by which he tests our hearts. How we respond to the myriads of situations involving money speaks louder than words as to their condition. If greed is revealed, God will "turn up the heat" in an effort to extricate it from our lives. It's a long and painful process, but it's necessary if we want to be made pure.

Peter tells us we have trials "so that our faith—of greater worth than gold, which perishes even though refined by fire—may be proved genuine" (1 Peter 1:7). Just as gold is devalued if it contains anything other than pure gold, our character is flawed if we are less than authentic.

Money works as a test at every income level. Christians who are wealthy actually have more tests as they need to work through issues of self-sufficiency, generosity, greater stewardship responsibilities, and fears of financial reversal. Believers who struggle with lack must overcome coveting, frustration, and discontent. All of us battle greed in one form or another.

Every day we are confronted with opportunities to make decisions about money. Every choice is a test. Will we follow God's principles? When the heat and pressure is applied, what comes out of us? Only when our financial backs are against the wall do we discover what our values really are.

"When he has tested me, I will come forth as gold." Job 23:10

The Key to Success

"Do not let this Book of the Law depart from your mouth; meditate on it day and night, so that you may be careful to do everything written in it. Then you will be prosperous and successful." Joshua 1:8

With the proliferation of self-help books on the market today, the world's number one best seller still remains the best kept secret to knowing how to live a successful and prosperous life. How can this be? Simply because people aren't reading it—or if they are, they are rejecting its message.

Also, the Bible's criterion for success is fundamentally different from the way the world defines it. Our culture measures success by the amount of money one has. To be *prosperous* is to be visibly wealthy, as displayed by the house one lives in, the car one drives, and the clothes one wears—the status triad.

When Joshua took over as Moses' successor to lead the Israelites into the Promised Land, God gave him one of the most inspiring pep talks in all of Scripture. He assured him of his presence, victory over his enemies, and all the land wherever he set his foot. These promises came with a condition: Joshua and the people must be obedient to God's laws. Their success depended upon their faithful adherence to do what the Lord had said.

We are living successfully when we are walking with God in the light of his Word and fellowshipping with him. It has nothing whatever to do with our income or the outward trappings of our lifestyle. It has everything to do with how well we know the Bible and how much of what we know we're putting into practice. Part of every day should be spent reading and studying what God has spoken to us through Scripture. We are to memorize it. Meditate on it. Write it in our minds and on our hearts.

Most of all, we're to obey it. Obedience is the key to success.

Father, thank you that you have given me clear direction for my life in the Bible. Open my understanding to it and help me to be careful to do everything in it. I ask in Jesus' name. Amen.

Patience Equals Profits

"The plans of the diligent lead to profit as surely as haste leads to poverty." Proverbs 21:5

Patience is not only a fruit of the Holy Spirit, it is our ally in saving money. Think of all the purchases you have made that turned out to be totally unnecessary simply because you were unwilling to wait.

Our culture is geared towards a hurry-get-it-now mind-set of shopping for everything from cars to food. We're busy people; we reason it's easier to pick things up when we see them rather than shop around. We are exhausted just thinking about spending all that time at the car dealership haggling on price, so we pay what's on the sticker. Our habit of impatience is costing us.

For a big purchase like a vehicle or an appliance, never buy the first one you see. Do your homework. Check out several places, know your prices. See if a used item wouldn't make more sense. Pray about your purchase; God can connect you with someone selling what you're looking for. This all takes time. But when you do buy, you'll know you got the best possible deal.

We need patience to wait for things to go on sale. I've bought shoes only to see them go on sale later and I hadn't even worn them yet. I've picked up birthday cards a month in advance only to receive a coupon the next week that would have allowed me to get them for free.

Before buying anything that's not urgent, first see how long you can go without it. A cooling off period works wonders to keep us from rash actions we'll later regret. Don't replace anything until you've worn it out or used it up. Something better or cheaper could come along while the new item is sitting on the shelf waiting to be needed.

Patience will keep us from selling an investment too soon. Patience allows us the space we need to think over a purchase. Patience gives God a chance to work.

Give patience a chance.

Father, help me to cultivate patience in my money decisions. Teach me above all to wait on you. In Jesus' name. Amen.

You Shall Not Covet

"You shall not covet your neighbor's house. You shall not covet your neighbor's wife, or his manservant or maidservant, his ox or donkey, or anything that belongs to your neighbor." Exodus 20:17

The tenth commandment differs from the rest in that it is a sin of the mind. All the others—having other gods, making idols, taking the Lord's name in vain, keeping the Sabbath, honoring our parents, murder, adultery, stealing, lying—are committed externally in a tangible way. We can be guilty of coveting and no one would ever know—except God.

All sin begins in our minds with an evil thought. It's not a sin to *have* that thought; it's what we do with it once it's there. We can quickly reject it or we can entertain it. Entertaining an evil thought will lead to evil actions.

Covet means "to have a strong desire for." It is to wish for something enviously, to selfishly want what someone else has. It is the seed that sprouts the root of greed. Once it has been given the license to grow, it becomes a toxin that poisons our spirits. It will ultimately find its expression in the outward sins of idolatry, murder, stealing, and so on. God specifically singles out this inward sin that is so easily hidden, and he commands that we not allow it to harbor in our minds at all.

Coveting is flaunted in today's culture. People unashamedly want what their neighbors have, only their "neighbors" may be the celebrities featured on "Lifestyles of the Rich and Famous"—voyeurism of material goods at its most vulgar. The result is billions of dollars in consumer debt. It is kids killing kids to obtain a pair of sneakers. It is a multimillion dollar cosmetic surgery industry as women carve up their bodies in an attempt to look like a popular actress.

"You shall not covet." It's one of the Top Ten. Do we take it seriously? God does.

Father, with the help of the Holy Spirit, I will reject all covetous thoughts that come into my mind. I will avoid anything that would give it a foothold in my life. In Jesus' name. Amen.

The Sovereignty of God

"There is no wisdom, no insight, no plan that can succeed against the Lord." Proverbs 21:30

God controls people and nations and economies. Nothing is outside of his power. Our best laid plans can turn to ashes if they are not according to his purpose.

People today are very fretful over their retirement accounts, wanting to put their money in a safe place where they can earn a decent rate of return. With all the corporate bankruptcies, the downturn of the stock market, and interest rates of less than 2 percent, there's a lot of fear and insecurity in our nation. We want some assurance from someone. Listen to this:

"America's industrial situation is absolutely sound. Our factories are humming. Business is healthy. The economy is in good condition. There is nothing fundamentally wrong with our underlying business and credit structure. It's a good time to buy stock." Alan Greenspan? No, President Hoover, just before the stock market crash in October 1929!

All the financial experts were making soothing noises, telling the people everything was fine. Everyone but God was caught by surprise when the entire economy fell, bringing on the Great Depression. Was there anything anyone could have done to prevent it?

Absolutely not. It is God who orders events. It is God who is bringing history to a climax. The world's leaders may pretend they have the power to control their economies, but in truth no human will can prevail over the Lord.

What does this mean for our money? We need to release it to the sovereignty of God. We need to quit seeking worldly advice for ways to protect it and remember that God has promised to provide even if we lose it all. It wasn't until *all* the wine was gone at the wedding in Cana that Jesus showed his power. He is never too early, and he is never late.

To get answers, we are to go to God. He alone knows the future. Our minds can be at rest, for our Father is in charge.

Lord, what assurance that nothing catches you off guard! I will trust in you and not my own plans. In Jesus' wonderful name I pray. Amen.

Cornelius the Centurion

"At Caesarea there was a man named Cornelius, a centurion in what was known as the Italian Regiment. He and all his family were devout and God-fearing; he gave generously to those in need and prayed to God regularly." Acts 10:1-2

Roman soldiers are generally not well thought of by Christians; we think of their brutal treatment of Jesus at his crucifixion and are appalled. The centurions were commanders of military units consisting of one hundred men, and most seem to have been honorable. Jesus healed a centurion's servant and marveled at his faith (Luke 7:1-10). At the cross, after witnessing his death, a centurion confessed, "Surely this man was the Son of God!" (Mark 15:39). Considering they were Gentiles, these men had special insight into who Jesus really was.

God used a centurion to send for Peter and open the way for Gentiles to receive the message of salvation. What was unique about Cornelius that an angel would be sent on this special mission? In the words of the angel: "Your prayers and gifts to the poor have come up as a memorial offering before God" (Acts 10:4). He was a man of prayer known for his generosity. He was also obedient; he immediately sent to Joppa for Peter.

Cornelius had a crowd waiting to hear what Peter had to say. Before Peter finished his sermon, the Holy Spirit came upon those listening. After they were baptized, Cornelius showed hospitality to Peter and the six other Jews who had come with him.

"God fearing" was a term used to describe those who were not Jewish converts but who believed in the God of Israel and respected his laws. For all Cornelius' good deeds and acts of charity, it wasn't enough to save him. He still needed to put his faith in Christ.

When we hear of philanthropists who give generously to worthy causes, we must remember that without Jesus, they have no better shot at heaven than the unrepentant wicked. Salvation can't be earned.

Father, I praise you that you are no respecter of persons. Thank you that all who turn to Jesus may be saved. In his name. Amen.

The Grace of Giving

"And now, brothers, we want you to know about the grace that God has given the Macedonian churches. Out of the most severe trial, their overflowing joy and their extreme poverty welled up in rich generosity." 2 Corinthians 8:1-2

Why is it that the poor are often more generous in giving of their resources than the rich? Is it because they understand what it is to be in need? The Macedonian churches were extremely needy themselves, but they pleaded with Paul for the privilege of being able to contribute to the believers in Jerusalem. They disregarded the notion of the poor not being able to afford to give.

They gave "beyond their ability" (2 Corinthians 8:3), as much as they were able. And it wasn't from their excess or leftovers, it was money they needed themselves. How different from most of our giving! We give as long as it doesn't take away from our own comforts. We give, but we don't always give willingly or sacrificially.

The secret of their generosity can be found in the phrase "they gave themselves first to the Lord" (2 Corinthians 8:5). These believers were fully yielded to the will of God; they trusted him implicitly; and as recipients of his grace they became participants in the grace of giving.

Generosity is a natural result of joy. Hearts overflowing with love and gratitude to God for all he has given us can't help but give in return. If our hearts are cold, it is because we haven't grasped the depth of God's grace to us.

Giving can't be commanded any more than love can be. If we haven't abandoned ourselves yet to God, we're going about it backwards. It is in a surrendered life that we find God working in us "to will and to act according to his good purpose" (Philippians 2:13).

The Macedonian churches displayed the difference the grace of God makes in our lives and our attitudes. They gave freely, abundantly, sacrificially, demonstrating that no one should be deprived of the joy of giving.

Father, by faith I surrender myself to your grace. I trust your ability to sustain me as I participate in the great privilege of giving. In Jesus' name I pray. Amen.

Penny-Pinchers

"Do not eat the food of a stingy man, do not crave his delicacies; for he is the kind of man who is always thinking about the cost. 'Eat and drink,' he says to you, but his heart is not with you. You will vomit up the little you have eaten, and will have wasted your compliments."
Proverbs 23:6-8

Some people pride themselves on being frugal; they don't waste their money on unneeded luxuries and they live within their means. Being frugal is a virtue. Taken to an extreme it becomes stinginess, and the Bible doesn't have anything good to say about that condition.

Stinginess cuts across all economic levels. One can be poor or one can be rich and still exhibit this trait. It is the exact opposite of generosity; as such, it is anti-God. It is different from the spirit of poverty in that the stingy person quite often will spend freely on themselves, but they are unwilling to share what they have with others.

Children are naturally like this. It is part of our fallen nature. What parent hasn't been embarrassed by their child's refusal to share their toys? We are expected to grow out of this kind of behavior; some never do. "Tightwad" and "skinflint" are some of the unflattering adjectives their acquaintances use to describe them; because truth be told, they don't have many friends.

Stinginess is revealed in the refusal to give to anything that won't directly benefit the giver. It is selfishness that insists on keeping a tight grip on money and possessions at all times. It is greed at its ugliest.

Stingy people believe they're the richer for keeping their possessions all to themselves. Ironically, they end up impoverished. God cannot pour his riches into clenched fists.

Father, the only reason you give me beyond what I need is so I can share with others. Reveal any areas where I am exhibiting stinginess. For Jesus' sake. Amen.

Wealth, But No Joy

"God gives a man wealth, possessions, and honor, so that he lacks nothing his heart desires, but God does not enable him to enjoy them, and a stranger enjoys them instead. This is meaningless, a grievous evil."
Ecclesiastes 6:2

It is a tragic irony that so many affluent people have so little joy in their lives. They didn't plan it that way. When they began their climb up the ladder of success, they envisioned that their wealth and position would bring them contentment, happiness, and satisfaction. They never imagined they would be insecure, anxious, and unfulfilled.

They have the big house, but they don't enjoy it because they don't spend much time there. They're too busy working, too many responsibilities. The folks who really appreciate the place are those who are hired to care for it—the gardener, the housekeeper, even the pool service people who spend more time maintaining than the owner does swimming.

As a society, we need to step back and see where all this upward mobility is leading us. What's the point of having all this stuff if all our time is spent working to pay for it? What is driving us? We're in pursuit of the wrong dream.

Solomon is describing himself in this verse. When he asked God for wisdom, his request was granted, and more. As he discovered, those benefits are very hollow when joy isn't present. Would you want God to grant a request for wealth if you knew the result would be a restless, empty existence? If we're looking for fulfillment, we need to be sure we're looking in the right place. All the toys and trappings of the world won't make up for a life void of a sense of purpose.

Why didn't God give Solomon the ability to enjoy his vast wealth? Possibly as a consequence of his sin, or possibly to serve as a warning to the rest of us. As another wise person once said, you can never get enough of what you don't really want.

Father, I thank you for everything you have given me and I ask that you would give me nothing that would take away my enjoyment of life. In Jesus' name. Amen.

The Best Laid Plans

"Plans fail for lack of counsel, but with many advisors they succeed."
Proverbs 15:22

If we are to excel in our stewardship, we need to seek out advisors who can guide and educate us. Very few of us understand everything we need to know about investments, estate planning, taxes, and debt management. No one financial advisor is going to be an expert in all aspects of money matters and an honest one will admit that. Just as you need diversity in a portfolio, you need diversity in consultation.

Avoid getting all your information from just one source. No one is infallible, no matter how much you trust them. Professionals also have a tendency to suffer from tunnel vision. A tax accountant will advise against paying off your mortgage because they say you need the deduction. Consumer credit counselors will have difficulty understanding your commitment to the tithe when they see your debt load. Your entire financial picture must be taken into consideration as you make decisions.

Although you are ultimately responsible for what you do with your money, advisors help you to see things you might otherwise miss. Waiting to sell a stock until the next calendar year, for example, could save you thousands in taxes. Advisors can explain deferred giving, annuities, and whether it's wise to take a lump settlement in an insurance claim. Be careful when you are dealing with any financial professional who has a vested interest in what you choose to do.

Christians need to measure the advice they are given against Scripture. God is to have the last word. If it goes against biblical teaching, it's wrong, no matter how much "sense" it makes from an economic point of view.

Use advisors to help you navigate the financial maze, but never forget that it is the Lord we are bound to obey, even when his instructions seem to run counter to the facts. We are ultimately accountable to him.

Father, guide me to godly people who can give wise counsel when I need it.
Frustrate any financial plan that is not of you. I ask in Jesus' name. Amen.

How Much of God Do We Want?

*"When the people saw the thunder and lightning and heard the
trumpet and saw the mountain in smoke, they trembled with fear.
They stayed at a distance and said to Moses, 'Speak to us yourself and
we will listen. But do not have God speak to us or we will die.'"*
Exodus 20:18-19

This passage is a sad commentary on the nation of Israel's relationship with their God. They were afraid of him! This is different
from the healthy fear of the Lord, respect, and reverence every believer
needs to have. This was closer to terror, a feeling that God was vengeful
and was seeking to hurt them. They misunderstood God's nature and
sought to avoid contact with him. By asking for a mediator to stand
between them and God, they were saying they didn't want to know the
Lord intimately. Secondhand knowledge was good enough for them.

When it came to their physical needs, however, look at how
demanding they were! They complained they were thirsty; God gave
them water. They cried for food; God rained down bread from heaven.
They grumbled they had no meat; God sent quail. They didn't care
about seeking his face as long as they saw his hand.

Are we like them? Do we want God's provision but not his presence? There's nothing wrong with praying for material things when we
need them. God tells us to ask for our daily bread. But is that all we
want him to be to us—our provider? Men, how would you feel if your
wife wanted you only for your financial support, not your affection?
We often use God the same way.

Moses assured the people to not be afraid, that God simply desired
they would be kept from sinning by an appropriate awe of who he was.
But they remained at a distance. How hurt the Lord must be when we
keep him at arm's length!

He longs to be Immanuel—"God with us"—but it's up to us to
draw near.

*Father, you are so much more than a provider. I want to know you; I want to see
your face. I will come to meet with you every day. In Jesus' name. Amen.*

Blaming God

"A man's own folly ruins his life, yet his heart rages against the Lord."
Proverbs 19:3

It's one thing to blame other people for our troubles; it's quite another to blame God. It is accusing our perfect, holy Lord of wrongdoing against us. It's worse when we are simply reaping the consequences of our own foolishness.

We have dealt with people who thought that because they were tithing, they could spend their money any way they pleased and God was promise-bound to fund all their extravagances. When they couldn't pay their bills, they claimed God had let them down for not blessing their finances. This is twisting Malachi 3:10 to say something it was never intended to mean. Tithing is not a license to spend; nowhere in the Bible is that premise promoted. We are to obey the full counsel of God, not just bits and pieces thrown together to make up our own doctrine.

It's true that God allows things to happen for the purpose of showing us the error of our ways, but we have to realize when we have brought it on ourselves. He loves us too much to let us continue to do stupid things and he will not support us when we have wrong motives.

Greed led people to leverage their homes to purchase technology stock. When the market fell and the margin calls came due, it would have been criminal to shake a fist at God in anger, yet some folks did.

If we cosign on a loan and they default, we should not be surprised when the lender comes after us. Most of our financial foibles are clearly warned against in Scripture. If a child touches a stove after his mother told him it was hot, it's ridiculous for him to get mad at her when he gets burned. You can almost picture God throwing up his hands and saying, "What did I *tell* you?!"

Mature people take responsibility for their own mistakes and ask for forgiveness, not assign blame.

Father, help me to own up to the dumb things I've done with my money. Forgive me for being upset with you over them. In Jesus' name. Amen.

The Life That Is Blessed

"Blessed is the man who fears the LORD, who finds great delight in his commands. . .wealth and riches are in his house, and his righteousness endures forever. . .good will come to him who is generous and lends freely, who conducts his affairs with justice." Psalm 112:1,3,5

Godliness is the path to blessedness. What are the qualities of a godly person? Above all, they fear the Lord and obey his commands. If we aren't walking in obedience, we don't really love him (John 15:10). Godly people exhibit the same character traits of God— they are gracious and compassionate, generous and just. It is their relationship with God through his Son Jesus Christ that changes them into his likeness.

What are the benefits of being a godly person? The state of being blessed is more than an emotion; it is an overall condition of well-being and joy. It has nothing to do with money. As Seneca the Roman said, "Money has never yet made anyone rich." The wealth and riches in the house of the righteous can be material blessings, but the spiritual blessings are those that will endure forever.

Godly people trust God to the extent that bad news doesn't fill them with distress and fear. Their hearts are secure in spite of the circumstances around them. They are able to be generous and lend freely because they know their Father will always provide for them.

Read all of Psalm 112 and catch the vision of what God meant for our lives when he reached out to us and saved us. Isn't that all we really want, more than a large bank account? The Christian life was never promised to be problem-free, but it is meant to be wonderful! If it isn't for some believers it's because they're looking to the wrong things for their happiness.

Our God longs to bless us. Let's put ourselves on the path where he can.

Father, thank you that you are working to make me good. I'm realizing it doesn't matter what I have; it's what I am that counts. In Jesus' name. Amen.

October 1

Don't Be Impressed

"Do not be overawed when a man grows rich, when the splendor of his house increases; for he will take nothing with him when he dies, his splendor will not descend with him. Though while he lived he counted himself blessed—and men praise you when you prosper—he will join the generation of his fathers, who will never see the light of life." Psalm 49:16-19

My husband, an electrical contractor, gets inside a lot of large expensive homes in very exclusive areas. He tells me some of these bathrooms are the size of our living room. All I can think of is, "Who wants to clean that much tile?"

I am a firm believer in living a simple lifestyle; huge houses don't really tempt me. I would not want to pay these people's property taxes, their utility bills, or their upkeep no matter how rich I was because I would consider it a waste.

The psalmist reminds us that death is the great leveler of wealth; none of us can keep what we have once we pass from this life to the next. We are not to be "blown away" by someone's net worth because it's really meaningless in the eternal scheme of things.

Being impressed with the riches of another is one short step away from violating the tenth commandment. When we begin to covet riches in our hearts, we also begin to disdain the rich for having them because now we're envious. It's a vicious cycle; we aren't happy for them but we want what they have.

If we are striving to increase the splendor of our house, we need to ask ourselves why. So we can impress people? To receive the praise of men? Are we that insecure about ourselves that we need outward show to bolster our self-esteem?

We need to cultivate an attitude of gratefulness for all we do have, and realize that to many of the world's poor, we live in splendor. Count yourself blessed.

Father, thank you for my home. Teach me contentment with where I am, and help me to look forward to my eternal home in heaven. In Jesus' name. Amen.

October 2

False Fortunes

"A fortune made by a lying tongue is a fleeting vapor and a deadly snare." Proverbs 21:6

Solomon wrote the book of Proverbs 3,000 years ago, yet it is as up to date as today's newspaper. In the fall of 2001, the business world was rocked by scandal involving the country's seventh largest company. The end result was the largest bankruptcy filing in United States history.

Behind the whole mess were executives who were getting incredibly wealthy by using unethical accounting practices. It was revealed that documents had been destroyed to cover up the hoax. Those with seniority had bailed out of the company's stock well in advance of the crash while thousands of employees lost their savings. The perpetuators were brought to trial and now face prison. Their lies caught up with them.

Have you ever noticed that the people involved in these reprehensible acts are usually those who are already quite wealthy? They have so much to lose and so little to gain by playing their backroom games. For some it is a game, a high-stakes contest of winner-take-all, at the expense of their companies, their employees, their stockholders, and the public trust.

They are overcome by greed, and greed makes their decisions. They get caught in a web of their own making and soon they can't get out, even if they want to. Their lies have them trapped. Someone begins to suspect, and the fears get reported. The authorities close in, and soon it is all over. The game is up and they lost—big time.

God's truths are timeless. They work in every age, in every economy, in every political regime. We can't escape them by telling ourselves lies. We ignore unchangeable truth at our own peril.

Fortunes built and sustained by lies cannot last.

Father, I pray that all my business dealings would be pleasing in your sight. Help me to do what is right and fair in all situations. In Jesus' name I pray. Amen.

Trust and Rejoice—Regardless

"Though the fig tree does not bud and there are no grapes on the vines, though the olive crop fails and the fields produce no food, though there are no sheep in the pen and no cattle in the stalls, yet I will rejoice in God my Savior." Habakkuk 3:17-18

It's easy to say we trust God when things are going well, when we have a good job, money in the bank, and are paying our bills on time. But how do we respond when our financial boat is torpedoed through no fault of our own and we begin to sink?

Habakkuk's day was similar to ours. The nation of Judah was given over to immorality, greed, and injustice. God would use the evil Babylonians to punish his chosen people for their idolatry. The prophet foresaw a time of such devastation that there would be no food and no means of earning a living; houses would lie in ruins. There would be great suffering for the righteous and wicked alike. Yet look at his beautiful prayer of faith!

To be able to rejoice in times of hardship is pleasing to God because it is an indicator of how much we trust him to provide for us. Do we really believe Matthew 6:8: "Your Father knows what you need before you ask him"? He has promised to care for us no matter what state the economy is in, and he will come through with miracles if that's what it takes.

Notice that he never promised to protect our wealth. Many people grow bitter towards God when they lose their retirement savings or their business. Theirs is the "prosperity God" and they believe that he has failed them. Jesus warned us that terrible times would come upon the earth (Matthew 24:4-25) so we should be prepared.

We live in a very unstable world. We don't know what tomorrow holds. The Roaring Twenties were immediately followed by the Great Depression. But we can rest in the comfort that no matter what, God is there for us.

Father, thank you for your wonderful promises. Give me an unshakeable faith that will trust you in every circumstance. I ask in Jesus' name. Amen.

The Tragedy of an Undisciplined Life

"Diligent hands will rule, but laziness ends in slave labor." Proverbs 12:24

Successful people are willing to do the things unsuccessful people aren't. This is true in every area of life. Successful people write down their goals; unsuccessful people make excuses. Successful people are proactive; unsuccessful people procrastinate. The outcome of each is predictable.

It takes diligence to be a good steward. It involves keeping good records, careful planning, and discipline in sticking to a budget. It is saying no to today's desires in order to have a tomorrow. It's not something we do for a month or even a year; we persevere for the long haul. It takes painstaking effort.

Those who decide all this is too much work and let their money matters go can be assured of two things: One, that the natural law of entropy will cause their finances to become more disorganized and chaotic, and two, eventually the bills will come due and they will have to pay the piper.

By choosing the path of neglect, we find that what once appeared to be so attractive and easy when we set out has now become overgrown with thorns and thistles, and we have to work twice as hard to make our way. We may be forced into working more years than we care to because we can't afford to retire. We could be performing "slave labor," paying off our creditors and having no money to call our own. It's possible we could find ourselves penniless and dependent on others.

Discipline gets us to where we want to go in life. If we will end up where we want to be, we need to employ it.

Father, help me to commit to the job of keeping my finances in order, no matter how boring I think it is. Give me the discipline to do it right. I ask in Jesus' name. Amen.

October **5**

Disputes Among Believers

*"Is it possible that there is nobody among you wise enough to judge a
dispute between believers? But instead, one brother goes to law against
another—and this in front of unbelievers! The very fact that you
have lawsuits among you means you have been completely defeated
already. Why not rather be wronged? Why not rather be cheated?
Instead, you yourselves cheat and do wrong, and you do this to your
brothers." 1 Corinthians 6:5-8*

"Court TV" is a popular program today. While we are eating dinner
we can watch the plaintiffs battle the defendants over increasingly
ludicrous charges. There seems to be a competition among the judges
presiding over these shows as to who can be the most abrupt, curt, and
even rude in their treatment of those appearing before them. Frankly,
it gives me a headache. I turn it off.

The Corinthian version of "The People's Court" was a source of
embarrassment to the apostle Paul. Believers were taking each other to
the civil courts over property disputes, which would indicate their
motives stemmed from greed and retaliation. To argue these matters in
front of unbelievers was to discredit the power of Christ to practice
forgiveness and unselfishness.

The better way, Paul says, is to bring such disagreements before the
church and resolve any wrongs. Christians are fully competent to judge
each other in trivial cases, more so than a pagan judge who doesn't
view issues from a godly perspective.

Our policy should be a willingness to suffer a wrong rather than
sue an individual, whether they are a believer or not. This flies in the
face of everything we've come to expect as "our rights," but Christ calls
us to higher ground. God can make it up to us. If you are sued, you
have every right to defend yourself and trust God for the outcome. Use
it as an opportunity to be a good witness for your faith.

Settle your squabbles with maturity and love. Don't "take it to
court."

*Father, help me to trust you when I've been wronged and I long for revenge. Thank
you for being my advocate. In Jesus' name. Amen.*

October

Poor But Peaceful

"Better a dry crust with peace and quiet than a house full of feasting with strife." Proverbs 17:1

What happened to all the TV series that portrayed families as loving and loyal to each other in the face of hardship and monetary lack? "The Waltons," "Little House On the Prairie"—these prime-time programs used to be must-see TV. Maybe they were a little too idealistic, but they promoted solid values and left viewers feeling good about the human race in general.

They were replaced by shows like "Dallas" and "Dynasty," and although the characters were beautiful and rich, they were anything but happy. Not only did the families not get along, they plotted crimes against each other. Despite having every material comfort, they needed alcohol to numb their misery. Amazing that the secular media so accurately demonstrates the truth of what Solomon wrote in antiquity.

Does television mirror real life, or does it influence it for the future? The more America has prospered, the more American families have disintegrated. If people are looking to TV for what their lives should be, what are they seeing? The media has been blamed for the restless dissatisfaction rampant in this country. The middle class isn't content with being the middle class. Everyone wants to live in a McMansion and drive a SUV, send their children to private schools, and take exotic vacations. In striving to achieve this standard of living, all too often they sacrifice the relationships that make their lives meaningful.

We can't return to the days of "The Waltons"; our world has changed. We can do some critical thinking and observation, however, on what is really needed in life. It would seem that as long as families have love and concern for each other, they can survive anything. Add wealth to the picture and it appears to promote pettiness, bickering, and disharmony. Yet we believe wealth can scratch the itch we all have.

Maybe we need a dose of the old TV shows. We could use a reality check.

Father, I want to model my life on what your Word says, not what television portrays. Protect me from its negative influence. I ask in Jesus' name. Amen.

October 7

The Barter System

"Now let my lord send his servants the wheat and barley and the olive oil and the wine he promised, and we will cut all the logs from Lebanon that you need and will float them in rafts by sea down to Joppa. You can then take them up to Jerusalem." 2 Chronicles 2:15

Before there was money, there was bartering—the trading of goods by exchange. It began with food and animals and progressed to clothing items and other commodities. Solomon and King Hiram bartered for the wood used in building the temple. North African tribes traded gold for salt. Even after money became widely used, bartering remained a time-honored way of conducting business.

Farmers barter milk and eggs for produce; we trade clothes with our friends; kids exchange toys. Barter goes on all the time. If we are looking to save money, this is an excellent method of getting what we need without having to use our hard-earned dollars.

Services and skills can be swapped instead of cash. Baby-sitting can be done as a co-operative effort; car maintenance can be performed in return for yard work; haircuts can be given in exchange for pet care. By using our creativity and networking with our friends and neighbors, all kinds of arrangements are possible.

Even professionals use the barter system. My husband has a deal with our dentist—electrical work in exchange for our family's dental needs. He's also swapped his skill for legal services. Could your occupational talents benefit someone who has what you need? It never hurts to ask. People are often delighted to have work done that they've been hesitant about spending money on. However, services received should be counted as income, according to the IRS.

As prices for goods and services grow steeper, the need for bartering in our society will increase. We will need to loosen up and share our possessions with each other rather than run out and buy every item we may only use once. An added bonus is that we will get to know our neighbors better!

Bartering—it's a win-win for everyone.

Father, show me ways to be creative in getting what I need. Lead me to people who need what I have. Let this become a source of new friendships. I ask in Christ's name. Amen.

Hold Off on That Inheritance

"An inheritance quickly gained at the beginning will not be blessed at the end." Proverbs 20:21

Stories abound of young people who, upon receiving an inheritance or having a trust fund released to them, immediately set out to squander it. From the prodigal son in Luke 15 to today's spoiled offspring of multimillionaires, they live for the day when they can utter those four magnificent words: *Show me the money!*

It's not only inheritances and trusts that cause problems for young adults just starting out. As affluent parents age, they wish to reduce their estates before they pass away, to limit their tax liability. They do this by giving substantial cash gifts to their children each year. The kids come to expect—even demand—these outlays of funds and often have it spent before they receive it.

Capable people, who are economically supported by others, lack the initiative to work and earn their own way. They are likely to be "professional students" and chronically unemployed and are just as crippled as a frail child who is never allowed to walk on his own but is carried everywhere.

If you are wealthy and want your children to be able to stand on their own two feet, what's the best way to go about it? First, don't put ideas in their heads about how much money they will receive one day. Second, let them develop discipline and ambition by insisting they work. Third, set up your trust so they don't receive benefits until they're quite mature. Fourth (and best), give most of your estate to the Lord and his kingdom and don't burden your children with it at all.

Passing on an inheritance is a good thing. Seek God for wisdom on how to keep it from being too much of a good thing.

Father, help me to teach my kids to be frugal and hard-working. Keep me from interfering in their finances when they're adults. I ask in Jesus' name. Amen.

October

Status Seeking

"Your beauty should not come from outward adornment, such as braided hair and the wearing of gold jewelry and fine clothes. Instead, it should be that of your inner self, the unfading beauty of a gentle and quiet spirit, which is of great worth in God's sight." 1 Peter 3:3-4

All I wanted was a plain white shirt. All I found were white shirts emblazoned with logos. Designers claim the logo is essential; they can't sell clothes without them. Personally, I refuse to be a human billboard, but the need for status in our society drives most of the consumer markets. We are well aware we're being judged by what we wear and what we drive, and to be socially acceptable or even compete with coworkers, we can fall into playing status games.

Women are told their station in life is determined by their handbag, their shoes, and their watch, in that order. In some circles, it is socially humiliating to pull a drugstore brand lipstick out of that expensive initialed designer bag. What are we saying with this behavior? "I'm so insecure I need you to know how much I paid for this"?

People are so afraid of being perceived as "low class," they spend money they don't have to impress people they don't even like. They drive a certain kind of car just to be seen getting out of it when they park. They pay dearly for their status consumption. An equal quality shirt will sell for $30 more if it has ten cents' worth of designer name embroidery on it. In reality, most branded goods are almost identical to each other.

"We are what we buy"? No, God says we are each unique and valuable because he made us, and no outward adornment will change that. When we focus on the outside and neglect the inside, we become a swanky but shallow people.

If we need to express ourselves, let's do it with the light of Christ that is within us. Now *there's* a name we can be proud to wear.

Father, release me from my fears of being judged, and help me to not judge others by their outward appearances. I ask in Jesus' name. Amen.

October

Miraculous Provision

"During the forty years that I led you through the desert, your clothes did not wear out, nor did the sandals on your feet. You ate no bread and drank no wine or other fermented drink. I did this so that you might know that I am the Lord your God." Deuteronomy 29:5

I wonder if we fully appreciate what it took for God to care for Israel in their flight from Egypt. Three million people—who needed to be fed and clothed for a period of forty years in the harsh, barren environment of the Sinai desert. They needed protection from wild animals that roamed there and also from the hostile nations of the area that sought to destroy them. They needed miracles!

I live in the Sonoran Desert. Hikers are constantly being warned not to venture into areas without adequate provisions of food, water, sun protection, and snakebite kits. Death is common for illegal immigrants trying to make it across the Mexican border. Deserts are unforgiving and merciless places.

Unless God is with you! Look at what he did for his people:

- He fed them with manna from heaven every day.
- He provided water out of a rock.
- He protected them from the blazing sun with cloud cover.
- He kept their clothing and tents from wearing out.
- He gave them victory over their enemies.

Israel was completely without any means of self-support; they had to rely on God for absolutely everything to survive. He met their needs so completely they took it for granted; even became bored with it. Is that our experience? Do we value the Lord's provision?

First Corinthians 10:16 tells us, "Now these things occurred as examples to keep us from setting our hearts on evil things as they did." The day may come when we need God's miracles to stay alive. He's already proven he can do it. Will we learn from history and put our faith in him?

Father, I believe you can do anything. I rest in your promises. Your presence is my true protection. In Jesus' name. Amen.

Watch the Ants

"Four things on earth are small, yet they are extremely wise: Ants are creatures of little strength, yet they store up their food in summer."
Proverbs 30:24-25

God will often point us to the natural world for examples of behaviors we'd be wise to emulate. Ants have already been singled out as instructive to us for their work habits and their preparation for the future (Proverbs 6:6-8). Ants are savers. They gather more food than they need, not for the purpose of hoarding but to preserve for later use. Ants embody what has become known as the Puritan work ethic: thrift, hard work, and self-discipline.

In colonial America, people adhered to these principles. Ben Franklin wrote in *Poor Richard's Almanac* his famous sayings of "A penny saved is a penny earned" and "Neither a borrower nor a lender be." Debt was considered a shameful thing. It is only in recent history that installment credit has become "respectable."

Even during the Depression the U.S. personal savings rate peaked at just over 5 percent. During World War II it went to over 25 percent. From there it plummeted to zero in 1999 and today America actually has a negative savings rate, thanks to credit.

The new game in town is what Juliet Schor calls the "work and spend cycle." It is consuming everything you earn as you earn it. The only "saving" that is done is not paying full price for something. It's still spending; it's just not spending as much.

Surprisingly, the more education a person has, the less they save. Having a higher level of income does not lead to increased saving, as economists believed it would. To return to the lowly ant, a creature so lightly esteemed we think nothing of stomping them out of existence, it would seem their creator has endowed them with more wisdom than can be acquired by a graduate degree.

Truly God has chosen "the weak things of the world to shame the strong" (1 Corinthians 1:27). Can we humble ourselves to learn from a tiny insect? Wisdom is found in the most unlikely places.

Father, thank you that you use the things the world considers insignificant to teach us. Make my heart receptive to those lessons. I ask in Jesus' name. Amen.

Trustworthy

"And we are sending along with him the brother who is praised by all the churches for his service to the gospel. What is more, he was chosen by the churches to accompany us as we carry the offering, which we administer in order to honor the Lord himself and to show our eagerness to help. We want to avoid any criticism of the way we administer this liberal gift. For we are taking pains to do what is right, not only in the eyes of the Lord but also in the eyes of men." 2 Corinthians 8:18-21

It's been said that if you can trust someone with money, you can trust them with anything. I'm not sure about that, but it is true that financial integrity is one of the high marks of a person's character. It is mandatory for an elder or a deacon in the church (1 Timothy 3:8) and it should be for anyone who claims the name of Christ.

The apostle Paul in his letter to the Corinthians was assuring them that their contribution would be personally handled by men of well-known reputation. They need not worry that the money they gave would be in any jeopardy of being lost or "misplaced." Paul declined to take the offer to Jerusalem by himself; in this way no one could accuse him of pocketing any part of it.

This is an important precaution for all ministries in the administration of their finances. Never should only one person, especially the senior pastor, be in a position of overseeing all the funds. Accountability needs to be spread among people of the highest caliber of integrity, and those giving should feel confident their money is in good hands.

Unaccountability has brought down many large ministries; we can never think we are above such temptations. Money is dangerous. It has a corrupting influence that needs to be guarded against in every possible way.

The oversight of God's money is a solemn trust. We need to take pains to do it right.

Father, I pray for all the men and women entrusted to handle our offerings to you. Protect them from the temptations of the evil one. For Jesus' sake. Amen.

The Example of Jesus

"Do not take a purse or bag or sandals; and do not greet anyone on the road. When you enter a house, first say, 'Peace to this house'... "stay in that house, eating and drinking whatever they give you." Luke 10:4-5,7

Reading through the Gospels, I find it interesting that there isn't one instance where Jesus is mentioned handling money. I'm sure he did throughout his life, but during his three year ministry, his disciples were in charge of the group's finances, although Jesus is seen directing some transactions. He sent them to buy food in Samaria and told Peter to take care of paying the temple tax.

Are we to make anything of this? As the Son of God, Jesus owned everything. In human form, he had the need for money but chose to be dependent upon others to provide. Some sincere Christians have taken his example as their own, interpreting that "filthy lucre" is to be abstained from by a holy and set apart people.

Jesus demonstrated to the disciples that it was possible to live without such a dependence on money, to trust the Father to meet all their needs. When he sent out the seventy, he instructed them to not take any provisions, not even extra clothing, but to rely on the hospitality of the people to whom they ministered, as he himself did. They were to live entirely by faith.

Not everyone is called to this lifestyle; the apostle Paul was not. It is not a requirement for discipleship, although during seasons of our lives we may be asked to forsake our usual means of support in order to give ourselves to full-time ministry.

What we are to emulate at all times is Jesus' attitude towards possessions. He had a holy unconcern, resting in the Father's provincial care, free from worry, and enjoying his beautiful creation. We are to "put [our] hope in God, who richly provides us with everything for our enjoyment" (1 Timothy 6:17). That is how Jesus lived, and he is our model.

Father, give me the attitude that was in your Son. I want to live in freedom from worldly concerns. I ask in Jesus' name. Amen.

Wisdom Is Not Popular

"The way of a fool seems right to him, but a wise man listens to advice." Proverbs 12:15

Wisdom appears to be something everyone desires to have, at least much lip service is paid to its merits. When it comes right down to it, wisdom is often passed over in favor of popular opinion.

Why should this be? The thing with wisdom is that it is not loud and flashy. In fact, it appears to be boring on the surface. It is humble, quiet, and looks to the long-term as the best solution. It requires patience to follow it through.

Wisdom is out of step with our see-immediate-results society. We are impressed by advice that is shouted and touted by the media as the current "in" thing to do. How else do you explain the explosion of dot com stocks in the late 1990s? None of those companies were profitable, but everyone seemed to be buying into them anyway.

Wisdom goes against the flow of what it easy and desirable. Look at the credit card debt this nation has racked up in the last thirty years. We have been seduced by advertising that tells us we deserve to have what we want when we want it. It is a rare person who bucks the tide and saves up to pay cash for their purchases.

It is not that wisdom is hidden and inaccessible; it "calls aloud in the street" (Proverbs 1:20) but folly is more attractive to our flesh (Proverbs 9:17). Folly offers us immediate gratification whereas wisdom asks us to discipline ourselves.

Wisdom is no respecter of persons. It can be held by rich and poor, and it's available to all who would seek it and be willing to obey its counsel. We resist it because it takes courage to take the lonely road apart from what everyone else is doing. It can be difficult in the beginning, but in the end it bestows "riches and honor, enduring wealth and prosperity" (Proverbs 8:18).

Only a fool would turn down a deal like that.

Father, open my ears to hear your quiet voice above the shouting of the majority. I'm willing to be unpopular if I can be wise. In Jesus' name. Amen.

No Comparison

"Blessed is the man who finds wisdom, the man who gains understanding, for she is more profitable than silver and yields better returns than gold. She is more precious than rubies, nothing you desire can compare with her." Proverbs 3:13-15

The things that are truly valuable are intangible. Throughout Scripture, God likes to remind us of what we should really be pursuing instead of money. Today, let's meditate in the quietness of our hearts on these verses that tell us what is of inestimable worth:

- "Wisdom is supreme, therefore get wisdom. Though it cost all you have, get understanding" (Proverbs 4:7).
- "Choose my instruction instead of silver, knowledge rather than choice gold, for wisdom is more precious than rubies, and nothing you desire can compare with her" (Proverbs 8:10-11).
- "How much better to get wisdom than gold, to choose understanding rather than silver!" (Proverbs 16:16).
- "Because I love your commands more than gold, more than pure gold…" (Psalm 119:127).
- "My son, if you accept my words and store up my commands within you, turning your ear to wisdom and applying your heart to understanding, and if you call out for insight and cry aloud for understanding, and if you look for it as silver and search for it as hidden treasure, then you will understand the fear of the Lord and find the knowledge of God" (Proverbs 2:1-5).
- "For you know that it was not with perishable things such as silver and gold that you were redeemed from the empty way of life handed down to you from your forefathers, but with the precious blood of Christ, a lamb without blemish or defect" (1 Peter 1:18-19).

"…think on these things" Philippians 4:8.

October

Delusions

"We will not listen to the message you have spoken to us in the name of the Lord! We will certainly do everything we said we would. We will burn incense to the Queen of Heaven and pour out drink offerings to her just as we and our fathers, our kings and our officials did in the towns of Judah and the streets of Jerusalem. At that time we were well off and suffered no harm. But ever since we stopped burning incense to the Queen of Heaven and pouring out drink offerings to her, we have had nothing and have been perishing by sword and famine."
Jeremiah 44:16-18

Ishtar was a Babylonian goddess of fertility; the people of Judah had sunk so low they were worshipping her in rampant idolatry. They credited this "Queen of Heaven" with the prosperity they enjoyed under wicked King Manasseh. His grandson Josiah began to restore the temple and enact religious reforms in an attempt to turn the people back to the Lord, but it was too late. God was about to unleash all the covenant curses on his rebellious nation.

The prophet Jeremiah repeatedly warned them what was to come, but they accused him of lying. Against his word, some fled to Egypt to escape the Babylonians and died by warfare, famine, and plague. Others blamed their misfortunes on King Josiah's renewal of the covenant. The only thing they cared about was their material well-being.

Theirs was a classic case of misconstruing blessings with divine favor. God was not at all pleased with them; prosperity was his final mercy call to repent before his judgment fell.

We can be guilty of the same today—equating our national prosperity with the belief that all is well between our nation and God. We enjoyed a booming economy under leadership that was so immoral and corrupt it was shameful to even have to discuss it. We must not be lulled into a false sense of security. God still does not tolerate idolatry.

Are we listening?

Father, open my eyes to the true spiritual condition of my country. Keep me from delusions that all is well when it is not. I ask in Jesus' name. Amen.

The Discord of Greed

"A greedy man stirs up dissension, but he who trusts in the LORD will prosper." Proverbs 28:25

For an object lesson in greed causing quarrels, volunteer in your church's toddler classroom some Sunday morning. No matter how many toys there are to play with, at least two kids will decide they want the same one at the same time. Hysterical screaming commences when the first child to pick up the cherished item won't relinquish it, no matter how hard the second child tries to pull it out of his or her arms. War has been declared.

We laugh—at least until such behavior begins to wear on us, but there's nothing funny about adults who won't share. Behind every act of selfishness you will find greed pulling the strings. Greed has no regard for another person's feelings or rights. In a business deal, greed is quick to take advantage if it sees there's more to be made for itself.

Greed operates under what Stephen Covey calls "the Scarcity Mentality"—there's only so much to go around and if you get more, that means there's less available for me. Greed has the need to grab all it can before someone else can get there. It doesn't care who it steps on or hurts in the process of acquisition.

It's unfortunate that people who were once good friends can be estranged over money issues. A loan was given in good faith and never paid back. Partnerships fall apart when one party falls prey to greed and things are suddenly not fifty-fifty any longer. Trust is lost and may be forever destroyed. Greed can be cruel and ruthless.

The antidote to greed is to give. Giving frees us from the clutching and clinging of trying to keep everything for ourselves. Giving is an unnatural act; in our flesh we are like those little kids crying "Mine!" Giving requires us to be supernatural, manifesting the power of God to change us to live according to our new nature.

By replacing greed with giving, discord is defeated.

Father, my sinful nature always wants more; help me to see that there is such abundance with you, there is no need for greed. I pray in Jesus' name. Amen.

Caring For Widows

"If any woman who is a believer has widows in her family, she should help them and not let the church be burdened with them, so that the church can help those widows who are really in need." 1 Timothy 5:16

In biblical times, a widow had very few options available to her for supporting herself. If she had no family and did not remarry, she would be destitute. In Paul's instructions to Timothy, he tells him that widows over the age of sixty who are all alone should be cared for by the church.

This was on the condition that they had been faithful women and had led fruitful lives. The younger women were expected to remarry, so the church was not to support them. Widows with relatives already had support. It was a good system that made sure everyone was taken care of.

Today, what with life insurance benefits, Social Security, pensions, and government assistance, the church's role in caring for widows has diminished. Spiritual and emotional support is crucial, of course, but the church can also help its widows who are well-situated financially by helping her to protect what she has.

Financial counseling is especially important here. Widows are faced with many decisions and problems following the deaths of their husbands. Should she sell the house? What should she do with insurance proceeds? Are there debts to be paid? Often her children will have their hands out, wanting money for their own purposes. In her grief this can all be overwhelming.

The best advice to give a widow in this situation is that after paying debts, she should put the remaining money in an absolutely safe place and not touch it for a full year. It's almost impossible for her to make wise choices on these matters until she is over her immediate grief. Teaching couples how to put their affairs in order *before* a death are important preventative measures the church could undertake.

God cares deeply for widows and so should his church.

Father, thank you that through the church you have made provision for those who are bereaved. Strengthen us for this important ministry. I ask in Jesus' name. Amen.

Warnings to Kings

"The king, moreover, must not acquire great numbers of horses for him-self or make the people return to Egypt to get more of them, for the LORD has told you, 'You are not to go back that way again.' He must not take many wives, or his heart will be led astray. He must not accumulate large amounts of silver and gold." Deuteronomy 17:16-17

Moses' directions to the nation of Israel regarding the king they would someday demand are prophetic. This is exactly what Solomon did, with the predicted results.

It seems to be a defiant act of disobedience, the extremes to which Solomon went in breaking these commands. Every king was to write out a copy of the law for himself and read it continuously so there was no excuse for ignorance. Yet Solomon amassed:

- 12,000 horses imported from Egypt (1 Kings 10:26-28)
- 700 wives and 300 concubines, many of them foreigners who turned his heart to other gods (1 Kings 11:1-4)
- $20 million annual income in gold alone (1 Kings 10:14)
- Silver so plentiful it was considered worthless (1 Kings 10:21)

The reason God gave these directives was so the king would remain humble and not think better of himself than his brothers (Deuteronomy 17:20). He was to be a servant-leader, setting the example to his nation in obedience and reverence. Solomon broke the covenant, and as king, discredited the Lord in the eyes of the people.

What do we think of Christian leaders who live in luxury? Are they our role models—"Hey, if they can live like that, so can I"—or do we think of them as an outrage to the cause of Christ?

Wealth can distract us from pure heart worship of our God. It can turn us away from spiritual pursuits to worldly concerns. Solomon lost his peaceful kingdom. We need to be sure we're seeking the right one.

Lord God, guard my heart against the accumulation of anything that would lead me away from you. I ask in the name of Jesus. Amen.

Dreaming Doesn't Do It

"The sluggard craves and gets nothing, but the desires of the diligent are fully satisfied." Proverbs 13:4

All of us have dreams of what we'd like to accomplish in life, but some of us are better at implementing them into reality than others. The people who achieve aren't any more talented or creative than those who don't; they aren't smarter or "lucky"; they simply refuse to accept the status quo (literally, "same old rut") and they work to make things happen.

It's not enough to chart our course. Dreamers can excel at formulating plans and knowing exactly what they need to do. It's just that they spin their wheels when it comes time to actually do it. They procrastinate and make excuses. They can't summon the energy to move forward.

They crave financial success, but it eludes them, because their own laziness is holding them back. They can talk the talk, but they don't walk it out. Talk, as we all know, is cheap. If they put the same effort into action as they put into words, they would accomplish something.

Your dream of owning your own business, being a stay-at-home mom, or starting a needed ministry, will not happen unless you take the necessary steps. To do that you have to first have your finances in order. You can't get where you want to go until you have a clear picture of where you are now. What you want to do may not yet be feasible from an economic point of view, but you can begin working towards that day. Dreams should be exciting enough to give you the momentum to keep pushing forward for the long term.

There's nothing wrong with having dreams; some of them are given to us by God himself. But they're wasted unless we make the decision to get off the dime and make them concrete. If you're lazy, admit it. Then get motivated to change!

Father, help me overcome my tendency to be lazy. I know it doesn't honor you. Give me a strategy for change. In Jesus' name. Amen.

Giving in Secret

"So when you give to the needy, do not announce it with trumpets, as the hypocrites do in the synagogues and on the streets, to be honored by men. I tell you the truth, they have received their reward in full. But when you give to the needy, do not let your left hand know what your right hand is doing, so that your giving may be in secret. Then your Father, who sees what is done in secret, will reward you."

Matthew 6:2-4

The church in which my husband was raised would actually mail its members a list of how much every family gave that year. Was it done to shame people into giving more? Who can say? Everyone knew who gave the most and the least, that was for sure.

It's hard to imagine anyone actually announcing their giving with trumpets, but apparently the Pharisees made a great show of putting their money into the temple treasury, and when they gave alms they made sure everyone knew about it. Jesus denounced their piety as fake. The Father does not honor giving done in such a manner. It only exalts the ego and increases the desire for praise from men. If we are living to please God, it is enough if he alone knows.

The phrase "do not let your left hand know what your right hand is doing" tells us that our giving should be so much a part of our nature, we are unconscious of performing the act. Even if others are watching, we are unmindful of them because it is no great occasion to us—giving is simply something we do, like brushing our teeth. Our giving is "secret" because we don't call attention to it.

God looks at the heart. He rewards those who give in secret and don't keep score.

Father, let my giving flow out of my life that is hidden with you. I don't want the praise of men, only your approval. In Jesus' name. Amen.

Misplaced Faith

"Whoever trusts in his riches will fall, but the righteous will thrive like a green leaf." Proverbs 11:28

Money would have us believe it can protect us from problems. It poses as a savior that will deliver us from poverty, offers us a defense against anxiety, and desires to usurp the rightful place of God in our lives. Money as a religion is based upon fear—fear that if we don't pay homage to the almighty dollar, we will be penniless, powerless nobodies.

Like any cult doctrine, the creed of money disguises its poison with just enough truth to get us to take the bait. It's true we need money to live on. It's true that money makes us feel safer when we have it than when we don't. We begin to believe in it.

Once it has us hooked, money consumes us. Most of our waking hours are spent trying to get more of it, and because money cares nothing for our well-being it leads us into unhealthy behaviors. We have money, so we overspend. We overwork. We overeat. We do all kinds of things in an attempt to fill the empty void in our souls.

Money deviously neglected to tell us that it could not give us what we most long for—immortality. Money fails us at the point where we leave this life to enter into the next. When we stand before the God we did not know, it will be too late to renounce our allegiance to a false deity.

Jesus came to offer us what money cannot. The riches found in him are ours forever. He became poor for our sake so we could receive those riches (2 Corinthians 8:9). Was Christ a powerless nobody? Did he need money to gain influence, win converts, or change the course of history? No. There is a power available to us of which money knows nothing.

If we look to money to do for us what only God can, we will be disappointed. We are to place our faith in the one who is the only true security—Jesus Christ.

Father, I will trust in you alone. I renounce money as my master. In the powerful name of Christ Jesus I pray. Amen.

Our Lit in Life

*"Lord, you have assigned me my portion and my cup; you have made
my lot secure. The boundary lines have fallen for me in pleasant
places; surely I have a delightful inheritance." Psalm 16:5-6*

It's just my lot in life." Whenever you hear someone make this statement, it's usually in a self-pitying, negative tone of voice, stated to
gain sympathy or express frustration at the circumstances in which a
person feels trapped. It insinuates that in the great drawing of life, they
drew the short end of the stick.

David recognized that it is God who sets each of us in the place he
chooses for us. He took David from watching over sheep and set him
as king over Israel, but not without thirteen years of living as a fugitive
in between. Wherever he was, David rejoiced because the Lord was
with him.

Today, we are in the place God has assigned to us. It may not be a
place we would choose. Perhaps we're in a studio apartment and we
want more room, or we're stuck in the city and we long for the open
spaces and fresh air of a rural environment. We need to think more
broadly. If you live in North America, your boundary lines have fallen
in pleasant places. The squalid living conditions in India, where several
thousand people may share a single latrine, would make a trailer park
resident feel very blessed.

Why are we so privileged to live where we do, in a land of freedom,
with plenty of food and adequate shelter? Are we better than the
Christians in Ethiopia? No, but we're accountable for more because of
our great resources.

No matter where we live, if we're Christians we all have the same
inheritance—the Lord himself. We will all end up together with him
forever. The journey is different for each of us, but not the destination.

Our "lot"—our destiny—is secure. Our boundary lines may
change, our portion may increase or decrease, but our sovereign God
arranges the perimeters that will keep us safe in him.

*Father, thank you that my boundaries are in pleasant places. Give me contentment
where you have me now. In Jesus' name. Amen.*

Judgment Day

"Wealth is worthless in the day of wrath, but righteousness delivers from death." Proverbs 11:4

In an informal man-on-the-street survey, which do you think most people would choose if they could possess only one—righteousness or wealth? To the unbeliever, righteousness doesn't sound that appealing. They imagine someone who lets others walk all over them, or a goody two-shoes who offends everyone with their piousness. They don't see righteousness as doing them much good in a dog-eat-dog world where only the powerful rise to the top.

Wealth they understand. Wealth can buy you status and position. Wealth can open doors that remain closed to the poor. Wealth can bring every material comfort your heart desires. Wealth can attract a mate who wouldn't look at you twice before. Most people would choose wealth.

Those who choose righteousness take the long view. They understand that in the final analysis, who they *are* counts for everything; what they *have* counts for nothing. Righteousness is a robe they will wear into eternity; wealth must be shed upon departure from this life.

Worldly wealth is like the "funny money" issued by theme parks. You convert your dollars into their currency and you can spend it anywhere in the park, but once you leave it becomes worthless. No one will accept it outside the confines of that limited area.

The damned arrive at heaven's gate and discover that this is one door their wealth cannot open. It is invalid for redemption. Righteousness is the correct currency. It served its bearers well on earth; now it is the only "legal tender" God will accept as payment for our debt of sin.

Righteousness is not cheap. It cost Christ his own blood to purchase it for us. It's available to everyone, but some will choose not to accept. They prefer to clutch the wealth of the world rather than reach for eternal riches.

Judgment Day is coming. On which currency are we bankrolling?

Lord God, I choose the righteousness you offer in Jesus Christ. I trust in him only to deliver me from death. I pray in his precious name. Amen.

Arrogant Complacency

"You lie on beds inlaid with ivory and lounge on your couches. You dine on choice lambs and fattened calves. You strum away on your harps like David and improvise on musical instruments. You drink wine by the bowlful and use the finest lotions, but you do not grieve over the ruin of Joseph." Amos 6:4-6

The chasm between the rich and the poor is growing wider. Those in the middle class are drowning in debt in their attempts to live like the rich. Cable TV is now considered a "necessity." And the pursuit of luxury, known as "upscaling," can be measured by the changing standard of how much income people say they need to live "comfortably." That figure, according to the Roper Center, jumped from $40,000 annually in 1987 to $102,000 in 1994! We live on a planet where it is estimated that 1.2 billion people live on less than $1 a day; 2.8 billion on less than $2 a day. Survival is a daily struggle; the procurement of enough food to feed their families takes all their time. Meat is a luxury. Cattle need thirty acres per head for grazing, and the available land is needed for better uses.

The average American eats about sixty-eight pounds of beef a year. That's a lot of pastureland; rain forests in developing countries are being cleared to satisfy the demand. Our affluence is hurting the rest of the world. America makes up 6 percent of the world's population and consumes 33 percent of its resources.

The theme of the book of Amos is God's passion for justice. His "beef" with Israel's wealthy was their total unconcern for the affliction of the poor among them when it was the sin of the wealthy that caused this affliction.

We should feel uncomfortable. Besides giving money to causes that help, what can we do? Our family quit eating beef. We keep our air conditioner at 82 degrees. We drive fuel-efficient vehicles. All these things are a drain on the environment. Whatever you do to help the earth also helps your health and your finances.

Cut back on consuming! Learn the difference between luxuries and necessities.

Father, forgive me for my extravagances when so many people are suffering. Show me where I can change my lifestyle to make a difference. I ask in Jesus' name. Amen.

Wealth Is to Be Shared

"People curse the man who hoards grain, but blessing crowns him who is willing to sell." Proverbs 11:26

A famine was coming. Through Pharaoh's dreams and Joseph's interpretation of them, God had warned the king of Egypt that seven years of plenty would be followed by seven years of severe deprivation. It would be crucial that a portion of those bumper crops would be put into storage and preserved for the rationing that would follow.

Pharaoh appointed Joseph as his second in command to oversee the project. Joseph began to collect food; he "stored up huge quantities of grain, like the sand of the sea; it was so much that he stopped keeping records because it was beyond measure" (Genesis 41:49). There is a difference between hoarding and stockpiling. Hoarding is accumulation hidden away to keep for oneself. Stockpiling is preparing for an emergency when there is sure to be a shortage.

Egypt needed a man like Joseph who would not take advantage of his privileged position. He had the authority to do whatever he wished. He could have hoarded the grain for his own family or even limited its access to select groups of people. He did not. When the famine hit, he threw open the storehouses and all the world came to Egypt to buy food.

God gives abundance to some individuals as a means of bringing glory to himself. These people are not caught up in their own personal prosperity; they "open the vaults" to share their bounty where there is a need. If they're in business, they don't hoard; they don't drive up the price to make a greater profit off of someone's misfortune.

The world needs people like this whom God can trust with great wealth. People who have conquered greed and live their lives with their palms open. It takes a very special person to handle prosperity well.

Hoarding only creates enemies. God's favor rests on those who spread the wealth.

Father, bless those individuals who walk in humility and integrity before you. Multiply their resources so they can do more good. I ask in Jesus' name. Amen.

Faith in Action

"What good is it, my brothers, if a man claims to have faith but has no deeds? Can such faith save him? Suppose a brother or sister is without clothes and daily food. If one of you says to him, 'Go, I wish you well; keep warm and well fed,' but does nothing about his physical needs, what good is it? In the same way, faith by itself, if it is not accompanied by action, is dead." James 2:14-17

Faith without works is dead" is the overall message of the book of James. It is not salvation by works. Salvation is by faith alone, but true faith produces works.

If we believe what we say we do, we will act on it. If our actions are out of line with our words, then our faith should be called into question. If an orange tree produced anything other than oranges, we would rightly doubt if it were an orange tree.

James is getting after those folks who claimed that faith was enough, that nothing more was required of them. The truth is, faith in Christ will naturally produce works just as a fruit tree produces fruit. What good is our testimony if we don't reach out to people?

As Christians we are to be Jesus' hands and feet in our part of the world. He commissioned us to carry on his work. There is no "plan B" to default to if we fail him.

When we pray asking God to meet people's needs, we need to realize that he may be asking *us* to be the answer to the prayer. Sometimes we need to stop praying and start doing. Praying that God will take care of that homeless man we see on the corner every week isn't nearly as effective as taking the time to buy him a meal.

We have only this lifetime to use our resources to give aid to hurting and needy people. Once we stand before our Lord and Judge, it will be too late.

"Show me your faith!" says James.

Father, show me practical ways to put my faith into action. I will be alert for opportunities to act on what I believe. In Jesus' name I pray. Amen.

Kept Out of the Kingdom

"Do you not know that the wicked will not inherit the kingdom of God? Do not be deceived: Neither the sexually immoral nor idolaters nor homosexual offenders nor thieves nor the greedy nor drunkards nor slanderers nor swindlers will inherit the kingdom of God."
1 Corinthians 6:9-10

Almost lost in this explicit list of offenses that will keep people from entering into the kingdom is greed. Most of us, if we're honest, would not put greed on the same level as fornication. Yet Jesus, throughout the Gospels, came down on greed harder than any other sin. He was tender with the woman caught in adultery; he was gracious to the woman at the well in Samaria, knowing all about her immoral lifestyle. But greed he confronted head-on at every opportunity.

He was especially scathing in his indictment of the Pharisees. "Inside you are full of greed and wickedness" (Luke 11:39). Jesus knew that where greed resides there is no room for God. "You cannot serve both God and mammon" (Luke 16:13). Being bound to greed keeps us out of the kingdom because we are not free to serve God wholeheartedly.

"Greed, for lack of a better word, is good," proclaimed Gordon Gekko, the character in the film "Wall Street." His point was that greed is a catalyst for change; it "marks the upward surge of mankind" to continually better itself. Sounds good, doesn't it? Except he is using the wrong word; it is *discontent*—"restless aspiration for improvement"—experienced in the proper spirit, that stimulates improvement of conditions.

Greed is a cancer on our character. As a disease it eats away at our spiritual vitality; it is completely self-centered. Greed takes so much out of us—our compassion, our sense of justice, our very devotion to our Lord.

Greed, like homosexuality, is acceptable in our society, but Paul made it clear, that doesn't make it right. Those who practice such things should not profess to be citizens of the kingdom.

Father, help me to see greed as a serious offense in your eyes. Guard me against the deceitfulness of this sin. I ask in Jesus' name. Amen.

Selling the Truth

"Better a little with righteousness than much gain with injustice."
Proverbs 16:8

What price do you place on a clear conscience? Is it worth more to you than money? If it is, your integrity can't be bought and we need people like you not only in business but in our court systems.

Justice is not swift, due in part to the backlog of cases, but much of the delay has to do with the fact that the longer the situation is dragged out, the more money is to be made. The more appeals that can be filed, the more billing hours for the lawyers. It's legal, but is it ethical? Is it fair to the victims?

A friend of ours waited nine years to finally get her settlement resulting from a disability suit, and then she received only a fraction of what was rightfully hers. The lawyers got the rest. There's a reason why lawyers are one of the most picked-on professions when it comes to jokes!

Injustice is no joke. It exists because there is money in it. Lucrative incomes are earned through corruption. Getting to the truth is irrelevant as long as someone is making a profit. In some localities it is possible to make a nice living by accepting bribes under the table.

All through the Old Testament God thunders against injustice. "You who turn justice into bitterness and cast righteousness to the ground...you hate the one who reproves in court and despise him who tells the truth" (Amos 5:7,10). Such acts bring his judgment. Isaiah 3 details the consequences of crushing those who came to him for help. What does the Lord require? "Hate evil, love good; maintain justice in the courts" (Amos 5:15). He is just, and he demands that his people be just.

It's difficult to stand by and watch colleagues get the choice assignments, the promotions, and the perks, knowing they receive them through cheating and dishonesty. Better to keep our integrity before our God, however, and trust him to honor us for our uprightness, than to be counted among the wicked.

Father, help me to not desire unjust gain. I would rather have a little with you than the entire world without you. In Jesus' name. Amen.

The Prosperity of the Wicked

"This is what the wicked are like—always carefree, they increase in wealth." Psalm 73:12

With so much emphasis on material wealth in our society, it's hard not to evaluate people by their net worth. We observe who is prospering and who is not, and we make judgments based on what we know of them and their values. We have a formula that says the good guys should get the goodies and the bad guys should get the boot.

Asaph the psalmist felt the same way. Psalm 73 is his confession of his envy towards the wicked rich. They were enjoying all the world had to offer while he, a godly man, had struggles. He couldn't understand why God would reward arrogance and violence with health and wealth.

In every human heart there is a cry for fairness. Even as children we instinctively know what is unjust. We hate to see the school bully succeed because in our minds he doesn't deserve to. As adults it angers us when people who openly declare their disdain for God are seen enjoying their yachts. We can have a crisis of faith thinking God doesn't see or care.

If we feel this way, it is because we have lost our perspective. Aspah pulled out of his lapse while worshipping at the temple where it dawned on him that the wicked had already received everything they would ever possess. Nothing they were now enjoying would last. They would lose it all in that moment when death ushers them into an eternity without God.

The psalm ends with a beautiful prayer of praise and thanksgiving. Let it be our prayer today:

"Yet I am always with you; you hold me by my right hand. You guide me with your counsel, and afterward you will take me into glory. Whom have I in heaven but you? And earth has nothing I desire besides you. My flesh and my heart may fail, but God is the strength of my heart and my portion forever." Psalm 73:23-26

Suffering for What's Right

"When the owners of the slave girl realized that their hope of making money was gone, they seized Paul and Silas and dragged them into the marketplace to face the authorities." Acts 16:19

Paul and Silas were being followed around Philippi by a demon-possessed slave girl who earned money for her masters by fortune-telling. She was witnessing to their mission, with a subtle error. In the original Greek she was literally saying, "These men are servants of the Most High God, who are telling you a way to be saved" (Acts 16:17).

After a few days of this, Paul couldn't take it anymore and commanded the demon to leave her. Delivered from the spirit of divination, the girl no longer had the ability to predict the future. We don't know what happened to her after that, but her owners were so furious at being denied their stream of income they took it out on the missionaries. They brought them before the magistrates on false charges and had them beaten and imprisoned.

Anytime our convictions touch anything that affects someone's sacred cow of money, we can expect to be persecuted. I know of a man who lost his position at a law firm for refusing to assist on a case that would have him defending a purveyor of pornography. Not only did they fire him, they made sure no other law firm would hire him. Today he's a pastor.

At these times we need to recall Romans 8:28: "And we know that in all things God works for the good…." What was Paul and Silas' "good"? A slave girl was released from bondage, they witnessed to a jail full of prisoners, and the jailer and his household were saved.

Money should never be a factor for us in deciding what course of action to take. Who knows what we miss when we go for the gold instead of God's best? Our ease is never as important as God's purposes.

Father, help me to live by my convictions and do what is right, even if it costs me my income. I trust in your greater good. In Jesus' name. Amen.

The Day of Disaster

"Neither their silver nor their gold will be able to save them on the day of the Lord's wrath. In the fire of his jealousy the whole world will be consumed, for he will make a sudden end of all who live on the earth." Zephaniah 1:18

In 1666, the city of London was destroyed by a firestorm that raged for four days. People lost everything they owned. Unable to get their valuables to safety, they escaped with only their lives. This event had been preceded by a smallpox epidemic in 1665 that killed thousands. It had failed to arouse the people to repentance, so the Lord used more severe means to get their attention. This time it worked. The king issued a decree calling for a day of fasting and humility to petition God for mercy. London was rebuilt, but it was never again the most prosperous city on earth.

God in his righteousness cannot overlook sin. He punishes nations and cities that shed innocent blood, that wallow in immorality, that persecute his saints. He destroyed the world by water in Noah's day; he sent fire and brimstone on Sodom and Gomorrah; he brought down the Roman Empire. Is America next?

He has warned us. We've already had the plague of AIDS; we've had federal buildings bombed; we've had natural disasters of earthquakes, fire, and flood. We've had terrorist attacks on a scale never before seen. Yet all we seem to care about is our continued prosperity. We want leaders who will keep the good times rolling, regardless of their character. How much time do we have left?

Instead of seeking safe havens for our money (there are none), we should be seeking the Lord's face and praying for a spirit of repentance so that judgment might be delayed. We need to have our hearts in a state of readiness for whatever comes.

God goes with his people through the fire (Daniel 3:25). We need not fear the day of disaster.

Father, I will not fear, though the earth give way, and all the mountains fall into the heart of the sea. You are my refuge and strength. In Jesus' name. Amen.

Heads or Tails

"You will lend to many nations but will borrow from none. The LORD will make you the head, not the tail. If you pay attention to the commands of the LORD your God that I give you this day and carefully follow them, you will always be at the top, never at the bottom."
Deuteronomy 28:12-13

Scripture makes a strong correlation between debt and slavery. Perhaps we wouldn't be so nonchalant about going into debt if we saw it in that light. One of the many blessings God promised to bestow on the Israelites if they were obedient to him was that they would not be put into a position of having to borrow money from other nations.

To be "the head" is to be in control. It is a position of leadership and honor. "The tail" is subservient to the head. It is a position of weakness and powerlessness. It's obvious to see which nation will have the upper hand in a creditor/debtor arrangement.

We may believe that as citizens of the United States we are joined to the most powerful nation on earth, but are we really? Our national debt would say otherwise. We've gotten so used to it; the numbers are so astronomical it hardly seems real to most of us. But this is money that is legitimately owed to other governments and it will inevitably begin to affect our freedoms.

The United States had a balanced budget until the 1970s when we began to take on debt. It would take drastic measures to balance the budget now, sacrifices most Americans would not be willing to make. We have come to expect certain "services" from Uncle Sam, including government-assisted living.

Being a borrower can bring a curse, for nations as well as individuals.

Father, give me the courage to take a stand against government waste. Show me how I can do my part to help reduce the burden of debt on my country. I ask in Jesus' name. Amen.

November 3

The Wages of Eternity

"I tell you the truth, anyone who gives you a cup of cold water in my name because you belong to Christ will certainly not lose his reward."
Mark 9:41

He's gone to his eternal reward." We don't use that expression much these days when we refer to someone's death, and we probably don't really understand what we're saying when we do. Believers in Christ have the hope of heaven and being with him forever and that would certainly be reward enough. But God has more for us when our earthly life has ended.

The word Jesus uses in Mark 9:41 for "reward" is *misthos*, and it refers to wages, the same sort of wages an employer would pay for labor performed. He also uses it in Luke 6:33: "Great is your *misthos* [reward] in heaven." Did you realize you were on God's payroll?

The Bible also teaches that we will be repaid for the good deeds we have done. Luke 14:14 says, "you will be repaid at the resurrection of the righteous." The language is very straightforward; it means exactly what it says. God will reimburse us after we die for our service to him. According to Jesus, even the smallest, insignificant acts of kindness will be recompensed. A cup of water given (Matthew 10:42). Our private prayers (Matthew 6:6). Things we're not even aware of, God sees and credits to our account.

When we think of all God has already done for us, it seems incredible that we haven't even yet begun to receive everything he wants to give us. We must never fall into the trap of thinking our rewards are earthly, temporal things like a lot of money or a great job or a beautiful home. Those things are nice, but we can't enjoy them forever the way we will our real rewards.

When we get to heaven, we will be amazed at what God considered important to the kingdom. We have only this life in which to earn the wages of eternity. Make every day count.

Father, how awesome that you will repay us, your unworthy servants. Help me to live for that great day. In Jesus' name. Amen.

Spread Your Money Out

"Sow your seed in the morning, and at evening let not your hands be idle, for you do not know which will succeed, whether this or that, or whether both will do equally well." Ecclesiastes 11:6

To a certain extent, any of us can suffer from all-or-nothing thinking. When it comes to investing, we can react by doing nothing out of fear, or dumping our whole wad on one stock transaction. We can be torn between saving and paying off debt. What should we do?

Answer: Do both. The way we have handled the debt/savings dilemma was to divide the amount we had to work with in half. One half would be saved; the other would go towards the debt we were paying off, creating a win-win. It also eliminated all the wrestling with indecision about which is better.

With investing, it's never wise to put all your available money on one stock at one time. A better way is to purchase in levels. If your goal is to invest $6,000 a year, instead of buying all the shares at once, buy them in $500 increments each month. This is known as dollar cost averaging. It helps cut your risk as the price you paid for the stock fluctuates throughout the year. Instead of getting upset when the price falls, you can see it as a "sale" and know that you're getting more for your money that month. When the price goes up, you can be happy that you've made money on your previously purchased shares. Another win-win.

The key is to be consistent. We can overthink our strategies to the point where we're constantly changing what we're doing, and that will get us nowhere. Unless God is leading us definitively in a new direction, we should take a long-term view and not panic over market conditions.

Investments are uncertain. We're not to rely on anything except the only one who is certain, and that's our God. He will care for us no matter what happens to our money. We can only do the best we can—give and invest and leave the results to him.

Father, I'm investing to advance your kingdom, not mine. Show me a plan to follow. I ask in Jesus' name. Amen.

The Law of Reciprocity

"A generous man will prosper; he who refreshes others will himself be refreshed." Proverbs 11:25

We live in a visible world in which there are physical laws such as gravity that are immutable. As Christians, we also live in the invisible world of God's kingdom which has spiritual laws that govern it. One principle that transcends both physical and spiritual worlds is the law of reciprocity.

We see it at work in nature as cause and effect; for every action there is an equal and opposite reaction. We see it in human relationships as people respond to others either positively or negatively, based on how they are treated. Anger begets anger, but smile at someone and you will usually receive a smile in return.

We trust these principles to work because we see what they do. When it comes to applying it to our money, however, we often hesitate, believing the universe plays by different rules, but this is not true. God's precepts apply to every area of our lives; we just lack the faith to implement them.

When we use our resources to serve others, the law of reciprocity goes into effect to ensure that others will use their resources to serve us. This should free us from any fears of not having enough or of people taking advantage of us. Countless testimonies abound of those who gave out of savings they needed for a specific purpose, only to have the funds returned to them in sometimes supernatural ways.

"It is more blessed to give than to receive" (Acts 20:35); "Give, and it will be given you" (Luke 6:38). These words of Jesus are not just nice sentiments. He expects us to put them into practice. We refresh others, not only when we meet their physical needs but also through our friendship and encouragement.

By contributing to the well-being and happiness of others, we increase our own. This is how God in his wisdom established his kingdom to work. For those who live by its laws, the kingdom of heaven is now.

Father, thank you for your kingdom laws. Show me practical ways I can put them to use to bless others. I ask in Jesus' name. Amen.

A Beautiful Voice

*"My people come to you, as they usually do, and sit before you to listen
to your words, but they do not put them into practice. With their
mouths they express devotion, but their hearts are greedy for unjust
gain. Indeed, to them you are nothing more than one who sings love
songs with a beautiful voice and plays an instrument well, for they
hear your words but do not put them into practice." Ezekiel 33:31-32*

What is the purpose of preaching? Why does God have his
appointed spokespeople deliver his word in pulpits around the
world every Sunday? For enlightenment as to how we should live—not
entertainment, the way the exiles in Babylon treated Ezekiel's messages.
God revealed to his prophet that the people were coming merely
because they enjoyed listening to him, perhaps he was very eloquent.

It certainly wasn't the content of what he was saying—Ezekiel was
delivering a hard word of catastrophe and judgment yet to come. The
"hard word" in our day is what relates to our idolatry of money and
our giving habits, or lack of giving. Most Christians agree that materialism has infiltrated the church and people don't give the way they
should. But do they see themselves as part of the problem?

The giving pattern in most churches breaks down into 30 percent
of the families doing 94 percent of the giving, and the remaining 70
percent make up the other 6 percent. Something is really wrong with
this picture. These are people who are sitting under the same preaching
every week. Why such discrepancy? We can't blame the preachers if
they are faithful to bring forth the full counsel of God concerning the
tithe.

It doesn't matter how popular any Christian speaker is if their
hearers do not put their words into practice. If they're treated as entertainers, they haven't fulfilled their purpose. Len and I don't care to
counsel people who will not do what is asked of them.

A beautiful voice is in vain if we don't align our behavior with
what we are hearing.

*Father, open my spiritual ears to hear what you say through your messengers. Give
me a heart that will obey. For Jesus' sake. Amen.*

What Kind of Kingdom?

"Jesus said, 'My kingdom is not of this world. If it were, my servants would fight to prevent my arrest by the Jews. But now my kingdom is from another place.'" John 18:36

What a difference five days can make. When Jesus entered Jerusalem riding the donkey, people waved palm branches and shouted, "Hosanna to the Son of David!" (Matthew 21:9). When he appeared with Pilate before another crowd, they shouted "Crucify him!" (Luke 23:21). What happened in the interim that would constitute such a change of heart?

Jesus was not fulfilling their expectations of what Messiah was supposed to accomplish for them. They wanted a king who would overthrow the Roman government so they would be free from the tyranny of Caesar. They wanted all the material benefits they read about in the Old Testament, the prosperity and peace Solomon had once enjoyed. They wanted prestige as an independent nation again. They were oblivious to their greater need to be set free from the power of sin.

When people turn to Jesus today, what are they seeking? Do they want a Messiah who promises them financial success, immunity from life's problems, and then a ticket to heaven? When we offer the unsaved this kind of savior, what kind of disciples can we expect to raise up? A kind who will turn away as soon as their false expectations go unmet?

Jesus never offered people a visible kingdom. His rule and reign is in the human heart. His throne is over our wills that were once in rebellion against God. He promises to meet the deepest needs of our spirit, not the greedy materialistic desires of our flesh.

Our satisfaction with Jesus depends on the kind of kingdom we are looking for. If all we want is health and wealth in this earthly life, we will be disappointed. But if we want forgiveness of our sins, a personal relationship with God, and opportunities to serve our King, we will never go away empty.

Father, I look to the kingdom that is everlasting, eternal in the heavens. Take my eyes off earthly things to seek you first. In Jesus' name. Amen.

Live Like a King's Kid?

"Jesus replied, 'Foxes have holes and birds of the air have nests, but the Son of Man has no place to lay his head.'" Luke 9:58

Whenever the prosperity preachers appear on TV and exhort their followers that they should be living like "the king's kids," I always wonder what king they mean. The king of Brunei? Certainly he would be more in line with the lifestyle to which they're referring. The King and Creator of the universe did not lavish this world's goods on his only Son during his sojourn on earth. Quite the opposite. Born in the most humbling circumstances imaginable, he lived most of his life working as a common tradesman, and during his three-year ministry had no possessions save the clothes on his back.

It is a twisted teaching that insists God wants his children driving Cadillacs and living in splendor. It does not line up with the scriptures that warn against the deceitfulness of wealth and the folly of pursuing material gain. And yet some would offer the "promise" of prosperity as a motive to give your life to Christ. God forbid!

God does bless some Christians with great worldly wealth but it is not his desire for all of us. We should not be made to feel inferior or that we are harboring sin in our lives if we aren't rolling along on easy street. Ironically, it would seem many of God's purest saints have lived or are living with very little in material wealth. They submitted their level of lifestyle to him and they trusted him to provide for all their needs.

Just as he did for his Son.

Father, help me understand that my financial circumstances aren't an indication of my standing with you or as evidence of sin in my life. Your beloved Son emptied himself of material possessions to fulfill your purposes. Show me how to use my place in this world to achieve your mission for me. I ask in Jesus' name. Amen.

Selling Out for God

"So they pulled their boats up on shore, left everything and followed him." Luke 5:11

One of the astounding leadership qualities of Jesus is that people were willing to totally renounce their lifestyles to follow him. It is a testimony to his absolute authority; three words—"Come, follow me" (Mark 1:17)—and men threw aside their livelihoods to go after him to their deaths. The King James version states that they "forsook all"— pretty radical for career fishermen who have just had the catch of a lifetime! But Jesus had cast before them a grander vision. Instead of spending their time catching fish, they would be catching the souls of men—a far greater priority.

Such commitment to any cause can make us uncomfortable. We squirm and make excuses when it comes to answering our own calls. "We need to keep a balance and not become fanatical." This is luke-warmness; Jesus spews such talk out of his mouth (Revelation 3:16). If we are to follow him, we must empty ourselves of our self-centered desires, ambitions, and comforts; renounce the ways of the world; and humbly submit ourselves to God, no matter what the cost.

For some it may mean the loss of a lucrative career. It may mean going against a parent's wishes to take over the family business some-day. It may mean turning down a college scholarship. It may mean staying in college and getting a degree when we'd rather quit. There is no one method God uses to bring everyone into full-time discipleship.

One thing is certain: Once we catch the grander vision, money will pale in comparison to what Christ is offering us, and selling out for him won't seem like a sacrifice at all.

Father, give me a vision of the eternal significance my life would have were I to totally surrender all to you. I give you my life; do with it what you will. For Jesus' sake. Amen.

Pay the Hired Man His Wages

"Do not take advantage of a hired man who is poor and needy, whether he is a brother Israelite or an alien living in one of your towns. Pay him his wages each day before sunset, because he is poor and is counting on it." Deuteronomy 24:14-15

Every fall we have the palm trees in our yard trimmed; someone will ring the doorbell and offer to do the job for a price. If we hire him, we expect the work to get finished in one day, but sometimes it isn't. (It's a big job; we have a lot of palm trees!) If it isn't done, we will pay him the fair amount for the work that was done. Most of these guys need that money just to be able to eat and buy more gas for their truck. To withhold it all to the next day until the job is complete would be cruel.

We do know of homeowners who will not pay anything until the job is finished. They've found that once the fellow has a little money in his pocket, he never comes back, leaving the homeowner with a half-done yard. They want some insurance that the work will be completed.

However, this clearly violates the principle of the Old Testament regulation. It doesn't matter that God spoke this to Moses many thousands of years ago; it is as relevant today as it was then. The heart of the command is loving your neighbor as yourself and not putting your own interests first. The practice of most employers of holding back a week's paycheck is even questionable. Many people suffer financial duress waiting for that first check on a new job.

We need to look at those we employ through God's eyes.

Father, give me your heart towards the working poor. May I be able to bless them as I have opportunity. In Jesus' name. Amen.

11

The Cost of Integrity in Business

"What a man desires is unfailing love; better to be poor than a liar."
Proverbs 19:22

Integrity in the marketplace has fallen on hard times. There has been a large scale failure of moral courage among corporations as telling the truth is becoming the exception rather than the norm. CEOs look at the potential economic setbacks and decide to take the low road to quick profits rather than go the extra mile and produce a high quality product.

It is true that we sometimes take a financial hit by doing the right thing. Honesty can cost us a sale when we refuse to embellish the attributes of a product. We may lose the edge over the competition when we put the well-being of employees ahead of cost-cutting efficiency. Giving an honest estimate may mean not winning the bid. But if we are followers of Jesus Christ, our faith must extend into our businesses and careers.

Besides, ethics is just good business. After all, don't you want to work for someone with integrity? So does everyone else! Following ethical business practices can actually increase profits in the long run. It requires looking beyond short-term advantages gained by cutting corners that will increase the bottom line, but end up costing much more in the future.

Remember the Ford Pinto? The car company lost millions in lawsuits when it was discovered that the poor design of the gas tank caused it to explode in rear-end collisions, resulting in many unnecessary deaths. The costs associated with all the bad press, ill will, and lost trust are incalculable.

It is much better to be a little less profitable in your business and have a clear conscience than to be a smashing financial success by ripping people off. We do long-term damage to our character when we sacrifice it on the altar of commerce.

In the final analysis, the benefits of integrity far outweigh the costs.

Father, I submit my business practices to your lordship. Help me to be the same person on the job as I am in church. I ask in Jesus' name. Amen.

Clothing Issues

*"And why do you worry about clothes? See how the lilies of the field
grow: They do not labor or spin. Yet I tell you that not even Solomon in
all his splendor was dressed like one of these." Matthew 6:28*

It's hard to imagine anyone in America suffering from nakedness.
Perusing the yard sales, even in the poorest neighborhoods, you will
find makeshift racks groaning under the weight of all the clothes the
sellers are trying to unload. We always have more clothing than we can
give away at our outreaches. It's a nice problem to have, I suppose, but
it makes you wonder who is buying all these clothes in the first place.

Check out any department store; the vast majority of floor space is
dedicated to selling clothes. It truly is overwhelming. We each have
only one body we need to dress every day; how many garments do we
really have to have? Most of us wear only 20 percent of our wardrobes.
(That's true even for me, and I have just 25 articles of clothing in my
closet at any given time.)

Clothing is one of the first areas in a budget that can be cut back
or cut out. Unless you have growing children, you don't need to buy
clothes that often. This includes professional people. We need to get
over our fear of people judging us if we don't wear a new outfit every
day. I have one dress I love that I've worn to every wedding and graduation for the last two years, and if anyone doesn't like it, too bad!

Try it. See how long you can go without buying anything new to
wear. Make a game out of it. I went a whole year and bought only a
pair of sandals to replace the ones I wore out. God has abundantly
kept his promise to clothe us. We abuse his provision when we go
overboard.

Do your closet and budget a favor and keep your wardrobe reasonable.

*Father, thank you for clothing me so generously. Help me to stay streamlined by not
going to excesses and being overly concerned about fashion. In Jesus' name I pray.
Amen.*

Corruption At City Hall

"Both hands are skilled in doing evil; the ruler demands gifts, the judge accepts bribes, the powerful dictate what they desire—they all conspire together." Micah 7:3

A society is in trouble when the people in authority—politicians, elected officials, government employees, and administrators of justice—use their positions to achieve their own ends and to satisfy their greed. Their integrity is for sale to the highest bidder, they devise schemes to control the people under them, and they make sure nothing can be accomplished without money passing beneath the table to them first.

Construction in major cities often will not get done without a hefty payoff to the official in charge of issuing building permits. In this way, city officials can be sure that it is their "friends" who are awarded the big bids. It happens more often than you think, in more ways than you can imagine, even in small communities. Small contractors don't stand a chance against a system like this. They are helpless in the face of such injustice. How do you fight city hall?

In our own small town in Wisconsin, we exposed a property tax scam when our home was overassessed. The town office deliberately mailed the bill late so it could not be disputed. The situation escalated until we involved the media and contacted the governor's office to learn what our rights were. Other homeowners began to check their tax bills and suspected they weren't correct, either. It blew the lid off a can of worms that ended in the tax assessor being fired and all the assessments being rescinded. The town never got away with inflating property values again.

Throughout the ordeal we could see God working for us, giving us favor with people who could help. Not every injustice will have such a happy ending, but someday God will make all things right. Corruption angers him. Ultimately, no one in power is going to get away with anything.

Even if we're shut out from the halls of privilege, God is on our side.

Father, help me to keep my eyes on you and not the corruption around me. I will wait on you in confidence and trust. In Jesus' name. Amen.

Scorning Simplicity

"And his servants came near and spoke to him, and said, 'My father, if the prophet had told you to do something great, would you not have done it? How much more then, when he says to you, "Wash, and be clean"?'" 2 Kings 5:13

The Syrian commander Naaman had been sent to Elisha to be healed of his leprosy. Elisha sent word that he should go and wash in the Jordan River seven times and he would be clean. Naaman was furious at these instructions; first, that Elisha didn't come out and wave his hands over him while calling on his God for healing, and second, that he felt the waters of the Jordan were inferior to the rivers of Aram. Fortunately for him he listened to his servants, obeyed the prophet's directions and received the restoration of his flesh.

We find this attitude in our financial counseling. Because we don't tell people to do some "great thing," they often scorn what we have to say, convinced that someone with a degree in finance would give them better, more sophisticated advice. "Spend less than you make," is too simple for their tastes. Writing down every penny they spend to see where the money is going is beneath them. "Get out of debt and stay out" is too archaic for twenty-first century consumers.

We have often joked that what people really want us to do is wave a magic wand over them that will cure their financial cancers, and all they have to do is sit there and receive their healing. Sorry, not even God will do that.

The truth is, the best advice is often the simplest. This is not calculus. You do not need an MBA to manage your money well. Common sense is what's needed, not fancy rhetoric.

If you do what the Bible tells you to do, simple as it may be, it will work. Don't go elsewhere searching for some phony hocus-pocus.

Father, help me get off my intellectual high horse and submit to the simplicity of the Scriptures. Thank you for making it available to all who have ears to hear. In Jesus' name. Amen.

Asceticism

"For everything God created is good, and nothing is to be rejected if it is received with thanksgiving, because it is consecrated by the word of God and prayer." 1 Timothy 4:4-5

The practice of asceticism arose in the early church out of the heresy of gnosticism. The gnostics taught that the spirit is good and the material world, including the human body, is evil. It was a dualism that led to two extremes—licentiousness, that whatever you did with your body was of no moral consequence, and asceticism, that because the body was evil, it must be treated harshly.

Ascetics believe that by denying themselves physical possessions and pleasures, they can avoid sin. Strict ascetics live lives deprived of all but the absolute basic necessities. Even in food they will eat only what is bland and tasteless. They shun money; they deny themselves every convenience. Many ascetics in church history would live on top of poles or in the desert, away from the temptations of the physical world. In extreme cases they abused their bodies by beating, cutting, or attaching worms to their flesh.

Yes, these were Christians. But is that what the Bible teaches? Jesus is our example. Was he an ascetic? The Pharisees accused him of being a glutton and a drunkard; hardly compatible with an ascetic's lifestyle! Jesus attended parties and feasts and enjoyed his Father's good creation. He lived simply but did not condemn people for having wealth unless their wealth had *them*.

Living in austerity doesn't make us holy. It can, in fact, lead us into pride. We can become self-righteous about our self-denial and begin to judge others based on outward appearances. We can learn from ascetics; their uncluttered lives are a breath of fresh air amid the stifling materialism of our culture, but asceticism isn't the answer.

Neither is materialism which we will look at tomorrow, and seek a balance between the two extremes. God wants us free from both.

Father, I know that poverty is not piety and I can't impress you by choosing it. Lead me in the right path. For Jesus' sake. Amen.

Materialism

"A man who has riches without understanding is like the beasts that perish." Psalm 49:20

Materialism is a doctrine. By definition, it is a belief system that places the highest value on the physical world and discounts the spiritual. Its adherents seek fulfillment and happiness in things, not God. It started not in the twentieth century but in the Garden of Eden with Adam and Eve. When they chose to disobey the Lord's command and eat from the forbidden tree, they declared by their actions that God was inadequate to meet all their needs. They believed Satan's lie.

He has been busy ever since, attempting to convince human beings that "things" will make us happy. We see this played out every day as people who already have everything go from store to store buying yet more items they believe will contribute to their sense of well-being. It obviously doesn't work or they wouldn't have to keep doing it.

Materialism doesn't work because God has created us to find contentment in him alone. When we look to anything other than Christ to give our lives meaning, we are trying to treat a virus with antibiotics. It's not only an exercise in futility, but it is self-destructive, weakening our spiritual lives by hardening our hearts to things of eternal value.

John D. Rockefeller said, "The poorest man I know is the man who has nothing but money." Without a relationship with God, our lives are no better than those of animals who live only for their physical needs.

As Christians, we walk a tightrope between asceticism and materialism. Satan doesn't care which side we fall off as long as we fall. Keeping our balance is difficult. But like the tightrope walker who keeps his eyes fixed on one set point, we fix our eyes on Christ.

He will keep us from tilting to either extreme.

Father, help me to keep my balance in an unbalanced world that seeks to pull me down. I want to love people and use things, not the other way around. In Jesus' name I pray. Amen.

Equipped to Comfort

"Praise be to the God and Father of our Lord Jesus Christ, the Father of compassion and the God of all comfort, who comforts us in all our troubles, so that we can comfort those in any trouble with the comfort we ourselves have received from God." 2 Corinthians 1:3-4

But you just don't understand." This is often the response of hurting people to words meant to help. When someone is suffering through the pain of losing their home to foreclosure, they don't want to hear hollow expressions of sympathy from a debt free friend. Who would be in a better position to offer true comfort? Someone who has been there, who has had similar experiences and lived to tell about it.

This is how God can take our hurts, our setbacks, and our trials and use them for good. I think of Mary Hunt, who owed $100,000 in consumer debt and was at the end of her rope when she cried out to God for help. Today she is founder and publisher of *Cheapskate Monthly*, a financial newsletter that encourages responsible spending, and she is debt free. As she likes to say, no matter how crazy you've been with money, she's got you beat. People can relate to her, and they listen to what she has to say because she has personally experienced what they're going through.

Dave Ramsey had it all—until he lost it. His riches to rags story launched his new career as a financial counselor with a successful radio show, as he helps others learn from his mistakes. He is proof that yes, you can recover from bankruptcy.

These people and others actually have an advantage over my husband and me as we have no financial horror stories to share. Truthfully, we wouldn't be the best counselors for some people. They need to hear it from someone who has been wounded as they are.

Who knows, perhaps a ministry will grow out of *your* financial woes. You preach best on what you struggle with most! There is purpose in pain.

Father, thank you that you never waste a hurt. Use my financial follies to bring help to others. Help me be transparent in admitting my mistakes. For Jesus' sake. Amen.

Predators

"In his arrogance the wicked man hunts down the weak, who are caught in the schemes he devises." Psalm 10:2

Our electronic age—that makes it so easy and convenient for us to handle our financial transactions—has also made it easier for crooks to snatch our money without us even realizing it. Identity theft is the fastest growing financial crime in this country. All someone needs is a credit card number or a social security number to gain access to your accounts. People are even having their homes stolen from them, as it's become possible to apply for huge home equity loans over the Internet. If a thief can get information on you, he can clean you out overnight.

It's not a new problem. In 1 Kings 21 we read of how wicked King Ahab conspired with his wife Jezebel and seized Naboth's vineyard. Greedy schemers have always been with us, and they still choose for their victims the weak and unsuspecting.

The elderly are a major target for con artists. Telephone callers talk them into spending money they don't have for worthless products. And they are told of bogus investment opportunities or prizes they've "won"—anything to separate them from their money.

Are there ways to protect ourselves? Absolutely:

- Common sense. If it sounds too good to be true, it is.
- Don't do business with people you don't know.
- Get a password or PIN on all your accounts.
- Shred your mail and financial documents.
- Don't leave outgoing mail in the mailbox.
- Take your name off mailing lists.
- Check your credit report once a year.
- Watch your wallet!

If, despite your best efforts, you still get taken, know your rights. Report all fraud. Even if you don't get your money back, you may help bring the bad guys to justice. The Lord can make up your loss. Give your anger and frustration to him.

Father, I pray for those who are victims of scams. Restore to them what's been lost and call the guilty to account. I ask in Jesus' name. Amen.

Choosing the Good Way

"This is what the Lord says: 'Stand at the crossroads and look; ask for the ancient paths, ask where the good way is, and walk in it, and you will find rest for your souls. But you said, "We will not walk in it."'"
Jeremiah 6:16

Anything described as "old-fashioned" is seldom meant in a positive light nowadays. Whether we're talking fashion, morality, traditions, or architecture, the old is scorned in favor of the modern (unless you collect antiques). Books have been published with such titles as *The New Rules of Money, Men, Women, and Money: New Roles, New Rules,* and *New Rules For Financial Success.* The idea is that the world we live in is so different from that of our parents' and grandparents' day, we have to change the way we handle our money. And of course the Bible, as old as it is, is totally irrelevant.

Is this true? Do we have to play by a new set of rules now that we're in the twenty-first century? Have the basic principles of finances changed so much that the Bible's counsel is out of date? The authors of these books would have us think so.

The majority of the "new rules" are based on current trends such as low interest rates. As I write this, the real estate craze has peaked and that bubble will soon burst, hurting a lot of people who climbed aboard that train. What we need are principles that are timeless, that will work in any economy. This is what God offers us.

Paul warned that the days were coming when people would not put up with sound doctrine, but "instead, to suit their own desires, they will gather around them a great number of teachers to say what their itching ears want to hear. They will turn their ears away from the truth and turn aside to myths" (2 Timothy 4:3-4).

Don't be taken in by something "new" that's clearly "wrong." Go back to the Bible; follow the path that has stood the test of time.

Father, I will walk the ancient paths because they are true and right and good. You promise rest for my soul when I do. Thank you for showing me the way. In Jesus' name. Amen.

Watch What You Say

"But I tell you that men will have to give account on the day of judgment for every careless word they have spoken. For by your words you will be acquitted, and by your words you will be condemned."
Matthew 12:36-37

When I was a new Christian, these verses really scared me. Every careless word? I was in real trouble! What Jesus is saying is that our words, especially those that slip out when we're not thinking, reveal our hearts.

The words we speak are powerful. However, we must not slide over into the belief that we can change our financial destinies simply by what we say. This is the core philosophy of the "name it and claim it" teachings of the faith movement. The roots of this doctrine are not in the Bible but in nineteenth century metaphysics.

The precept is that God has set up the universe to operate under certain spiritual principles which he will not violate, so if we follow the correct steps, we can get God to do what we want. It reduces faith to a formula.

In practice, this doctrine means always maintaining a positive confession. Even if you're broke or unemployed, you should put on a happy face and pronounce, "I am prospering as God blesses me." It is to live in denial of reality. Instead of building our faith, it actually erodes it, because God is not a puppet we can make dance to our tune. Psalm 115:3 declares, "Our God is in heaven; he does whatever pleases him." He is not obligated to respond to our positive affirmations.

We aren't to delude ourselves and say something is true when it blatantly is not; we are to have confidence that with God all things are possible. "I can get out of debt with God's help," is a statement of faith that doesn't deny our situation, yet believes the power of God to effect change.

Careless words can trip us up, but they are more honest than rigidly parroting phrases we neither feel nor mean.

Father, keep me from falling into "mind over matter" thinking that would lead me away from faith in you. Let my words always be aligned with truth. I ask in Jesus' name. Amen.

Materially Rich, Spiritually Impoverished

*"You say, 'I am rich; I have acquired wealth and do not need a thing.'
But you do not realize that you are wretched, pitiful, poor, blind, and
naked." Revelation 3:17*

Of the seven churches in Asia Minor singled out to be the recipients
of John's apocalyptic letter, the Laodicean church was the only
one to receive no commendation from Christ; only rebuke. Laodicea
was an extremely wealthy city, a banking center about forty miles east
of Ephesus. Because of their wealth, the Laodiceans assumed God had
blessed them; their focus was on prosperity as the criterion for success.
They failed to take into account their spiritual indifference—luke-
warmness—and their compromising with the world. In reality, Christ
had no part in them. In graphic language, he tells them he will vomit
them out of his mouth (Revelation 3:16). That was how nauseating
their halfhearted efforts were to him.

A church is in trouble when it forgets that the purpose of its existence is to proclaim the message of Christ's sacrifice for the forgiveness
of sins. When they adopt a "country club" attitude, when acquiring
more land and bigger buildings and more opulent surroundings
become more important than lost souls, they can expect God to discipline them.

Christ's remedy for such a church is for them to assess their true
condition, to wake up to their spiritual need. He urges them to buy
gold from him that has been tried in the fire; in other words, to test
their faith through trials. He offers them white garments—symbolizing
his righteousness—to cover their spiritual nakedness. Finally he tells
them to anoint their eyes with salve to heal their spiritual blindness.

What's true for churches is true for individuals. Are we self-satis-
fied in our material well-being to the point of being apathetic towards
spiritual things? Has our fervency for the Lord cooled off in our pursuit of the good life? If so, we need to change direction and seek
Christ's riches, or we are in danger of him spitting us out in disgust.

*Father, I want my love for you to be hot and zealous. Remove anything from my life
that would be a hindrance to my walk with Christ. For his sake. Amen.*

Baalism

"How long will this continue in the hearts of these lying prophets, who prophesy the delusions of their own minds? They think the dreams they tell one another will make my people forget my name, just as their fathers forgot my name through Baal worship." Jeremiah 23:26-27

Who was Baal? Why were the Israelites continually throughout their history turning away from God to worship this idol? What was the attraction anyway?

The first mention of this false deity is in Numbers 22:41, when Balak took Balaam up to the high places of Baal in his efforts to get him to curse the people. Baal was the prime god of the Canaanites. His followers believed that a blessing from him guaranteed their prosperity. His name literally means "owner," or "master." Worship rituals included self-mutilation, ritual prostitution, and infant sacrifice.

Although the Lord demonstrated to his people time and time again that he was the only true God, Baalism persisted. It appealed to the flesh through its sensual nature, holding out to people an easy and enjoyable path to prosperity, in contrast to God's way of obedience to ethical and moral standards.

We may believe that we are too enlightened to fall for worshipping a false god, yet our actions may say otherwise. Have you ever considered that every time you deliberately choose to sin to please your flesh, you are indulging in a Baal spirit? How far are you willing to compromise your Christianity to ensure your prosperity?

Even though we may not call it by name, the Baal spirit is alive and well in our day. Compromised Christians are the norm now, as they have so adopted the worldview in how they live, they are indistinguishable from their unbelieving neighbors. This is exactly what happened to Israel. They were so absorbed into the pagan Canaanite culture that their God became just another one of many gods.

The same could be said of our generation.

Father, show me anywhere I am compromising my convictions and giving place to the spirit of Baal. You are my only God and I will look to nothing else. In Jesus' powerful name. Amen.

Fleecing the Flock

"This is what the Sovereign LORD says: Woe to the shepherds of Israel who only take care of themselves! Should not shepherds take care of the flock? You eat the curds, clothe yourselves with the wool and slaughter the choice animals, but you do not take care of the flock." Ezekiel 34:2-3

The shepherds of Israel" refer to the priests and spiritual leaders God had appointed to serve his people. They had the solemn and sacred responsibility of feeding the sheep in their care with God's truth, to minister to those who were weak or sick, and to bring into the fold those who were wandering and lost. Sheep *need* a shepherd. They are the most defenseless of animals, unable to find good pasture on their own, and with no one looking after them they wander off in every direction, easy prey for predators.

It's not difficult to see how this applies to a spiritual congregation of people. Israel's shepherds were self-serving; they were using the sheep for their own personal gain. They took their milk and their wool but were not providing protection and love.

Spiritual shepherds are neglecting their sheep today in pursuit of their own selfish ambitions. They take the money offered to the Lord and use it to fund their lavish lifestyles or they involve their flocks in projects that exalt their egos. We saw this in the 1980s when prominent Christians were building resorts and recreation centers. They went before their trusting people and demanded that they give because "God told me to build." They devoted all their time and energy to these projects, while the overburdened sheep, their spiritual needs going unmet, began to fall away from the faith.

We partake in this travesty when we send money to projects that have nothing to do with repentance and revival. If we had discernment and quit supporting shepherds who squander God's resources, they could not build their palaces.

Find a flock where you will be fed, not fleeced.

Father, give us holy shepherds who care more about your sheep than they do about brick and stone. Raise up those who will tend their flocks with love. For Jesus' sake. Amen.

Giving Thanks

"Enter his gates with thanksgiving and his courts with praise; give thanks to him and praise his name." Psalm 100:4

The American Thanksgiving holiday has come a long way from the days of the Pilgrims. For them, a day of giving thanks had more to do with fasting and prayer than feasting. The first national Thanksgiving Day was proclaimed by George Washington in 1789 to acknowledge the favors of the Almighty on the newly independent country.

A day of thanksgiving was celebrated erratically for the next seventy-five years until 1863, when Abraham Lincoln established the last Thursday in November as a national holiday.

Our modern Thanksgiving places so much emphasis on the food that we thank the one who provided it almost as an afterthought. We are so busy with our preparations in the kitchen, we have no time to kneel in worship and truly offer him a sacrifice of praise.

When our kids were in grade school, we started a tradition that each person had to write down five things they were thankful for and share it before our meal. I expected them to list things like "our dog Lisa" but was gratified when they put Jesus at the top as number one.

We have so many material blessings that they often get in the way of our relationship with the Lord. Maybe this year we can follow the example of our earliest countrymen and set aside Thanksgiving to fast and pray, then we would have a true appreciation for our food. Or we could do it the day after, while the rest of the country goes to the malls.

Whether you're all alone or have a household of family and friends with you this year, make sure you take the time to "enter his gates with thanksgiving and his courts with praise."

Father, I bow down in humble thanks to you. You have blessed me bountifully and I will offer you the fruit of my lips—a sacrifice of praise. In the name of Jesus I pray. Amen.

It's All About the Money

"Hear this, you who trample the needy and do away with the poor of the land, saying, 'When will the New Moon be over that we may sell grain, and the sabbath be ended that we may market wheat?'" Amos 8:4-5

Amos prophesied during a period of great prosperity in the nation of Israel. The times were also marked by immorality, idolatry, extravagant living, and corruption. Pretty much the same as our day!

We have "progressed" past Israel in that we don't cease commerce on the Sabbath or for official religious festivals as they did. Not that they were happy about it; their impatience to get back to business is indicated in Amos' indictment.

There were once "blue laws" in the United States that required businesses to be closed in observation of the Sabbath. Now Sunday is the biggest shopping day of the week, and the weekend following Thanksgiving is the busiest of the year. Retailers vie with one another as to who can get their doors open first on the Friday following the holiday. Six A.M. sales are common now. Some stores stay open until midnight; others simply never close—24/7 right through Christmas Eve.

The television newscasts are full of reports of how it's going in Consumerland; predictions of a "bad" Christmas with sales down from last year are supposed to motivate us to get out there and do our part to boost the economy. It's no joke; a single season of poor sales has sent many a store under. Don't feel guilty. It's not your fault they can't manage their debt.

In recent years there's been a backlash to all this. The International Buy Nothing Day targets the Friday after Thanksgiving as a moratorium on shopping. "Participate by not participating" is their motto. People wait until Saturday to shop, I guess.

Holidays have been reduced to how much money gets pumped into the retailer's coffers. We're addicted to economic growth at the expense of our savings, our souls, and our sanity. At what point will we decide enough is enough?

The Lord may step in and decide for us.

Father, forgive us for our indifference to spiritual things as we rush about this time of year. Gather our hearts back to you, for Jesus' sake. Amen.

Giving Away Your Best

"I have seen a grievous evil under the sun: wealth hoarded to the harm of its owner." Ecclesiastes 5:13

We either have possessions, or our possessions have us. How to tell the difference? Here's a very simple test: What is your favorite article of clothing? How would you feel about giving it away? Not selling it, but giving it to someone who could really use it. Does your gut wrench at the thought? Most of us, if we're honest, are very attached to our things. Our inborn greedy nature is loathe to give up anything voluntarily.

This is why it is so important that we develop the habit of giving things away. I'm not talking about getting rid of your old clothes when you clean out your closet; you'll do that anyway. That doesn't do a thing for your old nature. No, we need to give away items that really mean something to us, something that can't be replaced.

This is incredibly difficult, I know. It also reveals how deceitful and wicked our hearts really are. But this is all the more reason if you find yourself becoming attached to something to consider giving it away. We should reject anything that produces an addiction in us.

I admit I have a long way to go in this area. It doesn't come naturally for any of us. We need to *work* at making giving like this a regular habit, until it becomes part of our spiritual legacy. A man meeting Billy Graham commented on how much he liked his tie, and Mr. Graham took it off and gave it to him. Beautiful generosity.

God is our model. Two thousand years ago, he didn't buy us a present, he gave us a gift. He came down the staircase of heaven with a baby in his arms—his only Son. He gave his very best, an irreplaceable treasure. Can we not find it in our hearts to give up the world's trinkets for spiritual riches?

Father, thank you for your great generosity. Give me the strength to give up anything that has too tight a grip on my heart. I ask in the name of Christ Jesus. Amen.

The Priority of God's House

"Then the word of the Lord came through the prophet Haggai: 'Is it a time for you yourselves to be living in your paneled houses, while this house remains a ruin?'" Haggai 1:3-4

The Jews who returned from Babylon to Jerusalem were struggling with their poverty. For eighteen years they had labored trying to turn the wasteland Judah had become during their exile into a thriving community again, but they seemed to be getting nowhere. God sent Haggai to reveal why they were having such difficulty.

They had turned away from putting God first. The excitement of coming back to their homeland, of laying the foundation for the temple, had given way to the pressures of just trying to survive. The temple work was abandoned. Instead of making God their highest priority, they were putting their needs ahead of his interests.

Had setting God aside helped them get ahead? Haggai pointed out the results: The land was cursed with a drought; there was famine, inflation, and futility in everything they attempted. They forgot that prosperity was possible only by God's blessing. In ignoring him, they lost the one resource that was essential to their success.

In response to Haggai's message, the people set to work on the temple again. God's next words to them were of encouragement: "I am with you" (Haggai 1:13). They stayed on task until the temple was completed, and judgment was lifted.

God wants to bless us, but we have to obey him first. We cannot shamefully neglect him and his house without incurring his discipline against our house. This means our money is to go to his temple treasury before we redecorate or remodel. It is to go to missions before we invest in that backyard barbeque.

If we will just take care of God's business, he will take care of our business.

Father, I acknowledge that I can't succeed if I don't look to you and your interests first. I will make you my top priority. Thank you for my many undeserved blessings. In Jesus' name. Amen.

Unlimited Resources

"'The silver is mine and the gold is mine,' declares the Lᴏʀᴅ Almighty. 'The glory of this present house will be greater than the glory of the former house,' says the Lᴏʀᴅ Almighty. 'And in this place I will grant peace,' declares the Lᴏʀᴅ Almighty." Haggai 2:8-9

The post-exilic Jewish community had fallen on hard times. Their disobedience to God's command to rebuild the temple had resulted in a tough economy. It was into these less-than-ideal conditions that the Lord spoke to them, telling them they had neglected his house long enough.

Given Israel's checkered history, a truly amazing thing then happened. The people obeyed! Three weeks after Haggai spoke, they began work on the temple. Despite their poverty and depleted resources, they turned willing hearts and hands to what must have been a daunting project. They had to go to great lengths to acquire the materials they needed for construction and they also faced opposition from the surrounding Persian governors.

There's no hint that these Jews ever asked the question, "Where will the money to do this come from?" Not knowing the answer did not deter them. They seemed to understand that it was their responsibility to work, and it was God's responsibility to provide.

The resources came from an unlikely place. Judah's enemies had written to Darius, the Persian king, challenging the Jews' right to rebuild the temple. Their plan to stop the work backfired when Darius did indeed find Cyrus' decree that the house of God be repaired. Darius responded with a decree of his own: All the expenses for the work were to be paid out of the royal treasury.

Talk about a financial bonanza! The wealth of the mightiest empire on earth was at their disposal. God is not limited by our lack of funds. When he tells us to do something, we are to say yes before we see how. Once we commit to doing God's will, his supply will always follow.

Father, give me the faith to step out and do your will even when I don't know how it will be funded. I trust you to provide whatever is needed to do the work. In Jesus' name I pray. Amen.

Laying Aside Our Rights

"Was it a sin for me to lower myself in order to elevate you by preaching the gospel of God to you free of charge? I robbed other churches by receiving support from them so as to serve you. And when I was with you and needed something, I was not a burden to anyone, for the brothers who came from Macedonia supplied what I needed. I have kept myself from being a burden to you in any way, and will continue to do so." 2 Corinthians 11:7-9

The apostle Paul's ministry was exceptional in many ways. He was personally commissioned by Christ to carry the gospel all over Asia Minor. He performed miracles; he possessed supernatural revelation and discernment. If anyone had the right to demand financial support from those he was serving, Paul certainly did. He chose not to in the case of the Corinthians.

He did not exercise this right because of his love for them and the need to demonstrate the integrity of his ministry. The church there was plagued by division; false teachers were accusing Paul of not really being an apostle. They cited his refusal to accept payment for his preaching as proof that it was worth nothing.

Paul obviously was a huge target for Satan, who was constantly trying to discredit his apostleship. Money is an area where all of us are vulnerable; it would have been easy for Paul to take advantage of those among whom he was ministering. But to prove his ministry was sincere and genuine, he paid his own way and earned his living whenever necessary. He accepted freely given support from other established churches, but to the Corinthians—to whom he would have to defend his character—it was important that he exhibit selfless servanthood. Had he accepted money from them, it would have been more difficult for him to counter his critics.

Sometimes we need to lay down our right to receive financial support to serve a greater purpose. There are other compensations besides money when we are working for the Lord.

Father, purify my motives for ministry. If I get paid to speak, give me discernment to know when I should refuse payment. Let me hear you clearly on this matter. In Jesus' name I ask. Amen.

A Helping Hand, Not a Handout

"When you are harvesting in your field and you overlook a sheaf, do not go back to get it. Leave it for the alien, the fatherless and the widow; so that the LORD your God may bless you in all the work of your hands. When you beat the olives from your trees, do not go over the branches a second time. . . When you harvest the grapes in your vineyard, do not go over the vines again. . . Remember that you were slaves in Egypt. That is why I command you to do this." Deuteronomy 24:19-21

In all aspects of their harvest, the Israelites were commanded to leave behind food for the poor. Notice that they were expected to go and gather the sheaves, the olives, and the grapes for themselves. God didn't ask the landowners to set up a soup kitchen so the needy could come and stand in line for a handout. He was concerned about maintaining their dignity. Working even in some small way for our substance helps us feel productive and less like a victim.

The biblical way of expressing concern for the poor is by giving them a helping hand, not a handout. Most truly want to work, but they have little or no job training and limited education. Low wage jobs do not cover necessary living expenses.

The non-profit organization Habitat for Humanity has the goal of moving families out of poverty by helping to provide them with a decent place to live. But this is no handout; recipients are expected to put in 500 hours of "sweat equity" in building their homes. They are also required to attend classes on home maintenance and finances. When their home is complete they are given a 0 percent mortgage and must keep up the payments.

If your response is, "No one's giving *me* a 0 percent loan," ask yourself if you'd like to trade places with them. Just as God expected the Hebrews to show compassion for those who were economically disadvantaged, he expects us to also.

Father, soften my heart to care about the poor. Prosper all the organizations dedicated to giving them a helping hand. I ask in Christ's name. Amen.

'Tis the Season to Spend

"If you spend yourselves in behalf of the hungry and satisfy the needs of the oppressed, then your light will rise in the darkness, and your night will become like the noonday." Isaiah 58:10

The store decorations have already been up for weeks as retailers try to get us in the mood to shop. And boy, do we shop—for gifts, for food, for all the cards and wrapping paper, clothing…the lists are endless.

The Christmas season is the most difficult time of year for a lot of folks. They can't cope with the demands on their time, the demands on their wallets, and the pressure to produce a "good" Christmas for their loved ones.

It should be obvious why. Materialism has taken priority over the Messiah. Nowhere in Scripture are we told to celebrate Christ's birth. The holiday originated with the emperor Constantine in 300 A.D. When he converted to Christianity, he made it the religion of the state, but he didn't know what to do with the pagan celebrations. As a solution, he declared two major religious holidays to correspond with the old festivals. December 25 (Saturnalia, the birthday of the sun) would be celebrated as Christ's birthday (although he was most likely born in October) and his resurrection would be celebrated in the spring, to replace worship of the goddess of fertility.

With origins like that, is it any wonder we struggle with the "true meaning" of Christmas? I do know that if we are searching for meaning, we will not find it in the malls. We will find it by doing what Isaiah tells us—to spend *ourselves* in the work of meeting people's needs.

Instead of buying a bunch of stuff, use your money to spread the gospel. Take your kids to a nursing home and let them spread some joy to the residents there. Volunteer at a homeless shelter. Give this Christmas—of yourself.

Father, forgive us. We have so much and do so little. Show me how I can serve the people that you want to reach. I ask in Christ's name. Amen.

Riches in Christ

"Praise be to the God and Father of our Lord Jesus Christ, who has blessed us in the heavenly realms with every spiritual blessing in Christ." Ephesians 1:3

On those days when we're feeling poor in the goods of the world, it's beneficial to review the abundant riches we have in Christ that can never be lost, never be stolen, and never perish. Ephesians 1 and 2 lists some of these treasures:

- Chosen in him to be holy and blameless (1:4)
- Predestined to be adopted as sons and daughters (1:5)
- Freely given his glorious grace (1:6)
- Redemption through his blood for the forgiveness of sins (1:7)
- Lavished with all wisdom and understanding (1:8)
- Made known to us the mystery of his will (1:9)
- Marked by a seal with the Holy Spirit (1:13)
- Given a guaranteed inheritance (1:14)
- Power that raised Christ from the dead residing in us (1:19-20)
- Made alive with Christ and seated with him in the heavenly realms (2:6)
- Created in him to do good works that were prepared in advance for us to do (2:10)
- Brought near to God by his blood (2:13)
- He is our peace (2:14)
- Reconciled us to God through the cross (2:16)
- Given access to the Father by the Spirit (2:18)
- Made citizens of God's people and members of his household (2:19)
- Made a holy temple in the Lord, dwelt in by his Spirit (2:21-22)

"In Christ," we have all this and more. We should never feel poor when we possess Jesus. If we do, we don't understand our position as God's heirs. Open the eyes of your heart to the riches that are yours!

Father, I am overwhelmed by all you have given me through Jesus. Thank you that these riches are mine for eternity. In his wonderful name. Amen.

Restoring the Years

*"I will repay you for the years the locusts have eaten—the great locust
and the young locust, the other locusts and the locust swarm—my
great army that I sent among you." Joel 2:25*

Are you experiencing discouragement thinking of all the money
you've wasted over the years? Have the locusts of debt, impulsivity,
self-indulgence, and outright stupidity eaten away your finances to the
point where your future looks bleak? Do you want to kick yourself over
all the mistakes and bad decisions you've made in the past?

The locust plague God sent against Israel was in punishment for
their sin. It was meant to be a wake-up call, to move the people's hearts
to repentance. Our financial follies can be the result of either our own
disobedience to God's principles or just plain foolishness. Whatever the
reason, whatever effects we're living with today because of these follies,
God is willing to restore us.

When we confess our sin, God is quick to forgive our past and give
us hope for the future. The years of blight can be redeemed. In truth,
nothing is ever wasted with God. We learn more from our failures than
from our successes. Painful experiences teach us in no other way the
lessons the Lord would have us learn, and if we lose money in the
process, so what? It's only money to God.

I know from my own experience that it's difficult not to always be
looking back with regret at dumb purchases and wishing I could have
my money back. I've had to accept that I can't undo the past, resolve
not to make the same mistakes again, and move on. But now I understand my weaknesses; that's some of the fruit God has grown through
my losses.

God will bring good out of your situation. Your finances may still
bear the scars of your fiscal disasters, but you can look ahead with confidence to a new harvest. We can't make up our squandered stewardship to God, but he will make it up to us.

*Father, I'm so sorry over all you've given me that I've lost. Thank you that you
promise to put me right back on schedule. I pray in Jesus' name. Amen.*

The Mark of the Beast

"He also forced everyone, small and great, rich and poor, free and slave, to receive a mark on his right hand or his forehead, so that no one could buy or sell unless he had the mark, which is the name of the beast or the number of his name." Revelation 13:16-17

For decades, much hysteria has existed in the Christian community over this matter of "the mark of the beast." During the Tribulation period, the Antichrist will compel everyone to be marked with a distinguishing number identifying them as a beast-worshipper. Those who do not bear this mark will be cut off from economic survival. It is a frightening scenario. What is even more terrifying for some is that the technology is in place to do this very thing right now.

As the world moves towards a cashless society, it makes sense that each person would have one account number set up to handle all their money transactions. The problem with cards is that they can be lost or stolen. For this reason, one solution being talked about is for this number to be tattooed on an individual's hand.

Is this something Christians need to worry about? Think of this: If you belong to Christ, you already bear his mark on your forehead! The mark of the beast is Satan's counterfeit to God's seal on his servants (Revelation 9:4). Is God going to allow the devil to replace his mark with one of his own? I think not!

Believers need not fear experiencing financial boycott during the reign of the Antichrist. I personally believe Jesus will not leave his bride on earth to suffer his wrath towards those who have rejected him. This is not to say we will be spared hard times or persecution. The church in America is soft from prosperity, and we need to be taken into the wilderness with God to learn dependence on him just as the Hebrews did.

All we need to know is that God has promised that he will never leave us or forsake us.

Father, thank you that I am sealed as your child. Give me an unshakeable confidence in your power to sustain me at all times. In Jesus' name I pray. Amen.

Taking Pledges

"Do not take a pair of millstones—not even the upper one—as security for debt, because that would be taking a man's livelihood as security." Deuteronomy 24:6

A "pledge" was a token given to a lender. We call it "collateral" today, and it is requested in instances when the creditor is dubious about taking on an unsecured debt and wants additional assurance that he will be paid back. In Moses' day, only the truly needy would resort to having to borrow, and God gave detailed regulations as to how these transactions were to be handled so the debtor would not be taken advantage of.

It was common for a lender to hold something owned by the borrower as security for a loan; however, the item could not be anything that would interfere with the debtor's ability to care for his family or limit his ability to earn a living. Millstones were used every day to grind the grain for making bread; therefore, they could not be taken in pledge. If all a man had to offer as a pledge was his cloak, he was the poorest of the poor and the creditor was required to return it to him before sunset. Basic human rights were always to come before business.

The principle of not depriving someone of the necessities of daily life carries over into our modern laws. In Arizona we have the Homestead Act, which protects the first $100,000 of equity in a home. Not even the IRS can touch it. Bankruptcy laws often exempt the family house and car so people are not in danger of being thrown out onto the streets and so they have transportation.

God is concerned about the welfare of each individual. Everyone has the right to the resources they need. Those rights are not to be violated by creditors or by society in general. When we place limits on the opportunities of the weakest members, we are taking away their "upper millstone."

Let's develop our sensitivity towards "the least of these" so that nothing would be done to hinder their ability to prosper.

Father, thank you that you are concerned over the smallest details in our business transactions. Thank you for laws that protect us. I pray in Jesus' name. Amen.

December 6

People Pressure

"When Pilate saw that he was getting nowhere, but that instead an uproar was starting, he took water and washed his hands in front of the crowd. 'I am innocent of this man's blood,' he said. 'It is your responsibility!'" Matthew 27:24

Pontius Pilate's condemning of an innocent man to death, despite his conviction of the wrongness of the act, stands as an extreme example of what can happen when we fear people above our own beliefs. Pilate did everything he could think of to get Jesus released, but he finally knuckled under and gave the order. He tried to clear his guilty conscience by placing the blame on the people. He couldn't, of course. As governor, only he had the authority to make that decision.

So it is with us. The desire for approval from others makes us do things we don't want to do. How are you doing on your Christmas shopping? Are you spending money you don't have because of family expectations? Is the media influencing your decisions, as they make it sound as if everyone is buying a flat-screen TV for the holidays this year?

People pressure bears down on us all to a certain degree in our finances. Why do so many people spend more than they should to live at a level of affluence they're not even comfortable with? Doctors feel they must reside in a large home in a prestigious area among their peers, convinced that their patients would not feel confident in their abilities as a physician if they lived in a blue-collar neighborhood.

We are in full control of our spending habits. The decisions we make with money are our responsibility. We need courage to stand up for what we believe is right for us. God is the only audience we should seek to please. He won't accept excuses that our behavior is someone else's fault.

Pilate only *thought* he was off the hook. People pressure leads to compromised convictions.

Father, give me the honesty and humility to admit "that's more than I want to spend." Help me not be pressured by the expectations of others. I pray in Jesus' name. Amen.

Guest Lists

*"Then Jesus said to his host, 'When you give a luncheon or dinner, do
not invite your friends, your brothers or relatives, or your rich neighbors;
if you do, they may invite you back and so you will be repaid. But
when you give a banquet, invite the poor, the crippled, the lame, the
blind, and you will be blessed. Although they cannot repay you, you
will be repaid at the resurrection of the righteous.'" Luke 14:12*

This is one of my favorite weeks of the year. This is the week we
pack up our gas grill, 500 hot dogs with fixings, chips, and soda
and head to downtown Phoenix where we have a cookout for the people living on the streets.

This outreach grew out of our original "Covering the Homeless"
ministry in which we would take blankets and clothing to distribute to
those in need, but we wanted to do more. Our small group decided to
use what was left in our benevolence fund to purchase what food we
could and God truly multiplied that small amount. We fed 200 people
that year in the parking lot of the American Legion Hall, and the
response was truly gratifying.

"Man, I can't remember the last time I ate anything off a grill," one
man exclaimed as he wolfed down his second dog. Everyone loved it. It
occurred to me that these people live in the shadow of Bank One
Ballpark, smell the hot dogs and nachos, but never get to partake in
any of it. Such a small thing, yet it is so appreciated. "God bless you!"
we hear over and over again. We go to bless them, but we leave as the
ones who are truly blessed.

Now three small groups help with our December "banquet" and it
keeps getting bigger as we've added a worship band. People now
receive prayer, food, clothing, and hygiene kits. I know it blesses the
Father's heart. Is there a party you could throw for his uninvited ones
this season?

*Father, you desire that those who are well fed and clothed share with those who are
not. That is true hospitality. Give me Jesus' concern for the poor. I pray in his name.
Amen.*

Lovers of Gold

"If I have put my trust in gold or said to pure gold, 'You are my secu-rity,' if I have rejoiced over my great wealth, the fortune my hands had gained than these also would be sins to be judged, for I would have been unfaithful to God on high." Job 31:24,28

In his anguish of trying to understand why all his misfortunes had happened to him, Job defends himself to his friends by stating the sins of which he was not guilty. He asserts that despite his great wealth, his trust had always been in God alone. He recognized that to look to gold as his confidence would be spiritual adultery—reprehensible to the Lord, and worthy of his being punished.

Job was innocent, but as we have seen, one of the great dangers of wealth is that it seduces us into believing that as long as we have it, we are safe and protected. At that point, we have crossed the line and have begun to accept money as deity. Money worship taken to an extreme produces misers—people who love money for its own sake.

Misers start out as frugal people; they are savers with simple tastes. Somewhere along the line, the more money they save, the more it gets a grip on them, until they're stockpiling money just to have it. They hate parting with it. They stop heating and cooling their homes to avoid utility bills. They don't replace their clothes and go around in rags. They become too cheap to even buy enough food for themselves. By now they are recluses, shut off from people out of distrust that everyone is after their money. They die early and alone.

Satan will use money to get a foothold in our lives because he knows if it wedges itself deep enough into our hearts, it will destroy us. It is why we can never let down our guard.

Love of money, allowed to run unchecked, results in *"many griefs"* (1 Timothy 6:10).

"Miser" is only one letter short of "misery."

Father, guard me against putting my hope in money. Only you can meet my needs and are worthy of worship. In the name of Christ Jesus I pray. Amen.

Tax Rebels

"The weight of the gold that Solomon received yearly was 666 talents, not including the revenue brought in by merchants and traders. Also all the kings of Arabia and the governors of the land brought gold and silver to Solomon." 2 Chronicles 9:13

If you ever wondered where all Solomon's extreme wealth came from, here is part of your answer: taxes. His annual income in gold amounted to 25 tons through taxes alone. The tax burden Solomon laid on the people of Israel was so heavy that after his death they hoped to get some relief by appealing to his son.

Rehoboam came to the throne with a golden opportunity to win the hearts of the nation by lightening the load; instead, he threatened to increase the yoke his father had put on them. His despotism resulted in the division of the kingdom.

Rebellion has been the standard response throughout history of unreasonable taxation. The first British attempt to tax Americans directly—the Stamp Act of 1765—was the spark that ultimately ignited the Revolutionary War. The Boston Tea Party symbolized the rowdy reaction the colonists demonstrated to their monarch over their tax situation.

Governments still try to control people and their behavior through taxes. Do you remember the short-lived luxury tax which taxed yachts, jewelry, furs, and expensive cars? Angry consumers made their displeasure felt by boycotting the affected goods, and the manufacturers and dealers felt the pain. The tax was quickly repealed.

What about the "vice" taxes? Committed smokers get around that by buying their cartons online and out of state. It would seem that when taxes are involved, where there's a will, there's a way. It's difficult, if not impossible, to legislate morality.

Consumer behavior will change when people's hearts change. Social economists believe taxation by government will fix our spending habits. History teaches otherwise.

Father, give our leaders wisdom in managing the economy and passing tax laws. May they favor your principles and not promote immorality or rebellion. I ask in Jesus' name. Amen.

Meaningless Toil

"I hated all the things I had toiled for under the sun, because I must leave them to the one who comes after me. And who knows whether he will be a wise man or a fool? Yet he will have control over all the work into which I have poured my effort and skill under the sun. This too is meaningless. So my heart began to despair over all my toils and labor under the sun. For a man may do his work with wisdom, knowledge, and skill, and then he must leave all he owns to someone who has not worked for it. This too is meaningless and a great misfortune."
Ecclesiastes 2:18-21

Why are you working? Who are you working for? Your answers to these questions will determine whether you end up depressed like Solomon at the end of your life or joyful like the apostle Paul. If we work hard at building our personal kingdoms and leave God out of it, sooner or later we will arrive at the same conclusion: It's all a big waste of time.

The problem is one of perspective. We were made for eternity, so the things we look to for purpose and satisfaction—work, leaving a legacy, material possessions—cannot bring us fulfillment on a permanent basis. These all belong to the limited world of time; they are finite. To find happiness and meaning, we have to look to the infinite. We have to look beyond the mundane routine of our existence and find God in the middle of it. True pleasure is available only when we acknowledge God in our activities.

Lift up your eyes. Your life is more than work and toil that eventually death will separate you from. It really doesn't matter what happens to your earthly estate after you're gone. What matters is that God is glorified in all you do.

Eternity *will* be worth it all.

Father, enjoyment in life is impossible without you. Only in you can meaning be found. Help me to live out my days with you at the center. I ask in Jesus' name. Amen.

Using Godliness for Gain

"If anyone teaches false doctrine and does not agree to the sound instruction of our Lord Jesus Christ and to godly teaching, he is conceited and understands nothing. He has an unhealthy interest in controversies and quarrels about words that result in envy, strife, malicious talk, evil suspicions and constant friction between men of corrupt mind, who have been robbed of the truth and who think godliness is a means to financial gain." 1 Timothy 6:3-5

In the first century it was the accepted practice of traveling philosophers and religious teachers to demand payment for their instruction. An unwritten rule stated a teacher should receive compensation in proportion to the worth of his performance. Given the system they were operating under, whoever was the most charismatic, professional, and eloquent stood to be the most financially successful.

What nearly every false prophet or preacher in the Bible has in common is a love for money. Seeing religion as a means to make a profit, they were not concerned with truth or correct doctrine. They presented their rhetoric in a way designed to impress their gullible audiences, they used controversy to stir up the people (controversy sells!), and they loved to argue.

There are other, more subtle ways to use the pulpit as a paycheck. Some "career ministers" are pastors *only* because their father was, and his father before him, and they see the position as being a comfortable, secure occupation. They have not developed their own faith, but are going through the motions to earn a nice living. I had the experience of worshipping with a small, struggling congregation where only the for-profit preschool they operated was keeping the mortgage paid. Even though the church was going under, the pastor coolly gave himself a raise.

Even if we're not the clergy we can be guilty of using the church for our own personal gain.

Father, purify your house! Remove those who commit spiritual adultery while employed in your service, and lead them to repentance. I ask in Jesus' name. Amen.

The Father's House as a Marketplace

"In the temple courts he found men selling cattle, sheep, and doves,
and others sitting at tables exchanging money. So he made a whip of
cords, and drove all from the temple area, both sheep and cattle; he
scattered the coins of the money changers and overturned their tables.
To those who sold doves he said, 'Get these out of here! How dare you
turn my Father's house into a market!'" John 2:14-16

What does the Lord's house mean to us? Is it a place where we worship, give, serve, hear the word preached, and fellowship with other Christians? Or do we have another agenda in mind when we attend?

There are those who go to church not to give money but to make money. Their thoughts are on how many business contacts they can cultivate on Sunday mornings. They view the saints as potential clients for their practices or buyers for their products.

Purveyors of multilevel marketing or pyramid schemes teach their recruits that churches are a good source of prospective customers for their new business. It is common for someone to visit a church, take a directory, and call their way through it in an attempt to offer what they're selling. What's worse is the pretense involved, the insincere efforts at friendship before "moving in for the kill." If it's ever happened to you, you know how it feels to be manipulated and the loss of trust that occurs.

We make God's house into a marketplace when we use his people to further our careers or to benefit ourselves. Do you attend that small group because there are people with skills you hope to avail yourself of for free? Do you have a what-can-they-do-for-me attitude? How would you rate your motives?

The church has a high and holy calling. How dare we substitute sharing the gospel for some money-making opportunity. May we never use Christianity as a platform for our personal prosperity.

Jesus will pick up his whip and drive us out.

Father, take away all the money changers in your house. Do not allow your bride to be exploited by those out for profit. I ask in Jesus' name. Amen.

Simplicity or Selfishness?

"He who has been stealing must steal no longer, but must work, doing something useful with his own hands, that he may have something to share with those in need." Ephesians 4:28

Paul is telling us here that it is not enough to cease sinning; we must now turn around and do good. Instead of taking what belongs to someone else, Christians should earn enough to share some of their earnings with the needy. It is assumed that there will be excess to give and that generosity will be practiced.

The downshifting trend that began to catch on in the 1990s defined the simple life as working just enough to meet your needs. Adherents are urged to find fulfillment in having fewer possessions and to transform their relationships with work and money. It sounds very noble, this pursuit of a more deliberate lifestyle.

A closer look will reveal the inherent selfishness involved in this philosophy. If we earn only enough to care for ourselves and our own families, where is there any room for giving? Isn't it complete self-absorption to look only at *my* needs? Who is supposed to care for the poor and fund missions, if all the Christians are living hand to mouth by choice?

We can still live simply. Our problem is that we believe a six-figure income goes with a six-figure standard of living. It doesn't occur to us that we can earn a huge salary and live on just a portion of it, using the excess to fund the kingdom. John Wesley, in the 1700s, decided he would live on £28 a year, enough to cover his expenses. Everything above that he gave away. One year he earned £1400 and still only kept £30 of it. We, too, could set a cap on our lifestyles and give away our earnings beyond that. It is in line with what the Bible teaches. It sounds radical only because it's not popular.

With increased income, it should be our standard of giving that goes up, not our standard of living.

Father, you have blessed me with so much wealth. Change my heart so that I give according to my ability. In Jesus' name I pray. Amen.

Our True Home

"In my Father's house are many rooms; if it were not so, I would have told you. And if I go and prepare a place for you, I will come back and take you to be with me that you also may be where I am." John 14:2-3

Heaven is the Christian's hope, the permanent dwelling place where all believers in Christ Jesus will live forever. It is the residence we were created to inhabit; a real place, not some mystical dreamland. It is a perfect place; there will be no sin and no lack of anything we will need. Jesus himself is preparing it for us. How can we fail to be excited about spending our eternity there?

Yet by our lifestyles we are proclaiming that this earth is all there is, and we cling to it and its treasures as if we could actually keep them. We are under the illusion that our current address is our real home. We forget we are "sojourners and pilgrims" (1 Peter 2:11), temporary residents just passing through. If we understood this truth and lived by it, it would transform our relationship to our possessions like nothing else.

When you stay at a hotel, even if it's for several weeks, do you put much time and resources into decorating it to make it as nice as possible? No, your time is engaged in handling the business that requires you to be there, and it's only a hotel room! You don't put money into something that isn't yours and you can't keep. Applying the analogy to our homes, it's clear we should be more about the Father's business and less about keeping up appearances on something that is so transitory.

We have only this life to prepare ourselves for that "better country" (Hebrews 11:16) and the eternal existence God has planned for us. How we live *now* does make a difference. Let's be accurate in our appraisal of what really will last.

Father, help me to remember that heaven is my true address. Give me an eternal perspective so that I may serve you more faithfully while I'm here. In Jesus' name. Amen.

Your Personal Financial Counselor

"I will praise the Lord, who counsels me; even at night my heart instructs me." Psalm 16:7

Len and I are financial counselors, but we, too, have our own personal financial counselor. After I tell you about him you may want to consult him for yourself.

Ever since we got married, we have sought his advice on everything from job changes to buying a home to investments. He has never once led us astray. The mistakes we made were because we didn't follow his instruction. We have learned to trust what he says even if it doesn't make sense to us.

He looks out for our interests and protects us from bad deals by closing doors. He has arranged provision for us when it seemed we had no resources to turn to. He guides us in all our financial decisions, large and small. No detail is too unimportant for him to give his undivided attention to.

He's available every day of the week, every hour of the day. If I have a problem keeping me awake at night, I can talk to him about it and he's happy to hear from me. He assures me not to worry—he has everything under control.

Obviously, our personal financial counselor is God himself. He can be yours, too, if you are willing to put in the time to hear from him. Why do so many of us not do this? In truth, because of sin. Clinging to pet sins prevents us from hearing him clearly. God's way is first cleansing, then direction.

"Who then, is the man who fears the Lord? He will instruct him in the way chosen for him" (Psalm 25:12). The fear of the Lord is respecting his commands and obeying them.

When we're doing that, God is thrilled to give us precise direction. But it's up to us. It's our choice to go to him; he won't force himself where he isn't wanted.

The Lord God—PFC. Your Personal Financial Counselor.

"You guide me with your counsel, and afterward you will take me into glory" (Psalm 73:24).

The Undisciplined Life

"He who ignores discipline despises himself, but whoever heeds correction gains understanding." Proverbs 15:32

The parable of the prodigal son in Luke 5:11-31 has wonderful themes of forgiveness, restoration, and unconditional love. That all transpires on the prodigal's return home. I want to look at his situation when he started out.

It is clear that he was part of a wealthy family; the younger of two sons, probably in his teens. He makes a most unusual request. He wants to be given his inheritance before his father's death. Even more unusual, the father grants him his wish.

Why the hurry to get his hands on the money? His motives become obvious when "he got together all he had, set off for a distant country and there squandered his wealth in wild living" (Luke 15:13). He wanted to be free of parental control and live as he pleased.

Did his father know his impulsive son would waste his inheritance? Probably. But he also knew that often the only way for such a person to learn his lesson is to experience the consequences of his actions.

The inevitable day came when the money was gone and this formerly pampered rich kid found himself starving and having to take a job feeding pigs. "When he came to his senses," he decided to go home. He was truly contrite as he rehearsed his confession to his father. The classroom of dissipation had taught its lessons well.

Some people insist on behaving like rebellious teenagers all their lives when it comes to finances. Their money keeps bad company; it is blown on entertainments and pleasures. As long as they have income to sustain the party, they are oblivious to the fact that they are on the path to perdition. Solomon describes their fate: "At the end of your life you will groan, when your flesh and body are spent. You will say, 'How I hated discipline! How my heart spurned correction!'" (Proverbs 5:11-12).

The undisciplined life ends in physical, financial, and social ruin.

Father, you give us the freedom to go our own way. Yet you extend incredible grace and mercy to us when we come back to you. I choose to stay close. For Jesus' sake. Amen.

Leaving or Giving?

"For we brought nothing into the world, and we can take nothing out of it." 1 Timothy 6:7

It's an inescapable fact that whatever we own at the time of death is going to be left behind. Everything we own will fall into someone else's hands once we've passed into eternity. Wills and trusts are set up to assure ourselves that our worldly possessions will go where we want them to; therefore, we need to give serious thought to choosing exactly where our assets will do the most good—and when. Leaving everything to our children is not really the wisest course of action.

In the Old Testament, receiving an inheritance from one's parents was vital to a family's existence. Things are totally different today. Most inheritances are windfalls; the beneficiaries, unless they're minor children under the care of a guardian, don't need the money.

We need to understand the reasons for leaving an inheritance before we automatically assume it's the biblical thing to do. The Hebrews left their estates to their sons only. How many of us follow that guideline? For them it was a matter of provision—daughters were cared for by their husbands or remained in their father's household.

The question to ask is: If my children are financially independent from me, why would I want to leave them money and potentially cause them all kinds of problems when I could give it to God's kingdom *before* I die?

There is a vast difference between *giving* and *leaving*. Giving is a choice; leaving money is involuntary. It requires no sacrifice; it takes no faith. God isn't going to reward us for how much we kept during our lifetime to disperse at our death. What are we stockpiling money for in our old age when it becomes apparent we won't need it? We need to remember it's God's money, not ours. Is it right for our children to receive all of it? Set a time to discuss this with them and let them know your plans.

The time to store up treasure in heaven is while we're still alive.

Father, I need wisdom in deciding how much money to leave behind. Guide me in giving so your work for my generation will be accomplished. I ask in Christ's name. Amen.

The Proper Time for Prayer

*"Do not be anxious about anything, but in everything, by prayer and
petition, with thanksgiving, present your requests to God."*
Philippians 4:6

The first thing we should do when we find ourselves in a financial
crisis is often the last thing we turn to. Why do we wait so long—
until all our ingenuity and resources are exhausted—before we kneel in
prayer before the only one who has the power to do something about
our situation?

All Christians know they should pray. They know prayer changes
things. Most people have no inhibitions about coming to God with
their health issues, their worries over loved ones, or protection for their
children. But some subconsciously seem to think that money matters
are outside of God's realm of concern. Money is "dirty," unworthy of
the attention of a holy God. It is so secular; God deals only with the
spiritual. Therefore, they conclude it's up to them to resolve the problem. Prayer is finally taken up as a last-ditch effort after all else has
failed.

It's possible we haven't surrendered our finances to the lordship of
Christ. Knowing this, we feel uneasy about petitioning him about them
when in our hearts we really don't want him involved in that aspect of
our lives. As long as things are going well, we can rationalize this position. When they take a turn for the worse, we are greatly hindered by
our pride that stubbornly refuses to admit help is needed.

Paul tells us that anything that causes anxiety in our lives should
be taken to the Lord in prayer—as our *first* response, not as a last act of
desperation. God invites us to come and share our concerns with him
daily, not wait until a crisis has reached major proportions and we're
hanging by our fingernails. How we wound him when we attempt to
handle our trials alone!

Go to the throne room and present your requests to God. And
don't forget to thank him!

*Father, I'm so sorry I haven't always come to you with my money worries. From now
on I will run into your open arms. In Jesus' name. Amen.*

The Experience of Solomon

"So God said to him, 'Since you have asked for this and not for long life or wealth for yourself, nor have asked for the death of your enemies but for discernment in administering justice, I will do what you have asked...moreover, I will give you what you have not asked for—both riches and honor—so that in your lifetime you will have no equal among kings.'" 1 Kings 3:11-15

Imagine God appearing to you in a dream when you were twenty years old and saying, "Ask for whatever you want me to give you." What would most twenty-year-olds demand? Think of all the possibilities.

Solomon actually did have this encounter with the Lord at the beginning of his reign. He must have been feeling overwhelmed in his new duties, because he asked God for a "discerning heart to govern your people and to distinguish between right and wrong" (1 Kings 3:9). The Lord was so pleased that he promised to give him not only an understanding heart and exceptional wisdom, but also what he did not ask for—wealth and power. I've always wondered why.

Given money's ability to corrupt and become an idol between us and God, why did the Lord lavish riches on Solomon to the extent he did? Was it a reward for his unselfish request? We can't presume to know the mind of the Lord on this matter; we do know it is his nature to do far above and beyond all we ask or imagine (Ephesians 3:20).

Perhaps God was setting up Solomon as a case history to prove to us that money will never bring us happiness. Solomon was in the unique position of having an abundance of both wealth and wisdom, and was able to compare the merits of both. Wisdom was the winner. Without someone having experienced every material luxury the world has to offer and telling us about it (the book of Ecclesiastes), maybe more of us would be caught up in the empty pursuit of riches.

Too many of us still are.

Father, thank you that someone has gone before us and told us of the emptiness of wealth. We are the wiser for it. In Jesus' name. Amen.

"Occupy Until I Come"

"He went on to tell them a parable, because he was near Jerusalem and the people thought that the kingdom of God was going to appear at once. He said, 'A man of noble birth went to a distant country to have himself appointed king and then to return. So he called ten of his servants and gave them ten minas. "Put this money to work," he said, "until I come back."'" Luke 19:11-13

At least once every generation, a "prophet" rises up and announces that Jesus is returning on such-and-such a date and we'd all better get ready. The world was to end in 999 A.D. Obviously it didn't, but the belief was so widespread then that people sold everything, quit their jobs, and headed for the mountaintops to watch and wait. The same scenario has repeated itself many times since, despite Jesus' warnings that no one knows the day or hour except the Father (Matthew 24:36).

The last time this happened the prognosticators got quite creative. They reasoned Jesus didn't say "the month or the year" so they had him scheduled to return in September 1988. Even though I knew it was ridiculous, I remember feeling an excitement at the prospect. If anything, these false alarms serve a purpose in getting us to think about the Second Coming.

What are we to be doing while we wait? The Bible clearly tells us: We are to be about God's business as his faithful stewards. During Jesus' absence from earth, we are entrusted with his affairs. "Occupy," the KJV tells us. The Greek word used means "to trade, stay busy." Nowhere are we told to retreat and shut everything down. Keep earning, keep giving, keep saving, keep paying off debt. Some Christians live as if they're counting on the Rapture to bail them out of their financial woes!

Yes, Jesus is coming back. We don't know when; he's not going to tell us. His plan is for us to be engaged in the regular routine of living *while* we watch and wait. He will come when we least expect it. No one will miss it this time!

Jesus, I look for your glorious appearing! Give me peace about the future. I put all my trust and hope in you. In your wonderful name. Amen.

Making Many Rich

"For you know the grace of our Lord Jesus Christ, that though he was rich, yet for your sakes he became poor, so that you through his poverty might become rich." 2 Corinthians 8:9

Can you think of any stories where the rich hero or heroine voluntarily became poor? It's "rags to riches," not "riches to rags" stories that appeal to our culture. We never consider the opposite scenario—a rich man who decides by choice to live penniless among the weak and oppressed.

Yet that is exactly what Jesus Christ did. As we think about the incarnation at this time of the year, have we ever really contemplated all our Savior gave up to come and live alongside us in the flesh?

For one thing, he left heaven! Bill Hybels has commented that he doesn't even like to check out of a nice hotel. Jesus left the splendor of the celestial universe to be born in a barn. He entered our world as the most helpless creature imaginable—a human baby. He submitted himself to be nurtured by the very beings he had created. He laid aside all the glory he had with the Father in eternity and took on the appearance of an ordinary Jewish man. He gave up all his privileges as God to become a servant.

And Jesus died the cruelest form of capital punishment ever devised—crucifixion. He endured being cursed by God for those horrible hours, all so none of us ever need to experience separation from the Father.

In the resurrection Christ was restored to his place at the right hand of God, only now more highly exalted, and the riches he is heir to he now shares with us. He took our sins and gave us his righteousness in exchange. How can we not fall at his feet in worship?

This is the Christian paradox: "Poor, yet making many rich; having nothing; and yet possessing everything" (2 Corinthians 6:10). In Christ we are wealthy beyond belief. What a Savior!

Father, you sent Jesus, emptied of all his glory, so that we might possess eternal life. Open my eyes to how rich I really am. In his glorious name I pray. Amen.

The Good Life

"A man can do nothing better than to eat and drink and enjoy life and find satisfaction in his work. This, too, I see, is from the hand of God, for without him, who can eat or find enjoyment? To the man who pleases him, God gives wisdom, knowledge, and happiness, but to the sinner he gives the task of gathering and storing up wealth to hand it over to the one who pleases God. This too is meaningless, a chasing after the wind." Ecclesiastes 2:24-26

The message of the world is that you are not living the good life unless you have money. Lots of money. Or at least lots of leisure time, to spend in living any way you please. These two themes are entwined in our modern day obsession with accumulating enough money so we can retire in comfort and ease. Is this a worthy goal for a Christian? Is that why God left us on earth instead of taking us immediately to heaven once we got saved? What *is* the good life, anyway?

The good life is possible only if we live with God at the center. With him, it doesn't matter how little money we have, we can be fulfilled and content. Without him, it doesn't matter how much money we have, we will be empty and dissatisfied. Money is the devil's cheap substitute for real wealth. Money should have its proper place in our life—as our servant, not our master.

When we were first married, we had enough money to pay our bills and that was it. Now we have all the money we need and then some, yet nothing has really changed. We were living the good life then, and we continue to do so now. The amount of money we possess makes little difference in our enjoyment of life.

Pleasing God—that should be our purpose. When we work for that, everything else falls into place. If we're working only to earn more money, money is all we will have.

Money can't buy us the good life.

Father, thank you that abundant life is available to all who seek you. Only in you will we find true happiness. In Jesus' name. Amen.

All Scripture Is Profitable

*"All Scripture is God-breathed and is useful for teaching, rebuking,
correcting and training in righteousness, so that the man of God may
be thoroughly equipped for every good work." 2 Timothy 3:16-17*

God's Word is an incredible handbook for managing our financial lives as well as our spiritual lives. The two should not be separated. How we treat money has everything to do with how we treat God. We can't compartmentalize our lives into secular and sacred and still call him Lord. We must bring our finances under his authority.

From Genesis to Revelation, the Bible tells us how to do that. Are you surprised at how much God has to say on the subject? When he first gave me the idea for this book, I was enthusiastic, but overwhelmed. "365 days? Lord, how will I come up with enough material?" Friends assured me that an undated format would be fine; maybe three devotions a week. But the Lord was insistent. "365 days. You just show up and I'll provide."

The further I got into the project, the more the Scriptures opened up to me. He reminded me of sermons I'd heard in the past, books I'd read by godly authors. I am indebted to all my teachers. And I am still amazed at the vastness of God's revelation to us. Every financial situation I could think of is addressed in his Word somewhere. It is an inexhaustible gold mine; we just need to be willing to dig.

The wealth of God's Word is meant to equip us for everything we face in this life, including our finances. It is our instructor to teach us. It is our compass to show us when we go off course. It is a lamp to our feet and a light for our path (Psalm 119:105). God has not left us on our own to stumble in the dark.

Father, thank you for proving to me the adequacy of your Word. Help me to profit by what you've taught me. In Jesus' name. Amen.

The Gift of God

"Moreover, when God gives any man wealth and possessions, and enables him to enjoy them, to accept his lot and be happy in his work—this is a gift of God." Ecclesiastes 5:19

Christmas is a time to reflect. In our quiet moments, and even while all the hectic family activity of the holiday is whirling around us, we need to revere God in our hearts for all he has given us. Too much time and money are spent on the gifts we give others and the gifts they give us; we forget the Giver who makes it all possible.

People mean well, but often their gifts fall short. It's the wrong size; we don't like the color; we have nowhere to put it; we can't figure out what it is; it's not what we wanted; we already have three; how can we return it without hurting feelings? How often do we receive the perfect gift?

God's gifts do not disappoint. "Every good and perfect gift is from above, coming down from the Father of the heavenly lights" (James 1:17). His ultimate gift is his Son whose birth we are celebrating tonight. Where would we be without Jesus? "Thanks be to God for his indescribable gift!" (2 Corinthians 9:15).

Solomon notes in his spiritual journal that it is God who gives us the ability to enjoy our food, to enjoy our work, to enjoy our wealth and all that we have. Does it take the loss of these things before we know they truly are a gift?

Only in God can we find true enjoyment and satisfaction in life. It will never come to us in a gift-wrapped box under a tree, no matter how expensive. Read or watch *How the Grinch Stole Christmas* and remember that "Christmas doesn't come from a store. Maybe Christmas perhaps means a little bit more!"[2]

Father, thank you for the gifts you have lavished on me. Give me the gift of contentment this Christmas. I ask in Jesus' wonderful name. Amen.

At the Manger

"And she gave birth to her firstborn, a son. She wrapped him in cloths and placed him in a manger, because there was no room for them in the inn." Luke 2:7

This scene leads us to believe that Jesus was born into abject poverty, but that really wasn't the case. Joseph wasn't a poor peasant. He was a skilled tradesman, and he had the money in his pocket to purchase room and board for himself and Mary, but there were no rooms available. Len and I had the misfortune of passing through a city hosting a large convention one weekend and we ended up having to sleep in our car. No room at any inn, Holiday or otherwise, anywhere within fifty miles. It didn't matter how much money we had, we lived as vagabonds that night.

At least I wasn't about to give birth. Poor Mary! I wonder if she questioned what God was doing. The King of Glory to be born in a stable among beasts of burden? God in human form entered the world under the most unassuming conditions imaginable. No gilded palace, no servants in attendance, not even a midwife. God's Son was born in a place where the first to come and worship him would feel at home—shepherds, whom society looked down upon as outcasts.

Later, kings of the East would come and bring costly gifts—gold, frankincense, and myrrh. Both extremes of the social order—poverty and wealth, Jew and Gentile—came to pay tribute and kneel before the infant Messiah. Today, let us join them and bow down in adoration, offering Christmas worship to our King.

Shepherds, in the fields abiding, watching o'er your flocks by night,
God with man is now residing, yonder shines the infant light:
Sages, leave your contemplation; brighter visions beam afar;
Seek the great Desire of nations; ye have seen His natal star:
Saints, before the altar bending, watching long in hope and fear,
Suddenly the Lord, descending, in His temple shall appear:
Come and worship, come and worship,
Worship Christ, the newborn King.[3]

The Day After

"Forget the former things; do not dwell on the past. See, I am doing a new thing! Now it springs up; do you not perceive it?" Isaiah 43:18-19

The day after Christmas can be a real downer. The kids have probably broken at least one new toy by now, someone forgot to buy batteries, and everyone is getting on each other's nerves. Some of us have decided to brave the crowds and look for all those bargains on wrapping paper and cards for next year, or return the stuff we got that we don't want. The retail event known as the holiday season will go on until New Year's as everything sorts itself out and life returns to some resemblance of normality.

For me personally, the day after Christmas is when I get excited for the new year. We don't "charge" our celebration, so I don't have any nasty bills coming to depress me. I try to lay low and hear from the Lord what he has for me in the coming months. God would have us put the past behind us and move forward with enthusiasm.

Are there things you would like to forget about from this year? Some financial mistakes stay with us for years to come, others we can get over quickly. Whatever has happened, what's done is done. We can beat ourselves up over it or we can determine to overcome with the Lord's help.

Open yourself up to receive the "new thing" God wants to do in your finances. Meditating on what he says in Scripture about money has brought you to a fresh place where he can more effectively use you in the ongoing work of the kingdom.

God loves us too much to leave us where we are. Healthy things grow. Let the Lord refresh you today.

Father, I thank you now for everything you have for me to come. Keep me growing and let the wise use of my money be an indicator of my spiritual health. I ask in Jesus' name. Amen.

Adjusting Our Plans to God

"Commit to the Lord whatever you do, and your plans will succeed."
Proverbs 16:3

God has plans for us, and we have plans for us. Sometimes these plans are in conflict with each other! God is more than willing to guide us, but first we must be willing to surrender our personal agendas over to him.

The word "commit" used here means to "roll over onto someone else." It is the same idea conveyed in 1 Peter 5:7, where he tells us to "cast all your anxiety on him because he cares for you." We are to release the burden of trying to figure things out on our own and give it to the Lord.

Our oldest son wants to be a computer animator. A nearby private art college would train him wonderfully for that—to the tune of $56,000. He received a full scholarship to the local state university that also has an art college, but not as specialized. As the deadline to commit neared, the Lord made it clear he didn't want Brandon to be saddled with that much student loan debt. He went ahead and enrolled at the public university, trusting God with his future career.

We don't know what the outcome will be of this decision, but we do have peace about it, knowing that the Lord has confirmed it as his will. We get into trouble and make a mess of things when we form our own plans and take them to the Lord, asking him to bless them without ever consulting him first.

God will never go against his own word in Scripture. In our case, not only would there be a large debt incurred with no guaranteed way to pay it back, but we would have had to cosign the loans which is in violation of God's counsel. Providential circumstances guided us; the Lord was providing an excellent education at no cost. Even when the facts are so obvious, we still need to seek divine wisdom.

God's purposes are always greater than our plans.

Father, I seek to get my heart in a place where I have no will of my own. I commit all my plans to you. I pray in Jesus' name. Amen.

Standing Firm

"So, if you think you are standing firm, be careful that you don't fall!"
1 Corinithians 10:12

Backsliding. It happens in the Christian's spiritual walk, but as long as we confess, repent, and come back when we fall, it's all part of the process of becoming Christlike. The danger is when we don't repent. We get comfortable in our sin and our hearts begin to turn away from God. This is a truly serious spiritual condition.

What about financial backsliding? We see it in our counseling. A couple will be doing really well and then they'll be back, mired in another mess. What happened is that they got smug; they got a handle on their money and began to see their way clear, so they let up. They got some relief and it felt good, so they celebrated in that American tradition of spending money they should have been saving. For some couples the slide backward is as simple as not writing down their transactions. Others do well as long as they have some accountability, but as soon as they get off on their own they sink.

The key to standing firm is to never forget from where you have come. Old habits die a slow death and one small action can be all it takes to resuscitate them. The discipline involved in keeping on top of your money is meant to be for the long haul, not a quick fix. It's like dieting. People lose the weight but as soon as they like the number on the scale, they go right back to the foods that made them fat. Soon they are overweight again.

Money is the same way. If you don't stick to your new habits for the *rest of your life,* you will fall right back to where you were. We have short memories, and we like immediate gratification. With the help of the Holy Spirit, we can overcome these tendencies. Determine you will stand firm going into the New Year and you will be well on your way to mastering your money.

Father, I know that when the pressure is off at last, I need to be more careful than ever. I look to you as my strong help. In Jesus' name. Amen.

Having Your Financial House in Order

"By wisdom a house is built, and through understanding it is established; through knowledge its rooms are filled with rare and beautiful treasures." Proverbs 24:3-4

This week between Christmas and New Year's Day is a great time to evaluate how you're doing in your stewardship. Following is a checklist to help you take inventory of your finances:

- Do I reconcile my bank statement every month?
- Do I have a written budget?
- Do I know how much I'm spending?
- Do I keep good records?
- How much do I owe?
- Have I been faithful to the tithe this year?
- Have I been saving regularly?
- Do I have an investment portfolio?
- What tax planning do I need to do for the coming year?
- Did anything change this year that would require an adjustment?
- Do I know and understand all my insurance policies, and am I adequately covered?
- What major expenses do I see coming next year that I need to plan for?
- Do I have my will or trust prepared?
- Is all my paperwork in order—important documents, tax papers for the last three years, car titles, account numbers—and can I access them easily?
- Does my spouse know and understand all of the above?
- How are we doing at training our children to handle money?
- What are my financial goals for the New Year?

The peace of mind from being able to check off each of these items is well worth the effort it takes. Do it as soon as you can, and go into next year prepared to be a great steward.

Heavenly Father, you have entrusted me with so much and I want to be worthy of your charge. I will put my house in order. For Jesus' sake. Amen.

Setting Financial Faith Goals

"Now faith is being sure of what we hope for and certain of what we do not see." Hebrews 11:1

It's been estimated that only 3 percent of Americans have written, measurable goals. Guess who the successful people are? Writing down a goal makes it real to us. Our thoughts go from our heads to our hands to our hearts. But our goals must come from God; otherwise we're just wasting our time, operating in the flesh.

What is a financial faith goal? It is asking God his plans for our finances and committing to carrying them out. Faith is involved because we usually can't see how we will be able to achieve the vision he gives us. When we focus on our present resources we forget that God is not limited.

The first step, then, is spending time with him to find out what direction he desires for you. Keep asking, and write down what you feel he's saying to you. When husbands and wives do this separately, the Lord will usually tell them the exact same thing. After this happens, you have all the assurance and confirmation you need to proceed.

Now you can set a measurable goal. If it's not measurable, how will you know when you've achieved it? "Paying off the credit cards" is a measurable goal. Saving a specific amount for a down payment, giving to your church's building fund—all measurable.

Next you must take action. Begin setting aside the money, even if you don't know where it will come from. We are called to walk by faith, not by sight (2 Corinthians 5:7). You trust God to supply; after all, it is *his* goal. And when the goal is reached, he will get the credit. You will have grown spiritually and have stronger faith for having been tested.

Everyone's financial goals are unique. God treats us as individuals. He may lead you to change a goal halfway through. Be sensitive to what he tells you, even if it looks impossible. "Now to him who is able to do immeasurably more than all we can ask or imagine" (Ephesians 3:20).

Father, what would you have me do? Guide and provide direction even as you increase my faith. I ask in Jesus' name. Amen.

Trust and Put Him First

"Trust in the LORD with all your heart and lean not on your own understanding; in all your ways acknowledge him, and he will make your paths straight." Proverbs 3:5-6

We've come to the end of another year. Astonishing how fast they roll by! How was this year for you? Did you mature in your Christian walk? Are you experiencing more of the power of God in your life? Did he stretch you, take you out of your comfort zone?

He certainly did me, in the writing of this book. Living what I've learned is not easy. I've always believed the Bible to be the ultimate authority on life because of who the Author is. Who would know better than the Creator of all things how to manage what he has given us?

We've come full circle; in the end, all we are is stewards. We own nothing. We can get so caught up in being financially successful we forget this. Success isn't measured by the size of our bank accounts. Are we in any bondage? Are we free from greed? Generous, lacking in fear? Are we financially mature, able to give up today's desires for tomorrow's benefits? These are what make us successful.

All spiritual growth begins with a decision. God is looking to anoint disciplined, self-controlled people for the work of his kingdom. Fruit is grown by making consistent godly choices on a daily basis. Our decisions determine our destiny. The longer term your perspective, the better decisions you will make.

As the above verses tell us, God is there to help us when we put him first. We can't lean on our own understanding; we don't know enough. We never will. But when we do it the Lord's way, he will make our paths agreeable and pleasing. He longs to bless us from the heart of a Father. He loves us so much. If you ever doubt that, look to the Cross.

In *The Message*, Proverbs 3:5-6 is paraphrased: *"Trust God from the bottom of your heart; don't try to figure out everything on your own. Listen for God's voice in everything you do, everywhere you go; he is the one who will keep you on track."*[4] Amen. Let that be our prayer today.

Notes

1. THANK YOU Words and Music by Ray Boltz. Copyright 1988 Gaither Music Company. All rights controlled by Gaither Copyright Management. Used by permission.
2. Geisel, Theodor Suess. "How the Grinch Stole Christmas" (New York: Random House, 1957)
3. "Angels, From the Realms of Glory" by James Montgomery
4. The Message, The Bible in Contemporary Language © 2002 by Eugene H. Peterson (Colorado Springs, Colorado: NavPress)

Scripture Index

Meditations on Money
Order Form

Postal orders: Meditations on Money
4816 W. Laurie Lane
Glendale, AZ 85302

E-mail orders: MoneyMeditations@aol.com

Online orders: www.MeditationsOnMoney.com

Please send *Meditations on Money* to:

Name: _____

Address: _____

City: _____ State: _____ Zip: _____

Telephone: (_____) _____

Book Price: $22.99

Shipping: $3.00 for the first book and $1.00 for each additional book to cover shipping and handling within US, Canada, and Mexico. International orders add $6.00 for the first book and $2.00 for each additional book.

Or order from:
ACW Press
1200 Hwy 231 South #273
Ozark, AL 36360

(800) 931-BOOK

or contact your local bookstore